(Continued)

Restructuring Schools for Linguistic Diversity

Linking Decision Making to Effective Programs

Ofelia B. Miramontes
Adel Nadeau
Nancy L. Commins

Foreword by Eugene García

Teachers College
Columbia University
New York and London

Published by Teachers College Press, 1234 Amsterdam Avenue, New York, NY 10027

Library of Congress Cataloging-in-Publication Data

Miramontes, Ofelia B.
    Restructuring schools for linguistic diversity : linking decision
making to effective programs / Ofelia B. Miramontes, Adel Nadeau,
Nancy L. Commins ; foreword by Eugene Garcia.
        p. cm. — (Language and literacy series)
    Includes bibliographical references (p.) and index.
    ISBN 0-8077-3604-X. — ISBN 0-8077-3603-1 (pbk.)
    1. Education, Bilingua—United States—Case studies.
    2. Linguistic minorities—Education—United States—Case studies.
    3. Second language acquisition—Case studies. I. Nadeau, Adel.
    II. Commins, Nancy L. III. Title. IV. Series: Language and
literacy series (New York, N.Y.)
    LC3731.M566   1997
    370.117'5'0973—dc21   96-40396

ISBN 0-8077-3603-1 (paper)
ISBN 0-8077-3604-X (cloth)

Printed on acid-free paper
Manufactured in the United States of America

04 03 02 01 00 99 98 97   8 7 6 5 4 3 2 1

This book is dedicated to all the children and families who have en-riched our lives with the spectrum of their languages and the diversity of their cultures . . . and to the many teachers, administrators, and university students who have helped us to learn and grow, have supported our work, and have continuously struggled to ensure that the voice of the linguisti-cally diverse child is heard.

Contents

Foreword

As teachers look at the students in their classrooms, they see a scenario much different from the classrooms of their childhood. Today, one in every three children nationwide are from an ethnic or racial minority group, one in every seven children speak a language other than English at home, and one in fifteen children were born outside the U.S. The linguistic and cultural diversity of America's school population has increased dramatically during the past decade, and it's expected to increase even more in the future. While three quarters of Americans now claim European descent, by 2050 only half as many will make that claim. The concept of a "minority" group will become obsolete—no group will form a majority (Garcia, 1994).

Educating children from immigrant and ethnic minority group families is a major concern of school systems across the country. For many of these children, American education is not a successful experience. While one-tenth of non-Hispanic white students leave school without a diploma, one-fourth of African Americans, one-third of Hispanics, one-half of Native Americans, and two-thirds of all immigrant students drop out of school.

Confronted with this dismal reality, administrators, teachers, parents, and policy makers urge each other to do something different—change teaching methods, adopt new curricula, allocate more funding. Such actions might be needed, but will be meaningless unless we begin to think differently about these students (Garcia, 1994; Figueroa and Garcia, 1994; Cole, 1995). In order to educate them, we must first educate ourselves about who they are and what they need to succeed. Thinking differently involves viewing these students in new ways that may contradict conventional notions, and coming to a new set of realizations.

This is particularly the case for educators and communities who are engaged seriously in today's educational reform efforts. In the last decade or more—beginning with the national report, *A Nation at Risk*—distinct policy developments at all levels have addressed issues of professional preparation, along with state and local organizational, curricular, instructional, and resource allocation reforms. These developments have made very clear that enhancement of educational achievement of all students is the primary target of these new reform endeavors (Garcia and Gonzalez, 1995).

Yet, policy changes will not make a significant difference unless we understand what reform means and can produce for these populations. This book provides us with such a road map. My remarks here will attempt to set a broader context and subtext for the text delivered in this significant volume.

Students from linguistically and culturally diverse families are often defined by a characteristic they share: a lack of English fluency. But such a definition masks their diversity, and underestimates the challenge facing schools. Schools serve students who are new immigrants, who know little of American life beyond what they have seen in movies, as well as African Americans, Mexican Americans, Asian Americans, Native Americans and European American students whose families have lived here for generations. Students representing dozens of native languages may attend a single school; in some school districts more than 125 languages are spoken by students. In many schools, a majority of the students come from immigrant or ethnic minority families. Some schools face a mobility problem; student turnover is high and the ethnic mix can shift radically from year to year.

How can schools cope with the diversity presented by their students? Should they look back to the model of education developed in the early decades of this century to deal with the large influx of immigrant youngsters? At that time, educators responded to increasing cultural and linguistic diversity among their students by attempting to accelerate the assimilation into the American mainstream. Their mission was to Americanize immigrants by replacing their native language and culture with that of the U.S. Educators confidently sought to fit newcomers into the American mold by teaching them the English language and literature, a sugar-coated version of American history, and a respect for the U.S.'s political system and civic life.

Although some recommended a similar approach today, it is no longer possible even to describe American culture with confidence. There is no single definition of American culture: multiple definitions have been informed by ethnic minority voices. When immigrant students become shining academic stars, their success is often attributed to the values and habits of their native culture rather than their Americanization. There is some evidence that assimilation may actually inhibit academic success. Studies of Mexican immigrants, Indian immigrants, and children who escaped from Vietnam by boat all suggest that those who maintain a strong identification with their native language and culture are more likely to succeed in schools than those who readily adapt to American ways.

Educators of earlier eras were selected not only for their formal credentials, but for their suitability as role models for the young. The impact of an educator on the life of a young person can hardly be overestimated. Education represents a link to the adult world of educated, successful professionals. For children of a different culture and language especially, education has a tremendous impact; schools are their critical links to society. Without the caring guidance of educators, these youth will have great difficulty getting into college and becoming engineers, playwrights, or educators themselves and serving as positive contributors to our social and economic well being.

This book touches upon many aspects of how education is meeting this challenge in the educational reform of today. It also provides needed analysis, a forum for dialogues that must continue, and the hope of educational reform for *all* students.

—Eugene García

REFERENCES

Cole, R. W. (1995). *Educating everybody's children: What research and practice say about improving achievement.* Alexandria, VA: Association for Supervision and Curriculum Development.

Figueroa, R., & García, E. (1994). Issues in testing students from culturally and linguistically diverse backgrounds. *Multicultural Education 2*(1), 10–24.

García, E. (1994). *Understanding and meeting the challenge of student diversity.* Boston: Houghton Mifflin. (pp. 156–182). Thousand Oakes, CA: Corwin Press.

García, E., & Gonzalez, R. (1995). Issues in systemic reforms for culturally and linguistically diverse students. *Teachers College Record 6*(3), 418–431.

Acknowledgments

The writing of this book has truly been a collaborative effort. Over the past few years, we have struggled to define our vision and to reach a common understanding of the concepts, terms, processes and ways in which we see our proposals playing out in the real world. The writing of this book has allowed us to synthesize and refine our views and perceptions regarding the education of linguistically diverse learners. Through this effort, our friendships have deepened and each of our professional lives have been enriched.

We have been very fortunate to have professional lives that have led us to work in a wide range of settings in which the struggle for equity and excellence in the education of linguistically diverse students is constantly being played out. We have received much help along the way. Many people have been instrumental in helping us to develop and present our ideas clearly, and in a way that will be of the greatest use to prospective teachers, practicing teachers, administrators and colleagues in higher education.

In the development of this volume, particular thanks is extended to Kathy Escamilla, Lynn Widger, and Carol Beaumont who each read drafts, challenged our thinking, and made important suggestions for improving the manuscript. To Eugene Garcia for his thoughtful foreword that sets this book within the current context of education for linguistically diverse students. To Rosalia Salinas, Kathy Adolph, Suzanne Sawyer-Ratliff, and Jose and Sandy Quezada for their ideas and unfailing support. And, to our editors at Teacher's College press for their hard work and clear thinking in guiding the development of the manuscript.

The writing of this book has been one of the most special events of my professional life. It could not have happened without the intense collaboration we participated in as part of the process. Sharing its conception, development, and completion with two people for whom I have a tremendous respect, and who have been so important to me as colleagues and friends over many years makes it an extraordinary accomplishment.

In life, the support and caring we receive from others often makes it possible for us to go far beyond what we ever expected of ourselves. To Bill, for always challenging my boundaries, extending my horizons, and helping me to achieve ever new goals.

—O.B.M.

To my husband Hank who has always believed in my dreams, and has encouraged those dreams with unwavering support and unfailing love. And to my children Tom, Rena, and Andy.

—A.N.

I am most fortunate to have had the opportunity to collaborate with Ofelia and Adel. I can think of no other friends or colleagues from whom I could have learned more nor with whom I would have embarked upon such a challenging adventure.

It is truly a precious gift to have a partner who is so unconditionally supportive. To my husband Ken who has believed in me and my dreams and to my son Alexander Saul, who hopefully one day will come to understand why mom was so busy so many evenings and weekends, I am forever grateful. I love you every second, every minute . . . (you know the rest).

—N.L.C.

Introduction

This book focuses on how decisions for using resources and personnel can be maximized to develop strong instructional programs for linguistically diverse student populations. A decision-making process, grounded in basic premises derived from research in first and second language acquisition, is used throughout the book as a framework for action. Given the complexities of program development and the variability in student populations, resources, political climate, and community support, it is neither possible nor desirable to write a how-to book that encompasses all situations. Rather, we intend to engage readers in the types of deliberations that must occur as program decisions for linguistically diverse students are made within a widely varying resource base.

The issues and topics discussed and developed directly address several of the major instructional and policy concerns in public education in this country today: the changing demographics of the student population; the adequacy of instructional programs for linguistically diverse students; the academic achievement of Latino students; and school governance, reform, and change. The framework provided in this book will be of use to prospective and current teachers, as well as to educational administrators and policy makers.

Program models have been the major focus for discussions of bilingual and second language programs over the years. It is clear, however, that a "models" approach to designing programs for this ever-growing population of students is inadequate. This points to the need for defining the elements that are fundamentally necessary to creating successful programs for linguistically diverse students, and of identifying a decision-making process for selecting, balancing, and implementing those elements within a total school context.

Planning and implementing programs for linguistically diverse students require a rethinking of the usual ways of doing business in schools. This idea fits naturally into the movements for school reform and restructuring that are a major thrust of current educational improvement plans. In fact, the demands of particular school contexts are also at the heart of the growing site-based management and school restructuring movements, and this book places programs for linguistically diverse students directly within these conversations on reform. The program planning discussed ranges from the full utilization of the primary language for literacy and content development to programs where only English is used as a medium for instruction. The strategies that are developed represent guidelines for rethinking staffing patterns and program structures, which can lead to better organization and use of resources. Approaches that support effective instruction are also discussed.

An overarching assumption of this book is that bilingual education is regular education. It requires, however, the added dimension of planning for second language acquisition. What we know about development for all children is linked and applied directly to the decisions made for linguistically diverse students in schools. Recognizing that programs that fully develop the primary language in school are not always possible in all settings or for all linguistically diverse students, we maintain that there is always a fundamental necessity to support the development of students' primary language. Regardless of resources, schools can always find ways to support students' home languages. In so doing, they support their social and academic development as well.

The importance of attending to the way two languages are used in bilingual instruction is a central theme of this book. Although there are certainly other factors that contribute to the academic difficulties of language minority students (Cummins, 1989; Ogbu & Matute-Bianchi, 1986; Trueba, 1989), the ways in which students handle language create expectations and often reinforce deficit perceptions about their cognitive and academic abilities (Commins & Miramontes, 1989; Diaz, Moll, & Mehan, 1986; Edelsky, Hudelson, Flores, Barken, Altwerger, & Jilbert, 1983; Hymes, 1974). Oral expression is the most visible and immediate vehicle for making judgments regarding student competencies. It is a major carrier of culture and a principle tool in the development of thought and mind (Mead, 1977; Vygotsky, 1978). Therefore, how each language is used and the opportunities for students to develop competency in each language across a spectrum of contexts play a significant role in the overall cognitive and affective development of the student both in and out of school.

Although several important and coherent philosophies and theories have guided the development of successful bilingual and second language programs over the years, the school as the unit of analysis and its efforts to improve and develop programs through a decision-making process have not been a major focus. In this book we: (1) present specific elements identified as critical in the development of programs and provide a clearly defined framework for program decision making supported by theory, research, and practice to guide program implementation; (2) focus on decision-making processes within particular sets of circumstances rather than on descriptions of program models; and (3) focus directly on the implementation of programs within a total school, rather than on describing the range of possibilities within isolated settings. Examples of this decision-making process are presented throughout the book.

This is not a book about theory per se; rather, it is a book that concretely presents ways in which theory directly informs practice. In addition, it rejects common practices that treat the education of linguistically diverse students as add-ons and peripheral to the functioning of a total school, and places them squarely in the mainstream of teaching, learning, planning, and educational change.

OVERVIEW OF CHAPTERS

This book is divided into three parts with a total of 11 chapters. Each chapter provides decision-making questions to guide readers in thinking through the information presented, and asks readers to participate in assessing their own situation by adding information in each area to profiles of their own schools. Part I: The Context for Decision Making (Chapters 1–3) introduces the theoretical framework. In Chapter 1, underlying assumptions are drawn from the literature. In Chapters 2 and 3, Basic Premises for instruction and program categories identifying four different levels of primary language use—from full to none—will be developed. In Chapter 3, a framework for decision making is presented. Part II: Premises in Practice (Chapters 4–8) presents specific information on how the Basic Premises apply to particular curriculum areas, assessment, and community involvement, and how they impact program decision making.

Part III: Decision Making in Practice (Chapters 9–11) offers three case studies, which give readers an opportunity to use the decision-making skills they have acquired. Chapters 9 and 10 challenge readers to use the information presented to make decisions about program planning and reorganization based on two case schools. These schools represent elementary and secondary, high, low, and no primary language use settings, as well as distinct features along the continuum of student populations and resources. As each case is presented, three possible organizational plans are outlined, with strengths and limitations of some of the plans discussed, and others left to the analysis of the reader.

In Chapter 11, a full case study of an actual school's decision-making process and program is presented. The case of Linda Vista Elementary

School in San Diego City Schools demonstrates a schoolwide staff development process that resulted in an exemplary bilingual program for students from several different language groups. The program that was developed by staff at Linda Vista school adheres to the Basic Premises of this book and reflects a variety of resourceful and innovative strategies to address the needs of a linguistically diverse student population in a complex setting.

Our hope is that this book will help guide, inspire, and support teachers and adminstrators as they continually challenge themselves to find better ways to serve the linguistically diverse populations they teach.

PART I

The Context
for Decision Making

CHAPTER 1

Theoretical Framework

For decades, educators have expended tremendous energy to improve educational programs for linguistically diverse students. Although several comprehensive philosophies and theories have guided the development of successful bilingual and second language programs over the years, these have not been widely implemented (California Tomorrow, 1994; Krashen & Biber, 1988). Despite all the best intentions, and some notably successful programs, overall achievement for the majority of language minority students has not improved significantly. Over the years many caring individuals have focused their efforts on trying to provide a sound instructional program for students in their classrooms. Along the way, they have had to overcome many obstacles in the form of attitudes, policies, and structures. In our work with teachers, parents, and administrators, we have encountered a wide range of issues, ideas, and feelings about the challenges and frustrations of trying to create effective programs for linguistically diverse students. Much of the frustration we have encountered has been expressed by individuals working alone in their schools, feeling disconnected and unsupported. On the other hand, the most positive comments I have come from educators and parents who work as part of a group to improve instruction for their whole program or school, not just a single set of students. The quotations following reflect the essence of things we've heard or been told.

> Every teacher in this building has his/her own idea about what's good bilingual education. So, they just want to be left alone to do their own program. (Fourth grade teacher)

> High school kids don't have time for bilingual instruction, they have to pass the competencies. (Secondary teacher social studies)

> I'm an aide, I'm not a trained teacher but I'm responsible for teaching ESL to all of the primary children in my school. (Paraprofessional)

I used to think parents in my school didn't care. Now I have parents in my classroom every day. (Seventh grade teacher)

I believe in heterogeneous groups so I think its better to translate than to put them in separate groups. (Sixth grade teacher)

I don't know what's wrong with these kids. They have had three years of bilingual education but they don't seem able to keep up. (Fourth grade teacher)

I know these students don't read English, but we have to get through the book. (Eleventh grade teacher)

Ever since we began to teach English speakers Spanish, kids get along better and the Spanish speakers use their Spanish more. (Eighth grade teacher)

I don't have time for portfolios, and anyway, in my district the only thing that matters is standardized test scores. (Fifth grade teacher)

I wouldn't have believed it, but a lot of the content teachers have been really cooperative. (Tenth grade teacher)

I've been a bilingual teacher for 15 years and every couple of years they want us to do something different. (Third grade teacher)

We're promising parents things that I don't think we're delivering. (Second grade teacher)

This shared decision making is really hard stuff, but I don't think I would ever want to go back to the way is was. (Sixth grade teacher)

Since we began using the primary language, the students are blooming. Where before they were quiet, they are now active and enthusiastic. (First grade teacher)

As active participants in the area of program development for linguistically diverse students over the last two decades, we are convinced that attempts to improve schools that serve linguistically diverse students are bound to fail unless an understanding and utilization of essential program elements is incorporated into school planning, and education for these students becomes a shared, schoolwide responsibility. Without a schoolwide vision and coordination, efforts at reform will inevitably continue to be frustrated, particularly if a framework for translating good principles of learning into coherent practice is lacking.

Addressing the demands of particular school contexts is at the heart of the growing movement to site-based management and school restructuring. Successful school-based efforts to improve and develop programs through a collegial decision-making process for instructional planning are based on understanding the needs of the immediate community of learners. Unfortunately, the needs of linguistically diverse students are usually seen as add-ons, and peripheral to the functioning of a total school.

Until their needs are placed squarely in the mainstream of teaching, learning, planning, and educational reform, it is unlikely that these students will have access to equitable educational opportunities. In order for school reform efforts to be successful, educators must understand how to include all students, weigh program choices, and anticipate and evaluate the consequences of particular decisions. This means recognizing both the external sociopolitical context and the internal pressures that affect how programs function.

Today, the questions that must be answered in order to assure comprehensive and successful programs for linguistically diverse student populations differ little from those of the past. They include questions about:

- *Placement:* For whom are bilingual and second language programs intended? What are their purposes? What is the role of native English speakers in a bilingual program? How do you distinguish a second language need from a handicapping condition?
- *First and second language instruction:* What is the balance between English and the primary language across the grades? How is the primary language used, that is, for what subjects, at what intensity? Is literacy part of primary language instruction? What is the level and focus of literacy instruction in each language? How are transition decisions made? How can instruction in an all-English environment be made comprehensible to second language learners?
- *Program Quality:* What constitutes good instruction? How is the continuity of a program guaranteed from year to year? What level of proficiency in language and teaching is required of teachers? Do separate instructional contexts have to be provided for each language? What is the nature of assessment in one language or both? Is just being in an all-English environment sufficient for the development of English second language proficiency?

These questions are not simply interesting to think about. How they are addressed directly impacts the outcomes and overall proficiency achieved by students. This implies the need for a systematic, monitored approach to curriculum planning that includes direct guidelines for program development *across* grade levels. Such educational planning necessitates an understanding of effective teaching and learning, as well as the ability to translate this knowledge into the practical, day-to-day activities that constitute a strong instructional program.

A MATTER OF CONGRUENCE

Poor congruence between theory and practice is expressed through contradictions regarding what is espoused to be good educational practice and the policies and instruction surrounding linguistically diverse students. These contradictions between what we know to be sound principles of learning and their implementation in schools result in the faulty practices that abound in the education of second language students. You may recognize some of these practices:

• Students are considered to have minimal or no language or cognitive abilities because they are not able to demonstrate them in English.
• Students are expected to achieve native-like English proficiency on a minimum of 15–30 minutes of English as a second language (ESL) pull-out a day with no second language reinforcement in the regular classroom.
• Students are exited from English as a second language services after two years, and expected to function fully across the curriculum as if they were native English speakers, although it takes far longer to become proficient.
• Students' potential for learning is tested, assessed, and judged, and they are labeled through assessments in areas in which they have had little or no academic experience. In essence, they have to bear the blame for their own lack of instruction.
• Students are always separated from English speakers for instruction or, at the other extreme, are never grouped by language proficiency, and always asked to perform in a setting in which they have to compete with native English speakers for the opportunity to express themselves.
• Reading and writing interventions ignore the need for the development of oral language and background knowledge in English.
• Students are asked to do their writing in their first language but are prepared for it in English, or vice versa.
• Students are taught in their first language by teachers with very limited proficiency in that language, or by paraprofessionals who do speak their language but may not read it and write it, and who are responsible

for student learning with little or no involvement or direction from certificated staff.

• Programs use translation as a substitute for a true development of thinking in the first language, or the first language is indiscriminately used primarily for directives.

• Critical masses of students of a particular language group are consistently split up and distributed throughout a school to provide a multicultural experience for other children—although their own educational needs are not be being met.

• Secondary students, because of their age and limited time left in school, are expected to magically meet graduation requirements in English with little or no primary language support—as though what we know about first and second language learning ceases to matter for older students.

These faulty practices have had tragic academic and life consequences for far too many students.

Why do these faulty practices continue? Much of the answer lies in the values, biases, and attitudes prevalent in the broader society. The creation of programs for linguistically diverse students does not occur in a vacuum. Much of the confusion, conflict, acrimony, and debate surrounding bilingual education, and other programs for linguistically diverse students, reflect the tension between social and political concerns and sound educational practice.

THE SOCIOPOLITICAL CONTEXT

Political and social concerns can act as distracters in efforts to improve instructional programs, and at times even supersede pedagogical concerns in program planning and implementation. Educators often react to the broader social issues over which they have little control in schools, instead of focusing on the areas of curriculum and school life over which they do have control. As a result, programs for linguistically diverse students become diluted. For example, in many schools children are transitioned as quickly as possible out of native language instruction, not because they can no longer benefit from it, but because the "public" perceives it to be counterproductive or unnecessary. Because social, political, and educational factors are integrally intertwined, they must ultimately be understood together in terms of their interactions and interrelationships. But, since each factor presents particular concerns, attitudes, and orientations, they must also be understood separately, helping educators to disentangle the types of arguments that derive from each.

Political Issues

Political issues that have significantly affected the social context in which bilingual programs must function include national language policies, control of the curriculum, immigration, and declining resources. National language policies are perhaps most clearly understood through an examination of movements such as English-only and English-plus. English-only movements have historically undermined efforts to provide primary language services for linguistically diverse students in this country. The English-only position asserts that using two languages diminishes an individual's opportunity to become English proficient. From an English-plus point of view, two languages are an enhancement because individuals will become fully functional in both languages if instruction is organized appropriately (Crawford, 1992a; Crawford, 1992b; Lyons, 1996; Padilla et al., 1991). Each position derives from a fundamentally different way of viewing the world. On one hand, affirming diversity is seen as a destabilizing force. On the other, it is seen as an absolute necessity for survival, providing individuals, their communities, and the nation a broader variety of ways to look at the world, assess problems, and pursue solutions.

Linked to the arguments about language are discussions regarding what students should be taught and who should be represented in the school curriculum. These struggles are exemplified by the debates about cultural literacy (Hirsch, 1987; House, Emmer, & Lawrence, 1991; Porter, 1990; Ravitch & Finn, 1987) and by the tension between such positions and those represented by multicultural, pluralistic education (Banks, 1994; Nieto, 1992). Specifically, issues revolve around whose cultural heritage should be the foundation for instruction in schools and what a so-called well-educated person should know.

As economic pressures increasingly become a reality in schools, xenophobia is another contributing factor that results in poor educational planning. In times of declining resources, immigrants become easy scapegoats. The cost of providing services to non–English speaking students causes concern in many regions of the country, especially if it is thought that some of those students are undocumented. Data that indicate that undocumented workers living in this country contribute substantially to the national economy are usually ignored (Undocumented Workers Policy Research Project, 1984). National immigration policies often create fear and tension for students. They may also impact schools and their resources. Nevertheless, resolution of such policies is not the immediate business of schools, whose daily job it is to teach children.

Social Issues

Social issues that are closely linked to the political issues discussed above have also made a significant impact on our perceptions of students in schools and have set the context in which bilingual programs must function. These include the status of students with diverse ethnicities, socioeconomic levels, and language registers *vis-à-vis* the majority society. The attitudes and general lack of understanding with regard to the interaction between students' culture and the culture of schooling have spawned cultural deficit and compensatory models in education. These have become the traditional mode of addressing educational concerns of linguistically and culturally diverse students, and directly influence curriculum selection and delivery.

Differences in status and power among ethnic groups are common in most industrial societies (Lenski, 1966), and to a large extent continuity of the status quo depends on the existence of ethnic boundaries. These boundaries are reinforced by theories that situate school learning problems in students' homes. Social class and economic stigmas have also contributed to compensatory traditions, and to the predominance of deficit views of children's homes, languages, and cultures. Although research such as that of Delgado-Gaitan (1990, 1992) clearly indicates that such a generalization is not only unwarranted but also unfounded, these perceptions of home-school relationships persist. In addition, deficit theories of intelligence and aptitude continue to surface (Dunn, 1987; Herrnstein & Murray, 1994).

Social class and cultural experience also play out in the differences between students from urban and rural backgrounds. In many countries, students from rural backgrounds have had limited schooling experiences. For a variety of reasons these students, and others who have had only intermittent opportunities to attend school, often find adapting to the culture of schooling in this country overwhelming.

Language differences can also become divisive factors. Although variance in the way language is used is normal, it becomes problematic in certain situations (Hymes, 1974). Cultural differences in the "ways of speaking" can lead to miscommunication and misunderstanding when members of different speech communities interact. This miscommunication seems to be characteristic of the relations among different ethnic and social class groups in the United States, and helps to maintain the unequal participation of ethnic minorities in societal institutions (McDermott &

Gospodinoff, 1981). There are clearly differential levels of acceptance of children who come from different language groups (Heath,1982; Labov, 1970), and it is clear that differences in social background and the way different communities use language can affect students' performance in school, and can lead to academic failure (McDermott & Gospodinoff, 1976; Trueba, 1989). This continues to occur, despite substantial research that indicates that with very few exceptions all children learn a mother tongue (primary language), that no language is any easier or any harder than another to learn as a mother tongue, and that all languages function equally well as a means of communication and expression of ideas (Halliday, 1975; Scribner & Cole, 1981; Slobin, 1979).

Language-related issues also include a dual standard with regard to who should have access to bilingualism. In this country, the general attitude is that if an individual is a dominant speaker of English, bilingualism is an economic and social benefit. However, the benefits of bilingualism are not seen to accrue to individuals whose dominant language is not English. Students without English are seen to have a deficit, rather than the same relative advantage toward bilingualism.

The factors discussed above affect our views of students' overall potential, the reasons for school failure, the search for better methods and strategies for instruction, and the kind of assessment data we collect. They are important to consider as we interpret and draw conclusions about student performance. In the decision-making process, the clash of values and beliefs among school staff often leads to abandoning discussions of controversial topics. But, as will be discussed in Chapter 3, exploring and understanding the sociopolitical positions school staff hold are critical to the process of change.

UNDERLYING ASSUMPTIONS

Decision making that aims to create effective programs for all students requires a firm grounding in the basic theoretical, practical, and research knowledge we have about teaching, learning, and bilingualism. Understanding the sociopolitical context highlights the fact that a variety of perspectives may be taken with respect to the education of linguistically diverse students. To be truly effective, educators must take stands on a wide variety of issues, and consciously act from these beliefs. This makes it necessary to clarify the specific positions, attitudes, and beliefs that guide educational planning. The following nine underlying assumptions reflect the stands we have taken, and the beliefs on which this book is grounded:

1. Learning is a process of development that is both dynamic and constructive.

2. The primary language, developed in the context of social interaction, is fundamental to the thinking, learning, and identity of every individual.

3. Students' first and second languages interact with one another. The instructional opportunities students receive in each language will play a critical role in determining their levels of bilingualism and academic achievement.

4. Bilingualism is a cognitive, social, and economic asset for all people, and schools can play a significant role in helping students from English and non-English backgrounds develop full academic bilingualism.

5. Individuals will need to function in a multicultural society. Students' knowledge of their own culture as well as the culture of others is important not only to their school performance but to their overall success.

6. The sociopolitical context has a direct impact on pedagogical decisions about education. Educators' underlying attitudes toward students' families, cultures, and languages shape their instructional approaches and can result in very different academic outcomes for students from differing backgrounds.

7. Schools can make a positive and significant difference for students when educators account for the complex interaction of language, culture, and context, and decisions are made within a coherent theoretical framework.

8. In all programs, there are ways to organize even limited resources to optimize student achievement. The most effective programs for linguistically diverse students result from a decision-making process that involves a total school community.

9. The pedagogical principles that arise from these assumptions set the vision for the school and hold true for all students.

In the following section, we explore each of these underlying assumptions and their implications for instruction.

Assumption 1—Learning As a Process

Learning is a process of development that is both dynamic and constructive.

Philosophies of learning can be divided into two distinct traditions. For some, individuals are primarily *reactors* to their environment—their behavior shaped by the consequences of their actions, and learning a conditioned response to stimuli. To others, individuals are seen as the *creators* of their environment and active participants in structuring their own experience.

For many years, educators' views of learning have been greatly influenced by theories that emphasize the mastery of the discrete elements of a task (assumed to be critical for the understanding of the whole) as the primary focus of instruction. For example, in reading, individual letters and sounds are viewed as the keys to unlocking the meaning of text (Chall, 1989), with meaning residing in the text as a puzzle that students are challenged to understand and acquire. Within this orientation to learning, the individual is primarily a passive recipient of a body of knowledge that has universal, acknowledged meaning. That is, the meaning, value, and importance of information are already established and reflect a set of norms and values that it is the individual's task to acquire. In this view, there is little room for the adaptation of knowledge to the learner's perspective.

A more inclusive and empowering perspective of learning focuses on the interaction of the learner with what is to be learned. In this view, meaning is not simply on the page, but rather is constructed in the interaction between the information that is being presented by the teacher and the learner's interpretation of that information as viewed through his or her experiences and understandings. From this perspective, learners are seen as active participants in the creation of their own knowledge and meaning. Both views have strongly influenced education. For those who take the latter, more interactive perspective, as we do, learning must be viewed within a broad context of experiences that include a person's home language and culture.

As individuals react to their environment, they do so from the context of previous experience, actively interacting with and integrating new information. It becomes axiomatic, therefore, that the importance of learning rests on individuals' ability to derive meaning from their experiences. What an individual comprehends, and subsequently does with this understanding, is the essence of "learning."

An important aspect of this constructive process is the interaction between learners and the people around them. In Vygotsky's (1978) view, social interaction is essential to cognitive development. Learning occurs when individuals receive assistance in moving beyond what they already know toward their level of potential development. In this process, they move through what Vygotsky terms the zone of proximal development (ZPD). The ZPD is not a fixed entity in the brain, but rather is an ever-shifting range between individuals' independent problem-solving capabilities and what they can do with the assistance of an adult or more capable peers. Working with someone more knowledgeable than themselves helps learners make the connections between what they already know and what is being taught.

The kind of active intervention or mediation that is necessary to support learners moving through their zones of proximal development has important implications for teachers. The teacher's role becomes one of actively guiding students through the process and providing opportunities for extended and meaningful educational experiences and discourse. Instruction is organized to call up or retrieve information already possessed by students, to furnish the information they don't already have, and to provide the means to connect the two (Moll, 1990a; Tharp & Gallimore, 1990). Oral interaction and instructional conversations in which teachers make the connections between words and meaning explicit, by providing structures, strategies, and examples, are key. In this role, teachers model a process for developing internal thinking and frameworks for asking one's own questions.

Assumption 2—Primary Language

The primary language, developed in the context of social interaction, is fundamental to the thinking, learning, and identity of every individual.

The development of language plays a vital role in the development and socialization of all young children. Although research is not conclusive as to the specific relationship between language and thought, the significance of this relationship is clear. According to Piaget and Inhelder (1969), language allows thinking to move from the personal, and allows it to be regulated by interpersonal exchange and cooperation. Mead (1977) suggests that the language process is essential for the development of the self, and Vygotsky (1978) saw language as the expression of human uniqueness, as "the most significant moment in the course of intellectual development, which gives birth to the purely human forms of practical and abstract intelligence" (p. 24).

Regardless of the specific place language occupies in the development of the individual personality, it is clear that it plays a fundamental role in naming, experiencing, and defining an individual's construct of reality. Along with the development of social and psychological knowledge, individuals also develop strategies for knowing and thinking, that is, problem solving and understanding. In discussing language and thought, both Mead (1977) and Vygotsky (1962) saw language as integral to the dialogue for thinking. In Mead's view, "thinking is a process of conversation with one's self . . . it is this inner thought, this inner flow of speech and what it means—words with their meaning—that call out intelligent responses; it is this that constitutes the mind" (p. 38).

In order to understand the implications of language and culture in the initial cognitive development of the individual, it is important to explore the development of an individual's sense of self and how children's parents and communities contribute to this sense of identity—an identity that creates a lens for viewing both the world in general and school learning in particular. The messages sent to children by significant caregivers and other individuals in their environment will help them develop their personality and their responses to life. Into this self come the feelings, the sounds, the smells, and the affect with which the infant is surrounded. Garcia (1982) defines socialization as the process through which parents and others transmit their culture to children in order to prepare them to interact with the world around them. These are not conscious teachings, but things parents do as a matter of course. Language is developing through these social interactions within the parameters of the family and culture of the learner. This social interaction creates the different contexts for language use (Heath, 1982). The development of language is a process of learning "how to mean" in the context of the child's culture (Halliday, 1975).

As they enter school, all children bring with them a fund of developed concepts and skills—ways of looking at the world and a sense of self. These skills represent a significant amount of cognitive, linguistic, and social skill. For example, by the age of 6, most children have the basic phonological, syntactic, and semantic skills acquired by most native speakers (Asher, 1982; Lindfors, 1987). As they learn the structure of their language, children also learn all of the social rules for putting it to use within their own speech community. As Hymes (1974) points out, the child learns *how* to say things as well as *what* to say. As children mature, they learn the referential and stylistic patterns that are used to convey their message. The rules for using language appropriately, then, are embedded within the social features of a child's environment.

Children's concept formation is also related to the interaction between themselves, their families, and their environment. As Ginsburg and Opper (1979) explain:

> Piaget's theory shows that by age 5 or 6 . . . [children] have developed remarkably sophisticated intellectual processes. By this age, most children already possess the intellectual prerequisites for understanding a good deal of what is taught in elementary school. . . . Given this notion, the educator can devise curricula which attempt to exploit the child's strengths. (p. 21)

The critical fact is that for all children, the meaning of these concepts and skills is encoded in their primary language, and embedded in their cultural experiences. This understanding of language and language development points out the absolute need to understand the context of students' lives if we are to teach them successfully. As students move from first language to second language, the task involves not simply learning new vocabulary, but rather a whole new system, expressing their knowledge and understanding.

When limited-English-proficient students enter schools in the United States, they enter a world that, by and large, functions on the assumption that the funds of knowledge students bring with them to school are useful only if they are encoded in English. If this prior knowledge is not in English, it is often assumed not to exist at all. Indeed, children who are not able to speak English cannot readily take advantage of initial instruction in English, except at minimal levels. However, if they are made to wait to develop new school-based concepts and skills until they have enough English, they are blocked from using their available cognitive tools to their full potential. The perception of language minority students' lack of competence in school, and the characterization of their having no language and of suffering from impoverished thinking skills, comes directly from exclusionary policies and practices that fail to tap the wealth of knowledge and skill children possess in their primary language.

Over time there are consequences to having poor instruction and being denied access to the primary language for instruction. Students can lose ground in the face of the increasing complexity and level of sophistication of instruction over the school years. They may be cut off from parents, thereby weakening family structures (Wong-Fillmore, 1991). Lack of appropriate instruction coupled with poor English as a second language instruction can also delay students' access to academic knowledge, and isolate students from full participation in school, contributing to a sense of alienation.

Assumption 3—Second Language

Students' first and second languages interact with one another. The instructional opportunities students receive in each language will play a critical role in determining their levels of bilingualism and academic achievement.

The fact that first and second language proficiency interact with one another suggests that second language development can benefit from, and build on, what students know and learn in their primary language. The challenge is how to create educational environments that allow students to develop their first and second languages in the most effective and beneficial ways possible, recognizing that students in any classroom will represent a range of levels of proficiency.

As discussed in assumption 2, students come to school with a set of cognitive, linguistic, and social assets. While this knowledge is initially encoded in the primary language, it can be accessed, though slowly at first, through another language. This is because individuals possess what has been called a common underlying proficiency of knowledge and concepts that develops as they learn and formulate their ideas about the world (Cummins, 1979; Oller, 1980). Once gained, this knowledge can be drawn on through any language a person knows or learns. In other words, the brain does not store what is learned in each language in different compartments, nor does information learned in one language have to be relearned in another in order to be useful. Just as people can sing in any language once they learn how to manipulate their vocal cords to allow sound to emerge in particular ways so they can also express their knowledge through any language when they can use its words and structures. For example, once students have learned the concept of shapes and that 3-sided shapes are triangles, which are different from 4–sided ones that are rectangles, they do not need to relearn what triangles and squares are to make use of this information in another language. Students will, of course, need assistance in learning new labels for already developed concepts, and practice in incorporating them into their developing second language repertoire. Similar assistance will be required in sociolinguistic and interactional competence.

As another example, consider how even young children are aware that certain things are not said to grandparents or that strangers are addressed differently from close friends and family. The knowledge that you adjust your language according to the listener is part of the repertoire of language-use knowledge that can be accessed as students negotiate the nuances of their second language. This is particularly true for students who have limited proficiency in each language and who are referred to as mixed dominant. These students need additional experiences, exposure, and practice with the full range of expression in each of their languages. The role of the teacher as mediator of learning is critical in helping students become aware of how they can make use of what they know, and in providing them assistance in practicing the new labels and discourse patterns needed to make use of their knowledge through either or both languages.

The shared access to concepts and information implied by a common underlying proficiency becomes a critical factor in developing appropriate instructional programs for second language learners. This is especially important in light of research that indicates that it takes a significant amount of time—five years or more—before second language learners develop the full range of proficiency they need to be successful across all social and academic contexts (Collier, 1987, 1989; Cummins, 1986). The fact that knowledge is added to an underlying proficiency or storehouse, means that time spent studying content and learning to read and write in the primary language is not time wasted. Rather, it is time well spent. The primary language can serve as the tool to expand students' conceptual foundation at a more rapid pace than is possible when only the second language can be used. The knowledge developed in the primary language can then be expressed in the second language as students gain proficiency and fluency in its words and structures.

For students who do not have the opportunity to develop first language school proficiency, but whose home and community environments reflect a strong use of that language, tapping the experiences, interactions, and underlying knowledge they have acquired in these settings is vital to overall academic proficiency.

The interaction and mutual support of each language for the other has implications for the nature of the curriculum and the coordination of instruction across languages. As discussed throughout this book, careful planning for the use of languages can enhance the power and potential of this interaction.

Assumption 4—Bilingualism

Bilingualism is a cognitive, social, and economic asset for all people, and schools can play a significant role in helping students from English and non-English backgrounds develop full academic bilingualism.

Throughout history, the human ability to communicate effectively in more than one language has been essential to developing interactions and interrelationships between groups of people from different language backgrounds. In most countries around the world, being bilingual (or multilingual) is the norm, and seen as essential for those who expect to participate most fully in the political and economic life of their society.

Because of our particular insularity (to some extent a function of geography), native English speakers in the United States in general have had few opportunities to develop bilingualism and to gain a broader understanding of people from other countries. Immigrant communities, and others who have maintained a long-standing use of a language other than English, tend not to be seen in a positive light, and their potential for providing a way of expanding cross-lingual and cross-cultural knowledge is ignored. While every student whose mother tongue is other than English represents a linguistic resource for the nation's future, their speaking another language is often perceived as a linguistic deficit in school. This is despite substantial research that has demonstrated that bilingualism not only accrues social and economic advantages but can be a cognitive asset (Diaz, 1983; Hakuta, 1986). That is, the full development of two languages can actually enhance cognitive flexibility and function (Ben Zeev, 1977). Especially in situations where there are sufficiently large populations of language groups, such as Latinos in the Southwest, the opportunities for bilingualism and biliteracy can be expanded for all students, including those from English-speaking backgrounds.

Bilingualism has generally been seen as important for the rich or a political elite. From time to time, it has also been recognized and promoted as an important national necessity with intense but short-lived efforts. As Crawford (1989) points out, "Disturbed by our growing trade deficit with economically developed countries like Japan, in 1988 the U.S. Congress created a $20 million program, on top of the $35 million it was already spending to promote the teaching of foreign languages" (p. 164). Ironically, Crawford indicates,

> That same year it appropriated nearly $90 million for Title VII programs of transitional bilingual education designed to *replace* other languages with English. In other words, while our government subsidized instruction in 169 "critical languages"—those deemed vital to national security, economic competitiveness, and scientific inquiry—it was encouraging native speakers of those tongues to abandon them as quickly as possible. This schizophrenic approach could be summed up as *additive bilingualism for English speakers and subtractive bilingualism for language minorities.* (pp. 163–164; emphasis in original)

As discussed above, understanding the sociopolitical climate can help explain this approach to language learning in the United States. Although across the decades immigration has contributed to the tremendous diversity of backgrounds and experiences in the population, it has also engendered a backlash reflected in recurring movements to make English the country's official language, and to eliminate bilingual education. Proponents of bilingualism, ourselves included, see it as an asset for all children. They also believe that speakers of other languages who are also acquiring English represent an important social and economic resource for this nation.

Bilingualism is also a vehicle for social, political, and economic inclusion. Because children's home language is their principal tool for learning and the foundation of their development, it represents the best tool for initial school learning, as the second language develops. English-only positions exclude large groups of people from effectively participating in the society. For native speakers of a language other than English, the cost of giving up that language, and thereby losing the ability to interact fully in their bicultural life, is too high a price to pay to become a "good" American. It costs the society as a whole to demand such an impossible and unnecessary sacrifice.

Assumption 5—Multiculturalism

Individuals will need to function in a multicultural society. Students' knowledge of their own culture as well as the culture of others is important not only to their school performance but to their overall success.

The world is shrinking. Both within and outside of our borders, the business of daily life is becoming faster, more varied, and more complex. Although the need for understanding and interacting with a broad variety of perspectives seems obvious, prevailing attitudes toward race, class, and gender in this country continue to be stumbling blocks to developing a respect for diversity. This is reflected in schools where the struggle over control of curriculum, and over whose point of view and experiences should be learned by students in this country, continues to rage.

From a monocultural perspective, it is argued that if we hope to maintain a strong national fabric, everyone should know a "common" history, literature, and cultural tradition. This common history, however, has been almost exclusively focused on Euro-western historical and cultural traditions. These traditions have come to represent so-called American values and culture, even though they tend to exclude the history, culture, and perspectives of many groups who have been an integral part of this nation since its inception. In this view, diversity is negative and assimilation into a narrowly defined national culture becomes a principle goal of education.

A multicultural perspective, however, acknowledges that this nation is composed of people from many different cultural and social traditions. Our common history and what we are as a nation is a reflection of the interaction of all these cultural groups. Truth regarding events, periods, and movements in history can be defined from multiple perspectives. The nature of these truths depends on where a particular group falls within the prevailing power structure. A principle goal of education, then, is understanding that these multiple perspectives exist and how each individual fits into the larger framework.

Multicultural education is often dismissed as lacking in substance and peripheral to the real business of schools. Sleeter (1991) suggests that this is "particularly a problem for people who know little about it, since many well-intentioned but superficial school practices parade as multicultural education, such as food fairs, costume shows, and window-dressing contributions by people of color" (p. 9). In reality, learning to think critically is the essence of a strong multicultural curriculum (Banks, 1994; Nieto, 1992). In discussing the need for developing strong critical thinking in students, Richard Paul (1990) argues that

> only if we raise children to think critically as a matter of course, about their use of language, the information they take in, the nature of propaganda which surrounds them, the multiple prejudices assumed to be self-evident truths; only if we educate children to probe the logical structure of thought, to test proposed knowledge against experiences, to scrutinize experience from alternative perspectives; only if we reward those who think for themselves, who display intellectual courage, humility, and faith in reason; only then do we have a fighting chance that children will eventually become free and morally responsible adults and hence help eventually to create, through their example and commitments, genuinely free and moral societies. (p. 47)

Multicultural education is not achieved by the mere presence of ethnically and/or linguistically diverse students in a school. Nor does the presence of students from different backgrounds assure the development of cross-cultural respect and understanding among students, an outcome that requires thoughtful and deliberate planning. The nature of learning and the type of student-teacher interaction, the topics of discussion, and the social interactions this perspective suggests can serve as guiding principles for a multicultural curriculum focused on empowerment. Used to its fullest potential, multicultural education can be not only an important vehicle for cross-cultural understanding, but critically important in achieving equity for a greater diversity of students within the society.

Assumption 6—Sociopolitical Context

The sociopolitical context has a direct impact on pedagogical decisions about education. Educators' underlying attitudes toward students' families, cultures, and languages shape their instructional approaches and can result in very different academic outcomes for students from differing backgrounds.

Our perceptions of students, influenced by our own racial, cultural, and linguistic experiences, will have a significant impact on the way we approach teaching (Kagan, 1986; Miramontes & Commins, 1991). To become effective teachers requires that we perceive students accurately. Attitudes toward social class, immigration, and languages other than English, for example, shape our decisions about the educational activities and opportunities students should have. This means knowing how our beliefs and values have been shaped by broader societal biases, understanding how our own positions within the sociopolitical hierarchy interact with our perceptions about students, and how, in turn, these affect our selection of the activities and experiences offered to students (Miramontes, Liston & Fletcher et al., in preparation).

Power relationships among groups with different status are carried out in day-to-day interactions (Schermerhorn, 1970). These interactions normally take place within the framework of the dominant majority group's status and institutions (Barth, 1969). An awareness of how these power relationships are carried out through social and linguistic interactions is essential when planning programs for students who, for the most part, are not part of the social and political mainstream. The context of schooling, that is, the attitudes, the predispositions, and the structure of instruction that results, has consistently been shown to affect the performance of learners worldwide (Erickson & Mohatt, 1982; Heath, 1982; Philips, 1983; Trueba, 1987). Studies of Korean students, for example, indicate that they tend to excel in U.S. schools, while their counterparts in Japan, where they are viewed as an inferior subgroup, tend to experience academic failure (Ogbu & Matute-Bianchi, 1986). This same phenomenon has been observed with Finnish children in Sweden (Skutnabb-Kangas, 1981).

The poor scholastic achievement and school failure of linguistically diverse students in this country echo the dominant sociopolitical arguments, and shape our responses to school improvement. Nowhere is this clearer than in the way deficit perspectives, based on theories of cultural deprivation, have negatively influenced the development of services organized for poor and linguistically diverse students. Services such as Title I have been organized to focus specifically on a compensatory framework of assumptions (Allington & Johnston, 1989; McGill-Frazen & Allington, 1993). In fact, these services were originally called Compensatory Education, thus perpetuating an emphasis on "catching up" rather than on "moving forward." It is not surprising, therefore, that teachers who have adopted these prevailing deficit perspectives usually see themselves burdened by the task of making up for what students lack, consistently ignoring the many resources that students bring to school learning and the tremendous academic progress they can make.

Unfortunately, the system is set up to blame students and families for their lack of participation and/or poor schooling achievement. As will be demonstrated in subsequent chapters, a lack of planning, organization, and monitoring often creates the conditions for failure. And, from a deficit or compensatory framework, student failure is a self-filling prophecy. Rather than assessing how the system might be failing the student, the failure is used as proof of an inherent weakness in the individual. Such arguments are not only evident in bilingual and second language education, they are also prevalent in other areas of schooling. They are demonstrated, for example, in perceptions regarding the math and problem-solving ability of girls *vis-à-vis* the competence of boys, and of many students with learning disabilities who can be capable learners when alternative strategies are provided.

When students are misperceived, opportunities for growth are restricted. The reductionist curriculum offered to many linguistically diverse students (Moll, 1988) will be replaced only when perceptions of students—and the attitudes, values, and roles of teachers—are reexamined. Although the situations in schools may seem somewhat bleak, the next assumption suggests that there is reason for optimism.

Assumption 7—Schools Make a Difference

Schools can make a positive and significant difference for students when educators account for the complex interaction of language, culture, and context, and decisions are made within a coherent theoretical framework.

For decades, educators and researchers have searched for ways to provide an equitable education for all youngsters regardless of their background. In the mid sixties, James Coleman and fellow researchers (Coleman et al., 1966) reported that factors related to social class, economic standing, and race were the most powerful determinants of student achievement, and since then the debate has centered on whether the schools that students attend can make a difference in determining their levels of academic achievement.

Some argue that the differences in educational achievement across groups are nearly impossible to overcome without major changes in the overall power structure, and that the disparity in achievement across ethnic and class lines is not only predictable, but essential to the functioning of an economic system that requires a great degree of stratification in the workforce (Anyon 1980; Apple, 1982; McLaren, 1989). Racism and prejudice against students from nonwhite and non–English speaking backgrounds compound the difficulties these students face in school. Despite these powerful arguments, however, research indicates that some schools are more effective than others in teaching students across the spectrum to think critically and to solve problems, as well as to read, write, and compute (Garcia, 1988; Lucas, Henze, & Donato, 1990; Snow, Barnes, Chanden, Goodman, & Hemphill, 1991; Teddlie & Stringfield, 1993; Tikunoff & Vazquez-Faria, 1982). It seems that teachers and schools can have positive effects on student learning that are just as powerful as negative ones (Grant & Sleeter, 1986).

In early school improvement efforts, five factors were identified as being associated with higher academic achievement in urban elementary schools: (1) a common vision about academic goals; (2) strong instructional leadership; (3) high expectations for achievement; (4) positive school climate; and (5) close monitoring and alignment of instructional programs. These factors were the core of what became known as the Effective Schools movement (Brookover et al., 1979; Edmonds, 1979). Unfortunately, not only was it impossible to generalize these results to all types of schools, but the overall disparity between mainstream middle-class students and low-income students from diverse backgrounds continued to exist. One reason for this may have been that for the most part these efforts were simply attempts to fine-tune traditional ways of teaching, and did not represent a rethinking of the fundamental *organization* of schools.

More recent work suggests that students' school success results from the interaction of multiple factors related simultaneously to children's home environments, the kinds of schools they attend, and (importantly) the kind of instruction they receive day to day in their classrooms. Ultimately, the factors that determine academic achievement can best be understood by looking at the interaction of multiple factors within the context of the larger community and its social and political climate (Cortez, 1986; Genesee, 1994; Nieto, 1992; Ogbu & Matute-Bianchi, 1986; Trueba, 1989). However, support for the view that schools can and do make a difference for children comes from a variety of sources. For example, Teddlie and Stringfield (1993) found that three factors—administrative appropriateness, teacher preparedness, and student readiness—combine to determine the effectiveness of any particular setting, and that no single factor alone can account for school outcomes.

Powerful evidence also comes from Snow et al. (1991), who conducted an intensive, longitudinal study of literacy development among a group of low-income students in an urban area in the Northeast. Through a complex rating system, both homes and classrooms were identified as being high, medium, or low in their ability to support literacy development. Their findings regarding reading comprehension, the area most closely tied to overall academic achievement, suggest that when students receive excellent instruction over time, the differences in their home backgrounds disappear as a factor in determining success. Even students with very little support outside of school made expected gains from year to year in these schools. Further, students from homes that were considered ideal in terms of their ability to foster reading comprehension could not always sustain academic success when they were confronted with poor instruction over time. We take the findings to mean that strong instructional programs can make a difference, and that the responsibility for providing sound programs clearly rests on the shoulders of school personnel.

While these results are extremely promising, it is clear that there is no universal formula for what makes a school effective. Rather than dictate what a school should look like, current reform efforts are aimed at critically examining the status quo and changing ways of looking at learning and assessment, organization and decision making (Barth, 1990; Clarke & Commins, 1993). Real change results from nurturing school improvement efforts indigenous to particular contexts, not when solutions are imposed from above (California Tomorrow, 1994; McLeod, 1996; Teddlie & Stringfield, 1993). The process that schools undertake to determine how to improve is as important as the steps that are finally decided on. This points to the need for people to work together within a community and school to clearly assess and understand the needs of students, to determine whether the strategies and methods they are using are effective *vis-à-vis* the population they are trying to serve, and how clearly they have articulated their goals and outcomes for students.

Assumption 8—Schoolwide Decision Making

In all programs, there are ways to organize even limited resources to optimize student achievement. The most effective programs for linguistically diverse students result from a decision-making process that involves a total school community.

The educational reform movement in the United States has illuminated ways to align educational institutions with the social, economic, and technological changes occurring as we move into the 21st century. As the area of school reform advances, however, it is clear that we are just beginning to understand how to incorporate the needs of English second language learners into this agenda.

While reform efforts provide a necessary broad framework for the process of decision making in schools, they lack a serious discussion of the kinds of decisions, programs, and guidelines that are necessary to the development of programs for linguistically diverse students (Gandara, 1994; Valdez, 1989). The strong research base that has been established about effective practices for English second language learners (Garcia, 1988, 1991a,b) has not been integrated into these policy discussions, displaced by the assumption of a "universal" teacher and the "universal" student (Zehler, Hopstock, Fleischman, & Greniuk, 1994). This universal perspective assumes an overriding solution inherent in the innovations themselves. It ignores the research and practical wisdom related to issues of second language acquisition and bilingualism. The exclusion of the needs of linguistically diverse learners is particularly ironic given the fact that they are among those students who are most marginalized by current educational practices (Valencia, 1991).

Innovation and change will fail if the basic tenets of educational practice that are grounded in research, theory, and ethical standards are ignored. In order to be effective, therefore, reform processes must recognize and incorporate key variables that are directly related to the instruction of students from linguistically diverse backgrounds. These variables include academic standards designed for the development of language acquisition, primary language development, assessment and accountability for instruction in the first and second languages, and organizational structure (August, Hakuta, & Pompa, 1994). In all cases, total school involvement increases the chances that these students' needs will be met, and that resources will be utilized effectively to support their academic achievement.

School reform is a process of inquiry, decision making, and innovation, all born out of the unique setting in which the reform is taking place. For example, in linguistically diverse communities a major distinguishing factor among schools and programs trying to improve academic achievement for English language learners will be the degree, intensity, and purpose of primary language instruction. The specifics of each school site, the composition of the community, types of language groups, numbers of students per group, resources, and so forth, will ultimately determine the kinds of programs that can, and should, be developed for students.

We share Follett-Lusi's (1994) belief that given the power to make decisions about what they do, people can and will produce effectively, even with meager resources. Often, however, the perceived possibilities far underestimate the actual potential for what a school might be able to do if all members of a school community were to work together to apply creative thinking and a visionary perspective and ground their thinking in action and inquiry. Incorporating parents and community members into the decision-making process increases the possibility that the specific needs of linguistically and culturally diverse students will be taken into account in reform efforts. These stakeholders are not involved merely by representation, but have a substantive investment in all aspects of the change process. This process requires that the entire school community take ownership of the changes, hold themselves accountable for these changes, and understand that negotiating change often engenders conflict. And, conflict and accountability must be understood as healthy processes. Seeing conflict and accountability as healthy for both adults and students increases the likelihood that they can be a means for growth and development. There are very few hierarchies in this kind of system, and all stakeholders—parents, community members, noncertificated staff, and teachers—think and talk together about curriculum, instruction, and other important issues related to school change. Members of the school community are continually involved in program analysis, self-assessment, generating questions, and seeking solutions.

Identifying and understanding the position of all individuals in a school will be important in understanding objections and sources of resistance. This can help create a setting for decision making that helps people hear each others' concerns and feelings as they work toward organizing effective programs for students. To achieve truly effective reforms, people will often have to take on new roles and decision making will encompass a wider range of issues than has typically been allowed at the school site. All the stakeholders will have to suspend business as usual and be willing to step outside of the bureaucratic boundaries normally imposed on schools.

In this kind of reform effort, members of the organization make their decisions in cross-grade collaborative teams, not only within their own cohort groups. For example, primary teachers will meet with upper-level teachers, classified staff with teachers, parents and business partners with each of these groups. In a school whose vision calls for high standards for all students, organizational flexibility becomes imperative. Changes in organization must be visible and allow for flexibility in staffing, resources, and services. For example, a school may have an innovative instructional program or assessment process, but if student grouping, equity of services, or staffing arrangements are highly traditional and rigid, then these innovative practices will be constrained. Staff must be empowered to design a new curriculum, make decisions on the mode of language use, and determine student groupings. In this process, it is critical that the discussions focus primarily on the needs of students, and not those of the adults.

Capacity building, though not heavily emphasized in the reform literature, is extremely important in efforts toward change. One aspect of capacity building is preparing people to make decisions by consensus. This means that decisions acceptable to all parties involved are arrived at through discussion and inquiry. This is not a linear endeavor, but one that requires constant inquiry, assessment, decision making, and reflection. Through the development of such skills, which increases the knowledge of the staff and the community, change can be sustained and refined over time. Through this process, a school community can be empowered to make decisions and create and maintain a unique program of excellence for all its students.

In summary, efforts to improve the education of linguistically diverse students *can* succeed. In order for these efforts to be successful, however, the parameters of the change process must include basic premises about teaching and learning, a strong decision-making process, flexible organizational structures, assessment tied to instruction, and across-the-board accountability. Change will not necessarily come easily, but the best decisions will be made when parents and community members work side-by-side with teachers, noncertificated staff, and administrators to truly meet the needs of all students.

Assumption 9—A Vision for All Students

The pedagogical principles that arise from these assumptions set the vision for the school and hold true for all students.

This final assumption is particularly important because of its assertion that all of the assumptions presented above, and all the Basic Premises that follow in Chapter 2, are inclusive of *all* school learners. In other words, they serve as the foundation for planning programs for linguistically diverse students regardless of age, prior instructional experiences, special needs, or handicapping conditions. Although it may be necessary to use specific techniques, or make adaptations for some students, the basic elements of program development and instruction will hold true for everyone.

It can be hard to trust the rhetoric of "for all learners," although the phrase is certainly popular. Too often when it comes right down to identifying who *all* students are, reformers, decision makers, and implementers begin to qualify their efforts in such a way that whole groups of students are excluded. How the range of students who constitute "all" in our schools—adolescents, students who require additional academic assistance, students needing special education services, and gifted students—fit within the framework of first and second language programs is discussed below.

Adolescents. Age introduces several additional factors to decision making for linguistically diverse learners. These are related to the ever-increasing range of background and academic experiences students bring to their learning. Linguistically diverse adolescents principally represent four distinct types of learners. In a single program there might be students who are bilingual, with fully developed literacy and content area skills is both languages, and others who are bilingual but not literate, not having been provided with either primary or formal second language instruction. There might also be students who are recent immigrants with a strong schooling background, and others who are recent arrivals with little or no schooling.

The range of backgrounds represented by linguistically diverse students must be accounted for in program planning and placement. The way schools are presently structured, however, leaves little room for the kind of flexibility needed to deal with this range in secondary schools. Schools seem to take for granted that after a certain age learning is the student's responsibility, and that little teacher support is required. At a certain point in time, for instance, schools begin to assume a uniform fund of schooling for all students, and certain prerequisite skills such as literacy are expected. Oral language development is assumed to have been completed, with no additional instruction needed. Many programs for adolescents also assume that primary language instruction is unnecessary, and that submersion in English will help them survive high school competency examinations. In the majority of junior and senior high schools, classes are discipline-based, departmentalized with little or no interdisciplinary connections, and the individual needs of students are often ignored (Patthey-Chavez, 1993). Instruction is didactic and decontextualized (Goodlad, 1984; Oakes, 1985). The organizational structure makes it difficult to integrate curriculum for students across content areas. Given the high rates of attrition in secondary schools (Fine, 1986; Kronick & Hargis, 1990), the practice of ignoring developmental learning principles for adolescents seems to have had severe consequences.

All of these practices ignore the fact that no matter what their background or how old students are, utilizing their cognitive and linguistic background knowledge is important. If adolescents are not literate, literacy must be developed. As with younger students, adolescent and adult students also need to have literacy development linked to meaning.

Another issue not usually encountered with younger learners is that because of their well-developed primary language system, older students will constantly want to rely on it for understanding. Their tendency is to want to use translation as a major vehicle to negotiate the languages. To become proficient in a second language, however, students need to have opportunities to use and practice English across the broad spectrum of contexts in which they will be called on to use it. They will find that reliance on translation will ultimately limit their proficiency and spontaneity in their second language, for example, their ability to fluently handle English in a job interview. Therefore, clear and distinct contexts are needed in which they can develop second language fluency in a safe environment.

Special Education Students. Special education covers a wide range of handicapping conditions. Some students may be challenged by physical disabilities such as polio, cerebral palsy, and so forth. Others may have difficulties hearing or seeing. Still others may be challenged intellectually. While each of these challenges interacts with a student's first and second languages in different ways, the benefits of primary language instruction or support are the same for students with special needs as for all students. In addition, instruction will have to support their acquisition of English as a second language. And, as for all students, parents' inclusion in program planning and decision making is vital.

When students are faced with physical challenges, the issues of first and second language development interact in much the same way as with all other students. With handicapping conditions such as blindness and hearing loss, however, issues that arise include in what language Braille or sign language will be taught, and how this choice relates to the language systems used by parents and other significant persons in the student's life (Miramontes & Baca, 1993). Such considerations should be made in relation to basic principles of first and second language interaction.

For students who have limited cognitive capacity, issues revolve around the perception that they lack the capacity to function bilingually. Research indicates, however, that this is an erroneous perception, and that such students can function fully as bilinguals at their own level of ability (Rueda & Chan, 1980). As much if not more than most students, students with cognitive disabilities need the strong connections, support, and understanding of their families. Therefore, access to the home language and access to bilingualism are of critical importance for them.

In the area of emotional disturbance, the tensions and uneasiness of having to function completely in a new language and cultural setting can severely impact some students. Frustration grows over time if students find they are unable to keep up with classmates, and begin to perceive themselves as falling further and further behind. This sort of emotional trauma may be compounded for immigrant students, for whom removal from the home country, relocation to a new country, and the potential loss of home language and culture may cause severe stress and anxiety. A lack of awareness, knowledge, and sensitivity to cross-lingual and cultural issues can limit the effectiveness of interventions for these students, and may lead to a compounding of their problems.

Most of the interactions between bilingual and special education are in the area of language disabilities and communication disorders, with misdiagnosis a major problem. Misdiagnosis can occur in two directions. One is the over-referral of second language learners for special education services when they simply have not had sufficient time or appropriate instruction to do "grade-level" work. The other is the failure to refer children with special needs because of the lack of services available in students' primary language (Gersten & Woodward, 1994).

The quality of programs in which students participate is a key to effectively identifying students who truly need additional assistance for learning within the context of public school classrooms. Poor programs actually create some of the conditions that make students seem to have difficulties and/or handicapping conditions. For example, where the language of instruction is arbitrary, spotty, and changed from year to year, students do not have adequate opportunities to develop the language proficiencies necessary to compete with native English speakers in an all-English environment. As they progress through the grades, and as the curriculum demands increase, they fall further and further behind, creating more and more of a discrepancy between abilities and performance. Many of these students are referred for "remedial" services because of their perceived problems, when in fact they have had relatively few consistent opportunities for substantive basic instruction. Determining whether students need additional learning assistance or whether they might have an inherent handicapping condition is extremely difficulty when schooling has been poor.

Another consistent concern has been that in order to receive special education services, students' typically lose existing primary language services. Special education services that are provided seldom include bilingual special education and are rarely coordinated with the student's bilingual program. Given this narrow range of possibilities, bilingual and ESL teachers are often reluctant to refer students to special education and a climate of distrust can result. Special educators often lack information about language acquisition and have negative attitudes toward bilingualism. On the other hand, bilingual and ESL educators lack information about the special education process, are unfamiliar with testing processes, and are often intimidated by the jargon. The traditional distance and isolation among the various program areas within a school continue to be major obstacles to program planning and coordination. Critical to this process of determining a handicapping condition is the existence of schoolwide involvement in the movement of students through first and second language instruction; clear and consistent criteria for transition; a child study team process where student problems can be discussed by all participating teachers; mechanisms for adjusting general education programs in order to provide appropriate basic education; and marshaling resources across the school to meet the needs of students before referrals are made with the idea of determining a handicapping condition.

A final area within the classification of exceptionalities is gifted education. As the research literature indicates, bilingualism can be a cognitive and intellectual asset, yet in most programs bilingualism is not available to most gifted students. Few bilingual-bicultural students are identified for gifted programs, and, in the rare instances in which such students are identified, they are usually forced to make the choice between a gifted program and a bilingual one. Forcing such a choice indicates a lack of understanding regarding the benefits of bilingualism and of the high cost of such choices, both to the individual and to his or her community.

CONCLUSION

Many individual attempts at reform fail to take into account the wide range of student needs in our schools. Plans for innovations and change are often not tested against this wide spectrum of needs, or balanced across often diverse and competing goals. The underlying assumptions presented in this chapter reflect a particular perspective and approach to the education of linguistically diverse students. They provide a base from which to think about instructional decisions. For example, if the primary language is fundamental to thinking and learning, program planning should seek to maximize the quality and substance of its use. If bilingualism is seen as an asset for all students, finding ways to include both majority and minority students becomes an important goal. If second language instruction in English is critical to students' academic and social well-being, attention must be paid to the development of full proficiency. If planning is a whole-school responsibility, all members of the community must see themselves as stakeholders. Throughout the following chapters, specific elements that are important to include if programs for linguistically diverse students are to be of high quality and appropriate to the learners will be described in detail.

The Basic Premises presented in the next chapter reflect the fundamental elements of teaching and learning that guide decision making for first and second language instruction. They move theory into practice and provide the foundation for effective program planning for linguistically diverse students and hold true for all students regardless of age, special needs, handicapping conditions, or prior instructional experiences.

CHAPTER 2

Basic Premises and Program Categories

The Basic Premises for first and second language program development discussed in this chapter derive from our underlying assumptions about teaching, learning, and the sociopolitical context outlined in Chapter 1. They create a framework of educational principles that are nonnegotiable if programs for linguistically diverse students are to succeed. They guide the decision-making process, regardless of the resources available, and constitute a bottom line against which ideas about possible levels of primary language support, goals, program configuration, and instructional strategies can be weighed.

Because the Basic Premises form the foundation for decision making, they will be revisited and extended throughout the second part of the book. Some Premises have broad implications across several chapters and are more fully elaborated in this chapter. Others are more specific to particular topics and are discussed in greater detail in the chapters corresponding to their topics. Following the discussion of each Premise, several questions are posed to help the reader focus on issues related to decision making and program planning.

The interaction between a student's first and second language is at the heart of instruction for linguistically diverse students. Because it is not always possible in schools to provide full primary language instruction to all students, in all language groups, decisions about the organization and allocation of language resources must be based on the resources available, the numbers of students to be served, the sociopolitical context, and the goals of the community. Depending on these factors, then, there is a range of options for the ways language(s) is used in instruction, and the organization of school resources.

The ability to utilize the primary language for instruction can range from its full use throughout all areas of the curriculum to no use directly for instruction. This range can, then, be conceptualized along a continuum of primary language use—from full to none. In the final section of this chapter, we delineate four program categories that distinguish points along this continuum in relation to primary language use. These categories will help guide thinking regarding the interaction between the

Basic Premises and program development across a variety of situations. Although we believe that the more the primary language can be used in instruction—as English language proficiency develops—the greater the potential for academic success, our primary purpose is to emphasize that if done well, programs in each category can contribute significantly to students' academic success. Success, however, will depend on adherence to Basic Premises related to the instruction of second language learners.

BASIC PREMISES

1. *Active Learning.* Knowledge is best acquired when learners actively participate in meaningful activities that are constructive in nature and appropriate to their level of development.

2. *The primary language foundation.* The more comprehensive the use of the primary language, the greater the potential for linguistically diverse students to be academically successful. There are always ways to nurture the primary language regardless of school resources.

3. *The quality of primary language use.* There is a difference between a token use of the primary language in instruction and its full development as a foundation for thinking and learning.

4. *Strategies for second language development.* Second language development creates an added dimension to instructional decision making. Instruction must reflect specific strategies designed to meet the needs of second language learners.

5. *Contexts for second language development.* Second language instruction must be organized to provide students the time, experiences, and opportunities they need to fully develop language proficiency. This requires a range of social and academic contexts in which both language and content are emphasized.

6. *First and second language environments.* Bilingual academic proficiency requires that clear, distinct, and meaning-enriched contexts for each language be created during instructional time.

7. *Transitions and redesignations.* Decisions regarding transition to formal second language reading and redesignations that exit students from programs cannot be made arbitrarily.

8. *Instructional assessment.* Instructional assessment must be based on students' first and second language development, rather than on grade level or predetermined criteria. An appropriate assessment plan should address language and literacy development, as well as content knowledge.

9. *Parents and community.* Parents and community must play a major role in the learning and schooling of their children.

10. *Planning for cross-cultural interactions*. Instruction must be organized to help students understand and respect themselves and their own culture as well as the cultures of the broader society. Planned cross-cultural interactions are an essential component of programs for all students.

11. *Sociocultural and political implications*. Sociocultural factors and political context must be considered in making decisions regarding every aspect of program planning.

12. *Teachers as decision makers*. Teachers are decision makers. As part of a learning community they are all equally responsible for decisions regarding the instructional program for linguistically diverse students.

Premise 1—Active Learning

Knowledge is best acquired when learners actively participate in meaningful activities that are constructive in nature and appropriate to their level of development.

This premise is based on the view that learning is a constructive process of development. Learning is not merely acquiring and practicing bits of knowledge, but rather is pursued most successfully through a process of experience, interaction, and mediation. A developmental continuum, broadly defined, exists for both first and second language, and must be taken into account when organizing instruction. In addition, a successful curriculum for linguistically diverse students presupposes a systematic coordination across languages and content.

Learning involves real-life experiences with peers as well as with adults. It is enhanced through comprehensive activities that provide an understanding of the whole by using and incorporating the parts. Through appropriate instruction, skills and knowledge are applied across subject matter. Throughout the process, students are always provided opportunities to weigh personal or group values against the material they are studying. An orientation toward active, participatory, and meaning-centered instruction can be situated within a range of approaches.

The teacher plays a very particular role in such a classroom. It is the teacher's responsibility to mediate or help students make sense of the instruction. This implies active involvement in the ongoing learning process, constantly providing examples and explanations to help expand students' conceptual base and to clarify their thinking. It means carefully crafting instruction to help move students from where they currently are to the next level or stage of development, or, in Vygotsky's (1978) terms, to try to fashion instruction so that it is in students' zone of proximal development.

For many teachers, teaching has traditionally been skill-oriented. From such an orientation, it is assumed that if students do not first acquire "skills" such as letter recognition in reading or computation in math they will not be able to learn. In addition to this focus on skills, activities are often teacher-selected, and activities are arbitrarily designated as belonging to one curricular area or another, rather than integrated across areas of classroom work.

In a meaning-centered curriculum, on the other hand, the development of ideas and thinking, and the ability to communicate those ideas, takes precedence over the development of skills, per se. Within this approach, overarching themes generally provide the context for learning. To broaden the relationships in learning, subject areas can be integrated into thematic units. The most appropriate themes are those that begin with or relate to students' prior experiences and build and expand on them. Learning about families, for example, might be the curriculum theme for an elementary class. Activities that incorporate science, social studies activities, and math concepts related to families would be provided, perhaps utilizing a centers approach, that is, a cooperative group math activity demonstrating how a family maintains a budget, or a science/social studies project comparing how families live and work in different communities. Community resources, trade books, and other primary source materials would be provided with which to explore, read, and write about the broad spectrum of families and their issues. Students could be asked to develop their store of knowledge about families by engaging in clustering activities, cooperative group discussions, and individual research. The knowledge gained about families could later be extended to the ways in which communities and nations function and interact. The entire process of learning is approached as a whole, and learning takes place in an enriched, continually mediated setting. Skills are taught as they are needed to gain meaning.

In planning for appropriate units that support students' levels of development, teachers can use district- or grade-level curricula to formulate topics and to support their instruction. District requirements can thus be satisfied by the ways in which their topic-centered instruction meets particular standards for language arts, math, social studies, science, and so forth. This also assures that the curriculum for second language learners parallels that of monolingual English speakers, allowing them access to the ideas and information that all students are supposed to acquire at a particular level.

Decision Questions. How can activities be made meaningful to students? How do you assure that students are active participants? How are activities tailored to students' first and second language levels? How do teachers become active participants in mediating students' learning?

Premise 2—The Primary Language Foundation

*The more comprehensive the use of the primary language, the greater the
potential for linguistically diverse students to be academically successful.
There are always ways to nurture the primary language regardless of school
resources.*

Perhaps one of the most basic educational concepts, and yet the most
difficult one for people to accept and act on when it comes to linguistically diverse students, is that students' primary language is one of their
principal tools for learning. The relationship of language, thought, and
social context discussed in assumption 2 speaks to the essential role of
the primary language for the development of thinking and learning for all
students, regardless of their language backgrounds. It is generally recognized that learning is enhanced by linking new to previous knowledge and
experience, and that knowledge is acquired most easily and effectively
when students can fully utilize their linguistic and cognitive resources. This
implies instruction that uses the primary language for thinking and learning over time. This, in turn, provides a foundation for academic achievement and English development (Cummins, 1986; Garcia, 1991b; Ovando
& Collier, 1985).

The range of options for primary language use—from full to none—
depends on the school resources available. Deliberation regarding program elements will be different depending on which of the four program
categories delineated in the final section of this chapter is being considered. The Basic Premises, however, remain the same. For example, regardless of the level of program that can be offered in school, the primary
language will always play a vital role in the lives of students who live in
bilingual worlds. One language is necessary for full communication within
the home and the community, the other is necessary for full participation in the broader society. A program that fully utilizes a student's primary language can provide the greatest resources for the successful academic achievement of linguistically diverse students. Such a program,
however, should provide a rich environment for the use of the primary
language across literacy and the content areas, accompanied by a strong
English as a second language (ESL) component.

In order to provide this firm foundation, a particular level and quality of development in the first language is necessary. In terms of literacy,
for example, if students have participated in a rich and diverse set of
activities, the broad range of understandings and skills learned will be
transferred into their second language learning. Conversely, if their primary language experiences are a limited, narrow range of literacy and
thinking experiences, that narrowness and lack of flexibility will be re-

flected in what is transferred. The same criteria apply to concept development in the content areas. Students who have opportunities to interact with a wide range of topics, and who are challenged to think critically about ideas, will have the strong conceptual foundation necessary for successful transfer. Various features related to creating a firm foundation are discussed in more detail in Premises 4 and 6, and in Chapter 4.

Beyond full primary language programs, the amount of instruction for, and access to, students' conceptual base in the primary language diminishes. Where students do not have access to primary language instruction, the use of specific methods can help students access information and concepts (see Chapter 5), but this will be a less direct process. Background experiences and knowledge encoded in the first language will not be immediately available to students. Neither will their developed expressive tools of language. The process of learning slows and narrows (Collier, 1995). In these programs, the role of parents and community becomes ever more important in helping students connect new to previous knowledge and experience. Educators can make a significant contribution to students' engagement in learning by actively pursuing ways to support the primary language in the home, and by encouraging parents to actively participate in school learning experiences, regardless of their own level of schooling (see Chapter 7). Schools have a responsibility to actively support parents' use of their language with their children, and to provide them with the necessary encouragement and tools to do so. Developing respect for and proficiency in a student's home language can help nurture family cohesiveness and student self-concept, in addition to enhancing academic achievement.

Decision Questions. Given the resources available, how can we support students' primary language development? What steps can be taken to actively involve parents in extending the primary language? How can we best organize the resources and personnel to provide optimal instruction in the primary language?

Premise 3—The Quality of Primary Language Use

There is a difference between a token use of the primary language in instruction and its full development as a foundation for thinking and learning.

From research and practice, it has become increasingly evident that the simple presence of the primary language in a program does not guarantee that it will be used to its full advantage (Escamilla, 1992, 1994; Legaretta-Marcaida, 1981). The integrity of each language and the quality of primary language instruction required for a strong foundation are essential parts of the content of this book. There are competing positions regarding the use of two languages in school settings. In fact, this is perhaps the most divisive issue in bilingual program development. The issue centers around the use of the primary language merely as a vehicle to understand English, a position closely tied to a compensatory framework. The token use of the primary language arises in a variety of different ways across various curriculum areas. It is most commonly seen in the use of translations as a quick fix. Although translation can be a very comfortable practice, it undermines the goals of developing a strong foundation and high levels of proficiency in each language.

One particular area of concern is literacy instruction. Some common but detrimental practices include reading something in one language and then reporting on it another, or receiving preparation to write about a topic in one language and being asked to write about it in another. Although popular, especially because they seem to offer students a degree of choice and access to background knowledge in the primary language, these practices can actually limit overall development. The following example demonstrates the point.

What Did Students Learn?

Ms. Ramos is bilingual and teaches a fourth-grade class of primarily Spanish-speaking students. Because the principal does not support instruction in the primary language, all formal instruction is in English. In order to help students, however, Ms. Ramos tells them to ask her if they don't understand directions. When they come to her she explains the assignment to them in Spanish. If the assignment is to write about a harvest festival, for example, she might explain,—*necesitan escoger un festival y describirlo. Si no saben que palabra usar yo les ayudo.* If a student comes up to her later and asks—*¿Cómo se escribe 'me gusta porque es bonito'*? she might write "I like it because it's fun" and the student inserts the sentence. If most students do not understand the assignment, she reviews the vocabulary of the lesson and translates it for the students. Because they are in an English-speaking environment all day, Ms. Ramos does not feel it is necessary to have a separate English as a second language development time, especially since she can help them understand through Spanish.

While this approach may serve to give students quick access to some of the ideas covered in the instruction, it limits their access to a more fundamental understanding of the concepts, truncates their creative expression, and inhibits the development of skills in either language.

—

Another example of this type of instruction is reported by Diaz et al. (1986). In observing fourth-grade students in an English-language reading group, they found that the students were able to report their understanding of a story they had read in *English* more clearly, and with greater detail, in *Spanish* than in English. Using the primary language offered teachers a glimpse into what students understood about the selection, and demonstrated awareness that students' performance in their second language did not provide the full picture of their literacy capabilities. However, as a long-term strategy for daily classroom instruction that responds to students' very different levels of expressive ability in each language, it falls short and can have several negative consequences. First, it does not solve the problem that students are not able to fully and fluently express their ideas in English, a task they will be asked to perform throughout their school years. Second, having students use one language to negotiate the other can limit their opportunities of learning to express their ideas in English, reduce authentic reasons for using English, and diminish their felt need to learn to express their ideas in English. Finally, this process asks students to bear the responsibility of gaining access to meaning and interpreting content across languages without support.

An additional common token use of the primary language is to present instruction in English, and then summarize what's been said in the primary language, or (seen less often) provide a verbatim translation. Both of these practices are also short-term approaches that limit language and concept development. When verbatim translation is used, students tend to listen only to the language they understand and not pay attention to, or try to understand, the instruction in their second language (Wong-Fillmore, 1982). This practice reduces authentic reasons for second language use, and because of the time it takes to say everything twice, the available instructional time is reduced by half. In programs that offer dominant English speakers the opportunity to develop a second language, translations weaken motivation, inhibit students' willingness to communicate in their second language, and often reinforce resistance and negative attitudes toward the second language.

The use of such practices also severely diminishes the status of the primary language. Because the focus is on English, such practices limit the development of the primary language by reducing it to a token that adds to students' lack of ability to express themselves fluently and fully in English. As discussed in Premise 2 (and more fully in Chapter 4), these students' potential for full bilingualism is inhibited. Their negative attitudes toward the use of their primary language in school is often evidence of this devaluing. Taking full advantage of the promise of bilingualism implies that a clear, distinct, and enriched context for the primary language is critical. In fact, their participating in such a context was the reason the students in the previous study were able to use their primary language skills to access second language material. The point, then, is not to pit one language against the other, but rather to emphasize the need for balancing languages and opportunities for language use across content, as will be discussed in the following Premise.

A final example of weakened language outcomes from the token use of the primary language is demonstrated in what sometimes happens at the upper grades (middle school and beyond) when teachers who want to be supportive allow students to complete assignments on their own in the primary language, even though it is not a language of instruction in the school or one that teachers can interact with effectively. For example, new English learners may be encouraged to complete a required research paper in their native language using whatever resources they can find in their home. When they bring their papers to class, students are then asked to explain their ideas in English. In this instance students must negotiate topics, decipher the parameters for research, and perform complex translations from one language to another on their own. In addition, there is no accountability for the nature or quality of their ideas, since no one in the school can understand their first language or knows what information they have actually discovered. While the intention of validating the primary language is commendable, the actual practice can be debilitating to students. The primary language is shortchanged, and appropriate second language support on how to conduct research in English may not be provided. These students would benefit more from a regularly scheduled opportunity to discuss academic concepts in the primary language, with a knowledgeable member of their language community, to gain a broader understanding of topics and issues (Chapter 7). Ways to organize for instruction that avoid the weakening of opportunities for language development, but that enhance both first and second languages, are discussed throughout this book.

Decision Questions. Does the program reflect rich and elaborated first language experiences? How can instruction be organized to do this successfully? How can you plan curriculum to avoid the use of translation? How can each language be used to its fullest advantage for student learning?

Premise 4—Strategies for Second Language Development

Second language development creates an added dimension to instructional decision making. Instruction must reflect specific strategies designed to meet the needs of second language learners.

Many educators mistakenly assume that by simply submerging (Porter, 1990; Rossell & Baker, 1996) their second language students into an all-English environment, they will be putting them on the fast track to academic achievement. The argument is that the more time spent in English, no matter what the setting or kind of instruction, the more quickly students will become proficient.

Indeed, many second language students begin fairly rapidly to function well in the basic social interactions of the classroom and school. Students' relative ease in acquiring communicative skills or their success in environments where their language does not need to be extensively developed or where abundant contextual support is available, however, can give a false impression of their ability to handle academic content. Although social discourse certainly requires many specific competencies—competencies that we usually take for granted in native speakers—these competencies do not guarantee success in school. Schools demand academic proficiency (Chamot & O'Malley, 1994; Heath, 1982, 1986).

Although second language learners arrive at school with the essential fund of language that English speakers come with, it is encoded in their primary language. They do not have the vocabulary or the thousands of hours of practice in English that can be counted on by their native English-speaking counterparts for approaching academic work (Asher, 1982). Because students must comprehend new material and master a new linguistic code, simple exposure to the target language is not enough to guarantee success. Second language learners require many, many hours of exposure to both oral and written input that is meaningful to them and that they can comprehend. Without special attention to making things understandable, an all-English environment can be nothing more than incomprehensible sound.

A focus on making instruction meaningful is key in the design of appropriate instruction for second language learners, no matter what level of services can be provided. Specific strategies will be discussed more fully in Chapter 5, but generally, comprehensibility is increased through the use of support materials such as visuals and realia, by having multiple opportunities to encounter concepts and vocabulary, and through activities that require students to act on and talk about the materials.

There are many ways that schools can create a strong language learning environment. The most basic is to adopt a total school perspective on how to meet the needs of linguistically diverse students. It is also essential to foster a climate in the entire school that respects and supports second language learning, and affirms the place of students from diverse linguistic and cultural backgrounds in the school environment (Miramontes, 1993b). Schoolwide involvement provides the context in which teachers can more easily find ways to plan together and coordinate curriculum. It also enhances teachers' abilities to organize instruction around thematic units through collaborative instruction, and promotes the use of cross-age groupings. This, in turn, allows for the articulation of the program across grade levels.

Decision Questions. What mechanisms are in place for building-wide decision making regarding the needs of second language learners? Is there a regularly scheduled, daily time for second language instruction? How can we determine whether strategies and outcomes are appropriate for second language learners? How are teachers throughout the school involved in the education of second language learners?

Premise 5—Contexts for Second Language Development

Second language instruction must be organized to provide students the time, experiences, and opportunities they need to fully develop language proficiency. This requires a range of social and academic contexts in which both language and content are emphasized.

For many people, an understanding of the requirements for developing a second language comes from a foreign language perspective. They think of their high school and/or college-level courses in Spanish, French, or German, where the stakes were not much higher than getting a good grade and the goals not more challenging than being able to order in restaurants on a trip abroad. The stakes are considerably higher for second language learners of English in school in this country. In order to have full opportunities for success, they must develop linguistic and sociolinguistic competence similar to that of native speakers, at the same time they are acquiring academic skills.

Because second language development in schools is a multidimensional process, a broad range of experiences and opportunities is required to gain full academic and social proficiency (Gibbons, 1993). Consider the kinds of tasks students in schools must be able to accomplish: handle topics at a conversational, nontechnical level; state positions and explain and defend them simply and clearly; articulate and develop subtle and complex ideas orally and in writing; answer questions and engage in a spontaneous interchange about academic topics; and so forth. For most of us, just dealing with a fully familiar topic in a second language is a challenge. To be successful in school, however, linguistically diverse students must be able to function in settings where the majority of the time cognitive demand is high and the language requirements are complex. At a time when they are in the process of developing basic underlying academic competencies, they are also expected to simultaneously master the linguistic code, as well as new content.

The difficulty or ease of any language task results from a combination of factors including the context of the interaction and the linguistic style that is required. The contexts of linguistic interaction range from simple to complex, for example, a conversation with a grocery clerk versus delivering an oral report to a group of supervisors. Linguistic style varies according to the need to control for the amount of slang or colloquialisms permitted as well as the need for grammatical accuracy. In a particular interaction, this style can be said to range from uncontrolled to careful (Ellis, 1986). These two dimensions of language use can be conceptualized as two intersecting continua, and any linguistic interaction can be characterized as falling into one of four quadrants.

This view of intersecting dimensions affecting language proficiency parallels Cummins's (1989) description of academic language tasks as varying according to both cognitive demand and the amount of contextual support in the environment. He suggests that the cognitive demands of an academic task range from simple to complex, and that all interactions occur in settings that have greater or lesser external or contextual support for their understanding. Settings in which abundant support is available to make sense of the task can be described as context-embedded. Those that offer minimal external support, such as a written text, are termed context-reduced. Figure 2.1 demonstrates the parallelism between these two dimensions of language use.

Linguistic tasks that call for the use of the vernacular or simple colloquial language are often those that are embedded in context and allow for the use of simple structures. School tasks, which over time become increasingly cognitively demanding and decontextualized, are also usually characterized by a more complex and careful linguistic style. In the same way, the ability to use abstractions will be initially easier in familiar contexts while even a seemingly simple linguistic task may become difficult if it is related to a complex problem.

It is important to recognize that in the developmental process more complex structures will first emerge in simple or familiar contexts and then, with practice, more regularly in more complex situations. Similarly, simple structures will initially characterize a more careful style and eventually complex structures will emerge. For example, first graders may be able to answer complex questions about motive and consequences in relation to a familiar fairy tale like "The Three Little Pigs," while being able to provide only a minimal description of the inner workings of a watch. Second language learners may be able to negotiate the rules and intricacies of a playground game of four-square, but be able to reply only in short phrases

FIGURE 2.1. Dimensions of language use (Cummins, 1986; Ellis, 1986).

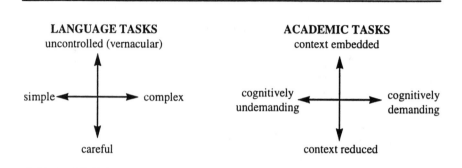

to questions about classroom content. Programs must be flexible enough to move students from their initial context-bound proficiency to the more complex language and structures needed to handle the decontextualized demands of academic instruction.

In other words, every effort should be made to assure that in organizing instruction, teachers keep in mind this intersection of the language requirements and degree of cognitive demand for any particular task. A successful second language teacher moves consciously among different linguistic and cognitive settings with the aim of creating independent learners who can function in the disembedded, cognitively demanding environment that characterizes high academic achievement. If the goal for students is learning instructional content, for example, then simplifying the linguistic load makes sense. If the immediate goal is linguistic accuracy, then both the stylistic and cognitive demands may have to be reduced.

Students can demonstrate only those language skills that they have had a chance to acquire and practice (Snow, 1992). Because of this, second language instruction should be a time when learners engage in a range of communicative and academic tasks. Without formal instructional experiences with the kinds of complex tasks demanded by academic instruction, students' language repertoire will center mainly on social interaction.

Decision Questions. What steps have been taken to coordinate and integrate existing curriculum? How can students receive the kinds of experiences necessary to promote success in the variety of contexts and uses of language they will be expected to master? How is attention being paid to students' underlying understanding of concepts and ideas, not just their surface presentations?

Premise 6—First and Second Language Environments

Bilingual academic proficiency requires that clear, distinct, and meaning-enriched contexts for each language be created during instructional time.

Students who live in bilingual worlds are required to have a more extensive language repertoire than monolinguals. For example, it is necessary for them to function in three distinct language settings, rather than just one. These settings represent the contexts in which they will constantly find themselves, both in their home communities and in schools. They are: (a) with monolingual primary language speakers, (b) with monolingual English speakers, and (c) with bilinguals.

Because of these intense requirements for linguistic competence, extended opportunities across a variety of contexts are critical to students' development of strong skills across languages and settings. Every activity in which students engage presents a decision regarding the language of instruction—a choice that should be based on a clear understanding of the linguistic and cognitive tasks for which students will be held accountable.

In all schools, educators organize and plan the instructional environment to provide the learning experiences they believe students need. In programs where two languages must be considered, there is an absolute necessity for explicit planning for the use of those two languages. A quality program for linguistically diverse students cannot be accomplished through a haphazard approach to language use. In order to understand why this is so important, let's consider what happens to each language environment when the other language is allowed to intrude.

The importance of this premise can best be understood in relation to the hegemony of English in schools (Shannon, 1995). It is not uncommon, for example, to encounter a 5-year-old monolingual Spanish speaker who, on meeting her teacher and being greeted in Spanish, will deny she knows Spanish, or a fourth grader who declares "Spanish isn't a language for learning things" (Commins, 1989). Children's rejection of their own language as a vehicle for learning points to the critical need to counteract these perceptions, and to create an atmosphere that validates and promotes the primary language as a means to acquire knowledge. A principal purpose of using the primary language is to create a firm foundation for learning. This strong foundation is critical in the development of full bilingualism and is necessary if students are to become sufficiently proficient in the primary language to be able to transfer their skills and understandings to their second language. In an all-English program, primary language support is also critical in order for the primary language to support parent–child interactions (Wong-Fillmore, 1991). The level, intensity, and quality of use of the primary language play a major role in the efficacy of programs for linguistically diverse students. An additive advantage must be consciously orchestrated in bilingual programs where there is differential status between the majority and minority languages. When the primary language is used, it must have its own time and space within the curriculum.

Organizing a rich learning environment in a language other than English in this country requires very particular planning. When discrete times and domains are established within the curriculum for each language, students are afforded the opportunity and encouragement to create and expand their language in the ways necessary for academic success. If an inviolable time is not designated for the primary language, English will almost always enter into the environment, in part because of habit, in part because of teachers' proficiency, and in part because of students' own internalized perceptions about the appropriate language for school interactions (Commins & Miramontes, 1989; Shannon, 1995).

Gaining access to the background information students know is very important in their development and extended understanding of ideas and topics. Providing adequate and appropriate activities for developing students' academic skills in the primary language creates the basic foundation for second language development. A concomitant opportunity to fully develop English language skills is also necessary. As with first language development, times for working in English also require a clear and distinct context to assure that students have the opportunity to practice talking, reading, and writing about the content of the curriculum in their second language.

As demonstrated in the following example, the simultaneous use of two languages in the environment can limit the quality of students' learning opportunities.

Concepts Underexplored

Mr. Franco teaches what is called a "bilingual" social studies class at fifth grade. Most students are native Spanish speakers who have been at this school for at least 5 years and have bilingual skills. The class is engaged in a brainstorming session in which they are trying to come up with everything they know about rain forests. The purpose of this activity is to check students' background knowledge and review ideas, and to prepare them to write an essay on rainforests during English language arts. During the discussion, Mr. Franco allows students to use whichever language they choose.

The discussion is brisk and many important ideas are expressed. Because this preparation for students' writing is done in either language, students do tend to use their most comfortable language and most of the interaction is in Spanish. Since students will eventually have to write in English about the rain forests, as students come up with the ideas, Mr. Franco writes the ideas down on a chart in English, summarizing their thoughts in a few words. For example, a point of discussion such as—*cortan los árboles porque necesitan proveer para sus familias, y los países extranjeros pagan mucho dinero por la madera que viene de los bosques*—[they cut down the trees, because they need to provide for their families and foreign countries pay a lot of money for wood from the rain forest] is summarized by the phrases "export pressures" and "economic necessity." A large and comprehensive chart summarizing the ideas covered is developed. Students can then use the chart to help them write their essays.

As the students switch teachers for their next period, they seem enthusiastic about the topic, and as they go into their all-English language arts class they see that Mr. Franco has given the teacher the chart they have just made. In this class they are considered ready to take the ideas they have discussed and developed on the chart to begin their essays on the topic. As they begin to write, however, they find that the categorizations on the brainstorming chart do not evoke the trains of thought that led to the interconnections during the discussion; many of the words are not comprehensible to them, and they do not know how to develop their ideas about the thoughts and discussion they participated in in Spanish, now through English writing.

If the students in the example above were in their native countries, or working in their primary language, discussions would have served the purpose of exploring background knowledge and developing concepts and vocabulary. The writing activities, done in their native language, would be a natural outgrowth of the discussion. Language, thinking, and task would be in synchrony. However, in this setting students' ability to express their background knowledge in their first language, although important, is insufficient for them to accomplish a writing task on the rain forests in English. What is missing is not only the vocabulary they might need in English, but the opportunity to hear and understand the discussion, arguments, and reasons in English, which they could then incorporate into their English writing. Without this, they have no models of English discourse and are left to rely on the quality of their individual translation skills to move from the Spanish oral discussion to the writing of the English essay. At fifth grade, writing essays is an important activity for which students should be prepared, but in this case they are not, and Mr. Franco's lesson does not provide help in succeeding at this task.

In planning for each area of the curriculum, it is important to ask what can be accomplished in this environment that can't be accomplished anyplace else and what specific opportunities to develop students' ability to use one language or the other are being enhanced. Throughout this book, it is emphasized that the primary language time should be used for expansion of conceptual development, and that second language time should be used for gaining experience, fluency and confidence in using English until the languages gain parity with one another.

Decisions regarding language use are very important in assuring that students will have the opportunities they need to make significant strides in both of their languages. This also has implications for the utilization of teacher resources. If the intent is to maximize the quality of the interactions in each language, the best person to create a meaning-enriched environment, especially in the primary language, should be selected for that job. Students will be unable to fully elaborate their thinking and language if their instruction is presented in minimal, grammatically weak fashion by someone who is less than fully fluent in the language of the lesson.

Decision Questions. How do you plan for the appropriate use of the two languages? What specific opportunities are created to enhance students' ability to use one language or the other? Are the best language models in each language working with students?

Premise 7—Transitions and Redesignation

Decisions regarding transition to formal second language reading and redesignations that exit students from programs cannot be made arbitrarily.

Transition periods have received little serious attention in the development of programs for second language learners. Although decision-making points are an element of the process, transitions are much more than a point in time. They are periods that mark a shift in the formal academic expectations placed on students, and in the relationship of one language to the other. Since they cannot be accomplished from one day to the next, they require time in which students are actively supported in accomplishing the extended tasks they are required to perform in their second language.

The points at which transitions begin and the nature of those transitions are somewhat different depending on the level of primary language service students have received. For students who are receiving literacy and content instruction in their primary language, there are two major transition periods: (a) when students who have been receiving formal primary language literacy only begin formal reading in their second language, and (b) when students begin to receive all of their instruction in English, without second language support. For second language learners who begin literacy in English, the transition period occurs when they are considered able to successfully handle an all-English environment (all content areas) without second language support. Criteria for these shifts are found in Chapter 7.

Transition periods are necessary because although students may have acquired literacy skills in their first language, as in programs that provide substantial primary language support, or at a basic level of oral and reading fluency in English, as in programs where little or no primary language support is available, it is unrealistic to go from being a new English learner one day to having native-like English proficiency the next. In fact, such a transformation takes years. Yet, in many programs, the "reclassification" of students from limited-English-proficient speakers to fluent English speakers happens by the stroke of a pen from one day to the next, often solely on the basis of oral proficiency assessments (Nadeau & Miramontes, 1988). To compound students' difficulties, communication among teachers about students' prior instruction is often limited, or nonexistent. To reflect on the issues raised by such decisions, let's think about Tien, an 11-year-old Vietnamese student.

By the Stroke of a Pen

Tien, a second grader, entered school speaking only his home language at kindergarten. He did not receive primary language instruction, but did receive an hour or so of ESL instruction per day with a certificated, trained ESL teacher. This was done through a pull-out ESL program that was orally based.

Because his state limits the funding for providing "special" services for linguistically diverse students to two years, now that he is in second grade, Tien has been "exited" out of the ESL program. Tien's classroom teacher understands this exit to mean that he is now a proficient English speaker and should be able to handle content effectively in English, though he has not yet received even informal literacy instruction in English.

As Tien has missed a good deal of classroom instruction by being pulled out for ESL instruction during the reading and language arts period, he is placed in a lower reading group so that he can catch up to the other students. After several months his teacher notices that he is not keeping up with his peers in reading and decides to refer him to the reading specialist. The reading specialist assumes (1) that Tien has received sufficient support in developing English skills, (2) that he is no longer a second language learner, and (3) that he has received a regular initial reading program, and has, therefore, had the necessary opportunity to learn to read in English. These assumptions lead the reading specialist to treat Tien as though he were a remedial native English speaker rather than the initial reader he may be, or the second language speaker of English he certainly is (adapted from Miramontes, 1993b).

Since Tien is not a native English speaker, many of the approaches that might typically be used for native speakers are likely to be inappropriate for him, and many of the experiences Tien needs, such as opportunities to develop oral as well as reading and writing fluency and planned instructional experiences with a wide variety of vocabulary and language forms, are probably missing (Allington & Johnston, 1989; Trueba, 1989). Without carefully defined criteria, based on Tien's competence in reading and writing as well as on oral fluency, and without assessment of the depth of his understanding of new content encountered through English, the determination of his overall academic competence in reading cannot be made.

Reclassification (or exit from second language support services) suggests that the transformation from limited English proficiency or bilingualism to monolingualism and native-like English proficiency is complete. Such simplistic thinking, of course, ignores the substantial period of time and the specific mediation needed to support students' adjustment to the new and escalating demands placed on them in the second language. Another example of the misunderstanding regarding transition periods is raised in the following example.

On His Own

Julio, a seventh grader, recently arrived from Argentina. He has strong academic and literacy skills in Spanish, but no prior exposure to English. There is a bilingual program available, but counselors decide that in addition to ESL they will put him into a remedial reading class in English, instead of primary language reading. They believe that because Julio's literacy skills are already strong, he no longer needs or will benefit from reading instruction in his primary language. In their view, he is ready for the transition to formal reading instruction in English.

In spite of the complexity of the task, many teachers expect that English second language learners who are literate in their own language can simply make the transition on their own. That is, that they can transfer the concepts and ideas learned in their primary language to their new language, effortlessly and with little or no support. Julio has but a minimal understanding of the English language, yet he is already being asked to try to make sense of and produce elaborated English text within days of his arrival. At the same time, he is considered a remedial reader.

Readiness. Another important aspect of the transition decision revolves around when students are ready to function fully and, more importantly, successfully in an all-English environment. As in the cases of Tien and Julio, a lack of defined criteria causes some students to be transitioned before they ever get a chance to receive services designed to address their needs as second language learners. At every grade level, faulty reasoning has been used to make decisions about "readiness." For students at the primary level, one argument that is often heard goes something like this:

> My non–English speakers are doing fine in kindergarten. They are well behaved and they are learning their colors and numbers. Although the alphabet is a little harder for them, they're doing just fine, and I'm sure, with practice, they'll get it. They're good listeners and don't act out. They're young and lack experiences, but they have time to catch up.

This kind of reasoning ignores the need not only for primary language development, but for focused second language instruction as well. Teachers in later grades understand (and achievement data support [Collier, 1995] that this is a shortsighted observation. Most non–English speaking students do not tend to "catch up" on their own as they progress through the grades into more complex curriculum. Without very specific attention to primary language and/or English language development, they actually begin to fall further and further behind (Escamilla, 1994). The impression of underlying competence results, to a great extent, from the types of skills kindergartners are expected to master. These skills are highly contextualized, usually involve content that is familiar to the child, and often require only rote demonstrations of learning. Such basic skill levels simply cannot sustain the more complex, decontextualized levels of understanding that will be asked of students as they move through the grades.

As indicated previously, students who live in bilingual worlds will have differential experiences across languages and perhaps differential skills between languages. These students will continue to need support for understanding and expressing ideas, even after they become seemingly fluent English speakers (Commins & Miramontes, 1989; Shannon, 1990). Attention focused on their understanding of content is critical to their academic success. Periods of transition are very important because as the tasks students are required to perform in English become more sophisticated, second language learners will meet new topics expressed in unfamiliar ways. For example, although they may be familiar with the ways in which people in communities support each other, they may have a difficult time understanding and discussing the complex hierarchical social structure of ancient Egyptian societies.

Primary Language Readers. The question of when students are ready for formal English reading is a question that causes a great deal of dissent in bilingual and second language education. This is primarily a result of a lack of understanding about the role of primary language literacy. As we will discuss in Chapter 4, literacy developed in the first language can provide the foundation for acquiring competence in second language literacy. Students will be able to transfer only what they have in the first language, no more no less. So the decision is not merely a matter of when, but also one of the quality and breadth of literacy experience students receive in their first language—the quality of the foundation.

The meaning of a "strong foundation" is directly related to what we consider a "good" reader. Although we always continue to grow and develop as readers and users of language in general, a strong foundation for reading includes, among other things, the ability to read a variety of different texts with meaning (narrative, expository, etc.), being able to answer questions both orally and in writing about what is understood, enjoying and creating stories and text, being able to present stories and ideas competently in writing, and reading text that is representative of literacy development for age and grade.

The Informal–Formal Reading Distinction. Making appropriate transition decisions requires a clear understanding of the distinction between formal and informal reading opportunities in the second language. In informal experiences with second language literacy, children listen to stories, experiment with "reading" new words; share experiences with their peers, and use ambient print. Through this informal interaction with English print, children learn a great deal that will help them to make sense of English text as they approach its more formal uses. In formal reading, students become responsible for acquiring information and using that information within the academic curriculum.

Students' interest in, and enthusiasm for, these informal experiences is not an indication that they are ready to handle the full range of tasks required for formal English literacy instruction. Students' natural curiosity and desire to learn make them want to explore the range of opportunities that surround them. And the powerful influence of the sociopolitical context draws them to English text, luring them away from the strong foundation they need to develop in the primary language. It is here that understanding and utilizing the distinction between informal and formal reading in a second language is critical. Many valuable and engaging opportunities for interaction with English literacy can be provided that do not require students to be responsible for academic literacy tasks in their second language until they have reached established criteria that reflect a sound literacy background (see Chapter 7). Understanding this distinction can help teachers plan more appropriate choices for students, choices that will allow them to enjoy their exploration of English books without undermining their literacy development in the primary language.

Decision Questions. Is there a planned transition period for the shift from primary language literacy to formal literacy instruction in English and then to all-English instruction with no second language support? What criteria are in place for determining when students are ready to make the transitions? Do all teachers in the school understand the criteria and can they explain the rationale for these criteria? What opportunities do students have to interact informally with English text before they are expected to enter into formal English literacy instruction?

Premise 8—Instructional Assessment

Instructional assessment must be based on students' first and second language development, rather than on grade level or predetermined criteria. An appropriate assessment plan should address language and literacy development, as well as content knowledge.

The purposes of assessment in education range from the measurement of individual student performance in the classroom setting on a day-to-day basis to the overall evaluation of the schools' performance through composite measures such as standardized tests. Within this range fall a myriad of other purposes: the standard grade reporting of student achievement to parents, curriculum development, statewide testing of individual and group performance, and various measures of student performance with criterion-referenced instruments created by districts and often for required district curricula.

The framework for assessment advocated in this book is derived from assumption 1—that learning is a process of development that is both dynamic and constructive. From this perspective, there is a dramatic shift from a deficit orientation that often accompanies traditional assessments to an advocacy orientation in both instruction and assessment (Cummins, 1989). Rather than focusing on the minimum students can accomplish, this more productive and useful view focuses on their demonstrated competencies as the starting point for new learning. For example, from a deficit perspective second language learners of English might be perceived as having no appropriate language skills, no experiences that relate to "American" values, and very little family support. From an advocacy perspective, these same students can be seen as having a fully developed native language and many rich experiences, concepts, and values on which to draw in organizing instruction.

The prevalent modes of assessment in schools exacerbate the problems faced by many students from diverse linguistic and cultural backgrounds. Given the deficit assumptions and biases of many test instruments, it is likely that students' abilities are underestimated by assessment processes developed for majority language students (Bennett & Slaughter, 1983; Figueroa, 1989; Merino & Spencer, 1982; Ortiz & Maldonado-Colon, 1986). Rarely do these assessments take into account the variation in skills bilingual students may have developed in each language, and their greater sensitivity to the setting or domain in which each language is used. In a traditional norm-referenced system, sorting mechanisms (such as IQ tests or other standardized achievement measures that assume some students will fail) are used to drive the educational process. When "some students" translates into many students, and when those students are members of diverse cultural and linguistic groups, assessment outcomes can become self-fulfilling prophecies. In contrast, when learning is viewed as a developmental constructive process, the framework for assessment shifts to being based on standards for the types of skills and abilities students should gain from schooling. Instruction and assessment are then designed to take students from where they are and move them forward, with all students seen as capable of reaching what Resnick & Klopfer (1989) have called "world class standards."

Assessment within an advocacy framework requires a comprehensive and in-depth orientation that can illuminate students' strengths and capabilities. In programs where development of the primary language is the foundation, student progress is assessed in both the first and second language, and all aspects of language, literacy, and content knowledge are monitored. Concurrently, the appropriate phases of second language development from oral language, through informal and formal reading, and finally to the full range of the curriculum are also assessed. Benchmarks for transition and redesignations are established based on this multifaceted perspective.

In order to determine underlying knowledge and competencies, the ongoing assessments of student progress should include multiple strategies, contexts, instruments, and approaches. An effective assessment and evaluation plan informs teaching and is tied directly to instructional planning. Students who are actively involved in their own learning should also be involved in the assessment and evaluation of their own progress (Palmer-Wolfe, 1989).

The following example shows two different settings that represent divergent approaches to assessment. In the first setting, judgments are made based on an external standard that has little to do with students' levels of development and how they interact with the instructional program. In the second, instruction and assessment are linked, and both focus on growth and development over time.

Little Room for Differences

Victoria, a shy but friendly 11-year-old, arrives from Mexico at the beginning of fifth grade. She knows no English and speaks so softly in Spanish that it's often hard to understand her responses to questions in her native language. Because the school has a bilingual program, she is assessed in Spanish using a standardized achievement test and she scores at the 10th percentile. The school relies heavily on results from such normative measures to analyze the effectiveness of the instructional program. Victoria is placed in the fifth-grade bilingual classroom and is pulled out for English as a second language instruction on a daily basis.

Over the year, classroom teachers assess Victoria's progress in primary language development and in English based on the requirements of the grade-level curriculum. At the end of the year, Victoria has made little progress on these measures. Given this lack of progress and her age, Victoria's teachers begin the process to refer her for special education testing. While documenting their rationale for a referral, the teachers discover that prior to arriving at their school, Victoria had had only one year of formal schooling. They are surprised that she initially scored as high as she did without much formal instruction, but proceed with the referral, thinking that Victoria still will not be able to succeed in the grade-level curriculum.

Given that Victoria's teachers are caring individuals, how is it that her failure to make progress led them to consider her for special education? While they may have wanted the best for her, their instruction and decisions about student progress were driven by an assessment process based on grade-level norms and standardized scales. The teachers' grades, which for the most part were based on skill-based activities, said very little about Victoria's capabilities. What she knew, or did not know, didn't fit into the fifth-grade curriculum.

Accounting for Progress

Victoria's family has moved to another part of town to a school where the staff has decided that the vision for their school will be based on a constructive perspective toward students. Classrooms and instruction are student-centered.

Victoria is placed in a multiage bilingual class, and receives her English instruction from a next-door team teacher. Her teachers provide opportunities for students to grow academically by actively including their language and experiences in the learning situation. The assessment process in this school sets high expectations for students, but allows for the fact that they all begin at different levels of school development.

Using portfolios, her teachers will be able to monitor her progress and development, and be able to reflect on her growth from a very different perspective. Victoria's work is examined regularly against criteria anchored by the school's standards and by other students' work. What Victoria needs to know is considered along with what she does know, and assessment is based on what Victoria has been taught. Even though she has had very little formal schooling, she is given the opportunity to relate her many experiences and ideas in her native language and regardless of how she acquired her ideas and experiences, they will be validated in this school setting and used to connect new knowledge and concepts. Teachers understand that if she does not yet have the necessary knowledge and skills taught in school, it is most likely because she has not had the appropriate instruction and does not have a command of the English language, and not because she is incapable or has a handicapping condition.

The assessment paradigm described in the second setting is very different from the one schools have embraced for many decades, and it will take time for it to take root in this country. The educational establishment at all levels, including the federal level, claims the goal is to respect and cherish cultural and linguistic diversity. Such a goal cannot be achieved, however, without comprehensive changes in assessment practices. Such changes must reflect setting high standards for all students; instructional interventions that are appropriate to every language, learning style, and developmental level of students; provision of authentic assessments to measure performance; and schoolwide accountability for student learning.

Decision Questions. What assessment tools are used to measure student growth across time? How is assessment focused on what students know and are able to do? How are authentic assessments integrated into the overall assessment plan? How are students involved in the assessment process?

Premise 9—Parents and Community

Parents and community must play a major role in the learning and schooling of their children.

All evidence points to the fact that when positive working relationships are established among students, teachers, administrators, and families, the school experiences of students across the spectrum of class and cultural backgrounds are enhanced and their academic achievement rises (Armor, 1976; Epstein & Dauber, 1991; McCaleb, 1994). When schools act in a proactive manner by orchestrating community outreach and inviting parents to collaborate in the educational process, they can help reduce the kinds of negative outcomes often experienced by students from linguistically diverse communities. A schoolwide vision that affirms the importance of engaging parents has implications not only for strategies that touch parents directly, but also for the overall school curriculum and teachers' day-to-day decision making regarding the content of instruction and the activities designed to carry it out.

The challenge for schools is how to reach out to a group of parents traditionally isolated from the schools because of language differences or a lack of knowledge or understanding of how schools in this country function, and what is expected of them by such a system (Delgado-Gaitan, 1992). Often, the strengths of parents from culturally and linguistically diverse communities are overlooked. For example, a lack of proficiency in English may be viewed as a deficit, and seen as preventing parents from supporting their children's academic development. Or, because of parents' lack of formal education, the life experiences and knowledge parents do possess may be ignored. Viewing parents from this deficit perspective can cause teachers to believe that non–English speaking parents can't really play a role in children's schooling.

What we sometimes forget is that the bond between parents and children is one of the most important relationships in society. Regardless of parents' own linguistic and academic backgrounds, they can and should play a significant role in supporting students' academic progress, and schools have an obligation to support families in this endeavor. Designing effective outreach strategies requires that we understand the ways in which members of different cultural communities view their roles in the learning and schooling of their children. In many cultures the responsibility for schooling is seen to rest with the teachers and schools (Delgado-Gaitan, 1992) and many parents' own value system dictates a deference to school personnel. An added challenge is that many parents would like to help, but they too may believe that they can't really support their children's academic development because of their lack of formal education or their limited English proficiency. The advice that many teachers give parents to speak English as much as possible reinforces this misconception. While well-intentioned, it may have the unintended result of cutting parents off from their children and their activities in school. Asking parents to function in a language in which they have limited proficiency diminishes the ties that bind families together and undermines the communication that is key in establishing strong relationships (Wong-Fillmore, 1991).

In order to change this dynamic, it is essential to view parents as partners who are to be included in the educational process. This can happen only when their native language skills and life experiences are viewed as an asset and are taken into account in school learning. The funds of knowledge (Moll, 1990b) that parents possess can be incorporated into the curriculum in ways that validate what they know as being important to the educational achievement of their children. From this asset perspective, parents are seen as allies in the educational process possessing wisdom and strengths that can allow them to assist in everything from student assessment, to instilling positive attitudes, to the design of curriculum, and to the governance of schools. A particularly critical role for families is to reinforce and extend basic conceptual knowledge in the primary language. This can also help to counteract negative attitudes students may have about their home language and culture and affirm the importance of the primary language as a tool for learning.

The level and degree to which parents become involved is influenced by the suggestions and guidance schools offer parents regarding their roles (Epstein & Dauber, 1991). If a school's vision is to reflect the needs and desires of all their constituents, specific outreach efforts must be organized so that eventually parents can take part in the decision-making process. Helping parents to become decision makers must be seen as a developmental process. The first step in this process is to build a foundation of trust and mutual respect. As will be discussed in more detail in Chapter 8, this can be accomplished in many ways, including reaching out in the language of the home, allowing parents to choose the level of involvement with which they feel comfortable, and including community institutions and organizations with which parents are already familiar in the school program.

A well-organized parent outreach program can impact the community in many ways. Not only does it benefit the students, but it can provide opportunities for the advancement of adults in their own educational and professional pursuits as well. In the end it can result in a stronger community and increased levels of participation in and support for schools in general.

Decision Questions. What kinds of opportunities are there for parents to become partners in their children's schooling? What strategies are in place to reach out to parents in their native language? What mechanisms are used to involve parents as decision makers?

Premise 10—Planning for Cross-Cultural Interactions

Instruction must be organized to help students understand and respect themselves and their own culture as well as the cultures of the broader society. Planned cross-cultural interactions are an essential component of programs for all students.

As we have discussed, many linguistically diverse students occupy a rather unenviable place in American society. They may be looked down on because of their limited experiences with English, their family's socioeconomic status may rouse compensatory perceptions, and their cultural differences may receive little tolerance from the society. Often, because we are unwilling to engage in serious discussions with students about the negative attitudes they might encounter, we leave students vulnerable to turning those feeling on themselves and thinking they are to blame for the reactions around them. Especially for older students, the need to discuss sociopolitical features of the environment is important to supporting their sense of self, and their taking on their role as informed citizens in the society.

Respect for students comes through actions rather than words. Teachers who are serious about helping students understand themselves and others take actions in the form of a curriculum that reflects the perspectives of the students' community (Cummins, 1994), as well as the contributions and interactions of the students' group in creating and contributing to the fabric of American society—its history, values, and perspective (Nieto, 1992). Making parents an integral part of the school and using students' language to support their academic achievement and family interactions are other ways to demonstrate such respect and caring.

Interaction in and understanding of programs for language minority students among teachers and the total school staff are crucial to establishing a safe, positive, and productive environment for students. Where there is little understanding of appropriate learning strategies and outcomes for second language learners, for example, false expectations and uninformed judgments can cause teachers to see students as lazy, unmotivated, and failing. A lack of criteria for second language accountability, and for movement between the stages of a first and/or second language program, creates situations where students are shuffled from program to program or back and forth between languages. The resulting lack of coherence in their instruction may hinder their academic progress. Often, rather than looking at the process that produced the failure, educators situate the problem within the students (McDermott & Gospodinoff, 1976; Trueba, 1989). As a consequence, the failure of program planning and coordination produces one more stigma that burdens students. Information, involvement, and discussion can help teachers avoid playing out their biases on students.

Expecting substantive growth and having high standards for students is important. Just as important is matching those high standards to a curriculum and instructional process that supports students in attaining those high standards. As demonstrated in the following vignette, high standards in and of themselves are irrelevant in helping students achieve academically.

The Limits of Good Intentions

In a group planning session, high school teachers were trying to come up with a way to integrate students' home and community experiences into their social studies curriculum. They decided that as a term project they would have the students select several important issues in their community and then interview a variety of community members to get their views on the issues. This, they thought, would really make the class relevant to students. The project began with a discussion with students on important community issues. Students then were divided into teams and assigned to do the interviews and write a report. About halfway through the semester, students were asked to turn in their notes on the project. The teachers were very disappointed in the results. Some students had made no progress on their interviews, and others had taken only the most cursory notes and were not able to draw conclusions from the material. Meeting again, the teachers decided that this assignment was probably too difficult for the students. Instead of having each student complete the assignment, they said it would be enough if each group brought in at least one interview. They then reviewed the basic organizational structure of the final paper students were to turn in and reminded them to think about what the content of the interviews meant in terms of solutions.

When the final reports were turned in, the teachers found that the issues had not been fully explored, that some of the interviews had wandered from the topic, and that students' ability to tie the comments they collected to meaningful solutions was weak. At the end of the semester, the teachers were discouraged. They concluded that the students hadn't worked hard enough on the assignment and that their experiment had not worked. The students, in turn, felt that the efforts they had made were not valued. Because they received so little direct support from teachers on this project, many students assumed teachers only gave the assignment to pay lip service to the importance of the community, but that they didn't really care about the very real issues that affected their lives. (Adapted from McQuillan, in press.)

Although the teachers are full of good intentions, their lack of guidance and direction contributed to the failure of this assignment to fulfill their goals. For example, when teachers noticed that the students were having difficulty doing the interviews, they might have: (a) helped them develop an interview protocol that focused on the important issues; (b) modeled an interview; or (c) helped them practice interviewing each other. Discussions to monitor progress and to help students interact with the information they were learning would have provided students opportunities to begin to organize the information they were collecting. Finally, helping students organize their thoughts and ideas, rather than concentrating on the organizational structure of the paper, would have supported their presentation of the material. It is often easier to think that students can't do the task than to plan ways in which to support their attainment of the goal. This robs students of opportunities to grow and expand their knowledge base. In addition, by paying closer attention to the substance of the issues raised, teachers could have created a greater basis for trust and perhaps have helped students direct their energy toward social change.

Involving students substantively in their own learning is a critical part of helping them understand and respect themselves as learners. Assessments that give students opportunities to realistically assess their own work, for instance, can help them participate in setting goals and seeing areas of concern as well as areas of progress.

Structuring Cross-cultural Interaction. Full inclusion of the diversity of students in our schools today continues to be one of the major challenges we face in education. Meaningful cross-cultural interactions for all students are necessary if they are to understand and participate effectively in the world around them. From the valiant efforts made for racial integration, however, we have learned that things do not change unless there are active efforts to make things change. Simply putting students together is not enough to help them come to understand and respect each other.

Techniques such as cooperative learning can be very effective in setting up authentic cross-cultural interactions, but unless they are carefully planned and organized they can be ineffectual and negative (Cohen, 1986; De Avila & Duncan, 1980; Rottier & Ogan, 1991). For example, unless the roles students take are balanced among students, some students may be left out. If tasks are far above the level of some students, they may be shut out and viewed as undesirable group members. Unless students get a chance to talk about group dynamics and process their interactions, resentment and misunderstandings may persist. Proactive measures are critical to overcoming long-standing differences and misunderstandings among different groups of teachers and students. These measures must include explicitly raising issues of differences, similarities, and misunderstandings; helping students understand the process of getting to know each other; paying close attention to the types of interaction students are having with one another; and creating meaningful interaction that helps students understand each other.

Regardless of good intentions, and exhortations to students to work together and respect each other, true change only occurs when opportunities to see and participate in respectful and empowering interaction are provided.

Decision Questions. What direct planning is there for successful cross-cultural interaction? How is respect for students' language(s) and culture(s) evident in the school? How are students engaged in understanding their place in the broader society?

Premise 11—Sociocultural and Political Implications

Sociocultural factors and political context must be considered in making decisions regarding every aspect of program planning.

The status of students' languages, circumstances of their incorporation into the country, and race relations in the community are all examples of external factors that impact students' and teachers' behaviors and attitudes. Hidden messages about which language/culture is viewed as having status are sent through the use of each language (Commins & Miramontes, 1989; Corson, 1990; Shannon; 1990) through grouping strategies (McGill-Frazen & Allington, 1993; Oakes, 1985; Sizer, 1984), and through the content of curriculum (Banks, 1994; Freire, 1985). Whether the primary language is used for instruction or simply for discipline, for example, conveys to students their teachers' values and expectations about that language. In a climate where English is promoted to the extent that all other languages are discredited, many students quickly get the message that their home language is of little or no value in school or in the broader society. Older students especially may initially reject instruction in the primary language, believing that it is insufficient for academic topics. Although we are fond of telling students how wonderful it is to be bilingual, and how proud they should be of their home language and culture, the structures of school and of society send a much more powerful message negating our words. Only by actively restructuring the environment in which students have to function do we have a chance to show that all those words may hold some truth.

The particular circumstances that necessitate the learning of a second language shape and influence students' motivation to learn the target language. The sociopolitical context, specifically the economic and social conditions in which learners find themselves, has a direct bearing on the acquisition process. This encompasses the power relations between the cultures of first and second language groups, including such factors as social dominance, integration patterns, how tightly knit each group is, how similar or different the cultures are, and the general attitudes of each group toward the other.

An important factor in this milieu is the significant gap between the public school population, which is minority, and the prospective teacher population, which is almost exclusively white, female, middle-class, and monolingual (American Association of Colleges for Teacher Education [AACTE], 1988). This plays out in the distance between teachers and students and their parents, and reinforces the idea that the few bilingual teachers available must be utilized judiciously in schools. It also highlights the fact that monolingual English-speaking teachers must be more actively involved in the effective education of the students they serve. Professional education must extend teachers' knowledge of first and second language acquisition, as well as their understanding of, and ability to work effectively with, students who are ethnically, culturally, and socioeconomically different from themselves (Liston & Zeichner, 1991). However, for many prospective teachers culture is a foreign concept. As one prospective teacher put it:

> I never thought of myself as having a culture. I always thought that I belonged to the dominant power group, and as such other groups possessed a culture. The word culture had a negative connotation to me because having a culture meant that you were not part of the dominant power group. Culture to me had more to do with skin color. Since I was part of the dominant power group, I always felt superior to those with a culture. I always thought that those with a culture felt inferior to the dominant power group. (Miramontes, Liston, & Fletcher, in preparation, p. 19)

The implications of this perspective about culture (and, by implication, language) seem fairly clear. This individual would consider culture and cultural activities compensatory, necessary only to make the inferior group feel better about itself. Although perhaps representing an extreme position, such attitudes about culture, language, and class clearly exist within a sociopolitical framework that supports these notions (see Chapter 1).

Because of the wide variety of experiences, values, and attitudes of school personnel, few decisions made in schools are easy. And yet the schooling of students requires constant decision making on the part of teachers—decision making that reflects their particular value positions. Even no decision is a decision. Often, it is the decision to abdicate responsibility for addressing the educational needs of linguistically diverse students. Critically, all decisions have direct consequences in the academic life of students.

Decision Questions. What are the attitudes of teachers, staff, and community with regard to language, culture, ethnicity, and social class? What attitudes and values do school policies and practices reflect? What opportunities exist for members of the school community to critically share, explore, and discuss the attitudes and values represented?

Premise 12—Teachers as Decision Makers

Teachers are decision makers. As part of a learning community they are all equally responsible for decisions regarding the instructional program for linguistically diverse students.

In an organization where all members contribute to the decision-making process and where work is accomplished through networks and flexible groups rather than hierarchies, responsibility for outcomes rests with each member, regardless of rank. In schools, this requires that teachers be responsible for the academic achievement of all students. Sharing power and responsibility necessitates a new definition of what it means to be a teacher (Schlechty, 1991).

Judith Warren-Little (1994), suggests that the new role of the teacher must be "grounded in a 'big picture' perspective on the purposes and practices of schooling, providing teachers a means of seeing and acting upon the connections among students' experiences, teachers' classroom practice, and school-wide structures and cultures" (p. 116). This challenges the common practice of treating teachers as individuals whose decisions focus narrowly on their own classrooms, independent of the total school community. The growing diversity of most schools makes the "big picture perspective" even more critical, since varying program interests must be brought together to form a cohesive vision.

Patterson (1994) argues that core values held by an organization are vital to arriving at what he calls fundamental rather than "symptomatic" solutions—band-aid remedies to isolated problems. The typical approach to program planning for English second language learners is to relegate the decision making to special programs people and to view the needs of these students as peripheral to the total school program. In a successful school community, however, teachers must make decisions about all students, regardless of special needs, on the basis of sound pedagogy, and within a perspective of high expectations for all. It is simply not appropriate or feasible for the education of the linguistically diverse students to be exclusively the responsibility of "special" programs (i.e., bilingual, ESL).

Within the context of linguistic diversity, operationalizing this Premise has some significant implications. Within such a shared decision-making process, it becomes possible to see why and how both monolingual and bilingual teachers have very important roles to play in the education of linguistically diverse students. For example, although language competence is a critical aspect in assigning primary language teachers, English monolingual teachers can contribute to students' English language development. If there is no process for nonbilingual staff to interact and help make decisions about linguistically diverse students' programs, we can hardly expect them to become invested in the needs of these students. Therefore, planning for both primary and second language instruction is the responsibility of the total school staff, not just the bilingual teachers. This means the overall literacy and content curriculum for bilingual learners is part of the school's overall curriculum, and at the same time, the overall school curriculum reflects the needs of bilingual students. The whole school is accountable for organizational planning that effectively mobilizes the necessary resources, staff, and materials to provide the best program for these students.

To say that teachers are decision makers with responsibility for aspects of the instructional program also means that helping second language learners develop English language skills is the responsibility of general education classroom teachers. This requires that monolingual English teachers incorporate second language acquisition strategies into their repertoire of practices. Asking teachers to take on the role of decision makers and to gain a broad perspective with regard to diversity requires a major shift in teacher preparation, as well as in how teachers view themselves and how they are viewed. Professional development programs, both pre-service and in-service, must provide ongoing opportunities for individuals to refine their "intellectual skill" and not just their skills as "technicians." This means opportunities must be provided to collaborate, to investigate, and to reflect on practice.

Warren-Little (1994) outlines several key practices and principles for the kind of professional development necessary for teachers to become decision makers within the reform context. She frames these principles as alternatives to the traditional training model. They embody a vision for professional development that engages teachers in intellectual and emotional practices both in and out of education, and provides ongoing opportunities for focus groups, collaboration, and networks that help teachers always see their practices in context. This development would foster the notion of dissent as leading to consensus building. Finally, it would place teachers at the center of the broader community, focusing them on introspection and inquiry. Contexts would be created in which they act as leaders and are accountable for the success of all students in their school community.

The inquiry process in staff development, teachers as learners and researchers (Sagor, 1993), implies that professional education must include an examination of beliefs about linguistic and cultural diversity, bilingualism, and the sociocultural and political context of the school community. This must be accompanied by authentic opportunities and the power to make effective program decisions. Through such a process teachers have the opportunity to see themselves as real agents of change—at the center of the process, rather than on its periphery. Ultimately, accepting responsibility results in being intimately involved in the decision-making process. The essence of this book is to provide educators both the theoretical framework and the decision-making tools necessary to establish a process whereby all the members of a school can work together to reach common goals of linguistically diverse students.

Decision Questions. Who makes decisions about second language learners in the school? How are programs for linguistically diverse students viewed within the context of the total school? How are regular classroom teachers who are monolingual in English involved in the decisions about second language programs? What resources and support do teachers need to take on new roles?

PROGRAM CATEGORIES

The Basic Premises discussed above provide the framework for translating theory into practice. Given the fact that student populations and the availability of resources will vary from school to school, decision making for program development should focus on how to best match the needs of the students and community with the resources available to meet those needs.

The differences among programs for linguistically diverse students are mainly determined by the level of primary language support students receive. Based on this, we have identified four different program categories that are distinguished by this variability in the use of students' primary language for instruction. Categories range from programs that provide full primary language (L1) support in school to those that provide none. These categories serve as guidelines for deciding what type of program will best serve the needs of the students in a particular school, and will be utilized throughout the rest of the book. They are: Category I: Full primary language foundation; Category II, Primary language support—literacy only; Category III, Primary language content reinforcement—no literacy; Category IV, all-English.

In most cases decisions will revolve around whether, given their circumstances, schools can provide a Category I or II program or a Category III or IV program. Given the range of populations and resources in some schools, it may be necessary to provide different levels of service for different linguistic groups, depending on student numbers, available instructors, materials, and so forth. For example, it may not be possible to provide the same kind of primary language support to all groups in the school population. The inability to serve all language groups fully, however, should not be the criterion for deciding to underserve particular groups at the maximum level resources allow. This is no different from the many other resource-allocation decisions that are made daily in schools. For example, a school staff would rarely make the decision to have no computers because it was not possible to give all students full access to them. Instead, they would find a way to maximize the experiences of all students with the computers available. Access to the primary language is much more fundamental to learning than is access to computers.

The program categories provide a way to focus the decision-making process on potential outcomes. Within a dynamic system of program development, enhancing programs is an ongoing process as needs and resources shift. Each category of program requires adherence to the Basic Premises of instruction if it is to help linguistically diverse students succeed academically.

Category I: Full Primary Language Foundation

Category I programs offer students full development of the primary language both for literacy and across content areas. Such programs are often tied to goals of expanded bilingualism, sometimes allowing 6 to 7 years or more for bilingual development. Sharing the goal of a strong primary language foundation, but *not* a vision for substantive bilingualism, other Category I programs (often called early exit) are on a more restricted time line, working to develop a firm foundation in students' primary language over a shorter period of time and requiring students to function completely in English more quickly (for example, with a minimum of kindergarten through third grade for elementary age children).

There are a variety of ways language and time can be organized using the Basic Premises as a guiding framework for decision making. A Category I program may be for second language speakers of English alone, or it may have as a goal bilingualism for all students, both native and second language speakers of English. Within two-way programs, all students become bilingual and biliterate across content areas. Because they address a broad variety of sociopolitical, curricular, and cross-cultural issues, these types of bilingual programs tend to provide the greatest opportunity for success (Collier, 1995).

Both long- and short-term Category I programs work best when there are sufficient numbers of students from a single non–English group, sufficient numbers of teachers who are fluent in the language of that group, and appropriate materials for both literacy and content instruction in both languages. In every type of Category I program, primary language development should be complemented by a strong second language component.

Category II: Primary Language Support—Literacy Only

With fewer resources, that is, fewer staff who speak the primary language of the students, and/or smaller numbers of students in any given primary language, a full primary language program across all curriculum areas may not be possible. In a Category II program, the primary language is used to develop strong basic literacy and academic thinking skills. Students learn to read, write, and explore new concepts in their primary language in order to provide a strong foundation for the eventual transition into all-English instruction.

Several conditions are necessary to be able to offer a Category II program. First, a substantial amount of time (at least two hours per day) must be provided for content-based literacy and language arts. This period of time must include a strong oral language development component, as well as reading and writing activities. A thematic approach and a strong second language component are also critical, especially because other areas of the curriculum will be taught only in English. The possibility of integrating content themes into literacy instruction is important, and sufficient materials must be available. Using a thematic approach allows for the organization of content in such a way that new concepts learned during the primary language time can be reinforced in all-English instruction and supported by English as a second language lessons (see Chapters 4, 5, and 6). Certificated staff with strong primary language and literacy skills must be available for instruction. Category II programs may be appropriate in schools where there are substantial but not large numbers of students from one or more languages other than English.

Category III: Primary Language Content Reinforcement—No Literacy

Primary language literacy development is not usually viable if only an hour or so of support during the day can be provided. With significantly limited resources in terms of primary language personnel, or with limited materials for literacy development, other ways in which the primary language can support the thinking life of the students must be found. Using the primary language for its greatest benefit to second language students, then, requires considering what it can offer as a tool for thinking and learning and how it can be used to help students connect new ideas to previous learning and experiences at home and outside of school.

A strong option in supporting critical thinking skills is to focus on content areas. In a Category III program the primary language is used to develop an understanding of the significant ideas related to content knowledge. In this way, the primary language can be utilized to link prior knowledge and experience to the content of the academic curriculum. Ideas and concepts that are abstract in nature and tied to critical thinking questions such as why, what if, and so forth; require a good deal of language to be explored. Although it does not involve literacy, Category III represents a substantial commitment in terms of daily instructional time, careful planning, and resources for concept development in the primary language.

A Category III program can be appropriate in a school where there are fewer than 14 students who are second language learners, across a grade level or multiple grades, or where there are several language groups represented in sufficient numbers to allow for groupings within or across several grade levels. In schools where resources and personnel are limited, a Category III program may be more appropriate than a Category II program for older students who already have a strong foundation in literacy in their primary language, supporting them in dealing with the ever more complex demands of the academic curriculum.

Category III programs are organized to ensure that students have well-planned, guided, daily instruction in their primary language. They may, in some cases, depend on the use of noncertificated personnel (paraprofessionals, native language tutors, or qualified community members). In such cases, providing instruction requires that certificated personnel be in charge of organizing and guiding these instructional services. These programs require flexibility in scheduling and a schoolwide planning process that allows for the concentration of resources to assure primary language support for as many students as possible. For example, students might need to be grouped across grade levels for primary language time. Or, if there is only one staff member who speaks the particular primary language, that staff member's time would be best utilized by concentrating on teaching in that language.

Finally, as discussed in Chapter 4, it is necessary to determine the way in which languages are used in students' homes and communities. If language loss is a factor, adjustments for using the primary language for reinforcement will have to be made.

Category IV: All-English

In a Category IV program, instruction is delivered completely in English with little or no opportunity to use the primary language in school. In all-English instruction, the strategies that can be used to foster second language development, such as sheltered methods and approaches to literacy development become the core of the program. These are discussed fully in Chapter 5. What is important to remember here is that an all-English program requires careful, long-range planning since it will take longer to bear results for most students. The success of the program will also depend on unqualified support for parents to speak to students in their most proficient language, the language of the home.

Although in a Category IV program there is no opportunity for consistent primary language development in school, the primary language still plays a major role in students' cognitive and affective lives, and ways should be actively sought to support it. In an all-English program, school or community resources may allow students to work with a primary language speaker of their language on a limited basis. This primary language reinforcement might be possible only at a minimal level, say 15–30 minutes three times per week. But even these limited resources can be very important in supporting academic development if used appropriately by focusing discussions on linking new to previous knowledge, and by extending students' thinking. The purpose of this time should be made absolutely clear. Using these resources for "quick-fix" translations or simply to catch up on homework can waste this opportunity. Instead, this time should be used to discuss, develop, and extend academic topics in the students' native language. In this way, students have a chance to access their underlying conceptual knowledge about the content, and to develop a sound understanding of the material.

In addition to what can be done in school, consideration must be given to how the primary language can be used to its full advantage outside of school. This requires that teachers give strong and specific encouragement to non-English speaking parents about their special role in helping their children achieve academic success. Parents and community members should be called on to help strengthen students' conceptual understanding in the primary language. This can be facilitated by informing them of content topics and providing them with suggestions about the kinds of discussions and questions that can be useful.

CONCLUSION

Throughout the rest of this book, we will analyze the implications for decision making of each aspect of program development in relationship to these four program categories. The implications of the Basic Premises across curriculum areas will be discussed as they are applied and analyzed for each type of first and second language resource. In addition, ways of organizing instruction for each program category will be presented in each chapter.

As you embark on the process of program improvement, it is critical to remember that the quality and effectiveness of the program will depend on two major factors. The first is the participants' adherence to the basic principles of teaching, learning, and language acquisition as outlined in the Basic Premises. The second is on the level of cooperation, coordination, and teamwork among school staff. The next chapter provides the framework for how to go about establishing procedures for working together to meet the goals of improved educational outcomes for linguistically diverse students.

CHAPTER 3

Decision-Making Framework

Basic premises have been presented as the cornerstones of programs for linguistically diverse students. As stated in assumption 9, the premises are pedagogical principles arising from a theoretical framework, and hold true for all students. Later in this chapter, there will be a detailed discussion of the importance of establishing a vision for schoolwide programs. For schools with linguistically diverse students, the premises form essential elements of the vision, along with the elements for successful action. The premises, however, cannot be applied or realized in actual programs without the inclusion of a framework for decision making. This chapter will provide such a framework.

Current movements for educational reform are energetically pursuing the agenda of systemic change in education from the perspective of school-level autonomy. These movements reflect the feelings of a society that views schooling as failing most students. At the same time, there is a growing realization that with the dramatic increase in the diversity of school populations, educational institutions are not effectively including disenfranchised groups, such as linguistically diverse students, in the mainstream of American education. The decision-making process presented here derives from these perspectives and suggests a process that can support substantive change.

At the very heart of this process is the notion that those who are responsible for providing the services within an organization should be part of the decision making about what they do. This means that school staff should have the responsibility and support to organize and implement programs for students. The goal of this chapter, therefore, is to provide the reader with the strategies needed to participate in this type of decision-making process. A perspective on change will be discussed, followed by key strategies fundamental to successful decision making. These strategies will first be explored by providing the reader with concrete examples pertinent to the education of linguistically diverse students.

Programs for linguistically diverse students fall along a continuum from the extreme of no identifiable organizational structure for second language instruction to a full two-way bilingual program with the goal of developing bilingualism and biliteracy for both native and second language speakers of English. Schools interested in beginning a new program, or improving an existing one, may be tempted to select a "model" along the continuum as the way to start. This may be particularly appealing since until now program models have been the major vehicle for discussions of bilingual and second language programs. There is a growing awareness, however, that a models approach to designing programs for this ever-growing population of students is inadequate. In a project conducted for the State of California, Berman et al. (1992) concluded that although there are broad models that can help guide the development of programs for linguistically diverse students, they are insufficient for the diversity of settings and needs of this population of students.

> The challenge is deeper than a simple choice of one model or another. The study found that the same model for the education of [limited-English-proficiency] students was implemented in different ways in different schools. The . . . models were not templates for replication, but rather a combination of programmatic decisions. . . . The challenge for schools was to adapt the program they had chosen—often because of their demographic realities to fit the needs of their students and their resources. . . . Rather than asking which model is superior, local stakeholders would identify those conditions under which one or some combination of approaches are best suited and then adapt the models to match their particular circumstances. (p. 7)

Many models do represent sound instructional planning. However, simply selecting a model that is considered exemplary does not guarantee a strong, systematic program. Often the label by which a school identifies its program masks very unsystematic instruction with little attention to sound principles of learning and language development. In addition, trying to fit into a model may discourage newly forming programs that on some intuitive level have begun making good decisions based on the perspectives outlined in the Basic Premises.

Since no one model can be translated directly into a specific setting, and all must be adapted to the population and context of the school, it becomes critical for educators to be able to understand, select, balance, and implement those elements that are fundamentally necessary to the creation of successful programs for linguistically diverse students. The ultimate success of the program will depend on the extent to which a total school staff is intimately involved in the process of decision making, and whether the plan they develop is based on common understandings of learning and language. Ignoring the interaction between the basic premises of learning and language, teacher attitudes and understandings, and particular schoolwide needs can result in developing an inappropriate plan that may isolate linguistically diverse students from the total school community, narrowing their opportunities to succeed.

A CHANGE PERSPECTIVE

Successful decision making within schools implies that the goal of change is improvement, and not simply a reorganization of personnel within existing structures. It is a process of systematically assessing needs and taking action to improve programs. The idea of "action as hypothesis" reflects a process in which action toward change is continually required, and is based on the reevaluation and renegotiation of the schoolwide plan. Within this framework, participation by all members and interaction between individuals and the team are paramount. Change must be systemic and pervasive. Real change will affect all members of an organization. Individuals are empowered within the organization in relation to how their efforts are directed toward the goal of student achievement. Goals are determined by the whole group and applied schoolwide. The following vignette illustrates this point. It also highlights the role of the formal leader.

Beginning the Change Process

An elementary school staff composed of bilingual and monolingual teachers is discussing ways in which they can provide primary language literacy to more students. There are five or six Spanish-speaking students per grade level, K–6, and currently the school has three teachers who are bilingual.

LEADER (L): OK, let's review why we think it's important to develop primary language.

BILINGUAL TEACHER (BT) 1: Well, we understand that if students develop a strong foundation in their primary language, their English skills will be much stronger.

MONOLINGUAL TEACHER (MT1): But we can't offer it to all of them. There aren't enough students at each grade.

BT2: What about multi-age groupings, with 10–15 per group? We could design a primary language program. Would the nonbilingual teachers be willing to team with us and teach the English curriculum?

BT3: I really don't think I can handle two or three grades—besides I've already got my program and curriculum set for the year.

L: Let's refocus. Why did we come together to discuss this?

MT2: Because we recognize that students are not making sufficient
   progress and need primary language development.
L: OK. What will be the consequences of not reorganizing for primary
   language instruction?
BT1: Students will continue not being successful academically.
BT2: I agree, I don't mind having two grade levels but I really want my
   own class. I'll teach the whole program.
L: Is this a program only to be conducted by the bilingual staff? I
   thought our vision speaks to total staff involvement.

How many of us have found ourselves negotiating between our own
needs and those of our students as in the above dialogue? Accountability for student achievement, however, must be the central concern of
school change, and the goals and programs developed must be generated not by individuals or special-interest groups, but by the team as a
whole, holding itself accountable for the success of all students.

Sticking to the Vision

T1: OK, if I end up with a sheltered class, I'm going to need help.
BT1: It has just occurred to me that we haven't discussed our special
   education students who are linguistically diverse. How will they be
   placed in the program?
RESOURCE SPECIALIST (RS): What do you mean? They have to have
   what is on their IEP!
T3: Doesn't our vision say for *all* students? And, don't the Premises
   apply to *all* our second language learners, including those with
   learning disabilities or other handicapping conditions?
LEADER (L): I think Teacher 3's point is well taken. Let's discuss ways
   that we can provide special services and also keep the program
   we've agreed to intact.
SPECIAL DAY CLASS TEACHER (SDCT): For one thing, I don't see why
   the special education students should not be able to receive
   primary language instruction just like the other students.
RS: The consultation team can indicate the need for primary language
   instruction on the IEP or a goal, but what about ESL? I have only so
   much time with the students.
T1: Remember, they will be getting all of their basic instruction
   through the sheltered program.
RS: Oh, that's right.
L: [to Special Day Class Teacher] Do you think you or your aide could
   do the ESL instruction within your program, or should your three
   students join a regular class for ESL?

T4: I think that since we are also striving for more interaction among students, the three special day class students should come into one of our classes for ESL.

SDCT: Between primary language and ESL, that might be too much moving around for these students.

L: Obviously, we have gotten to the point that we are able to make these decisions together and we are really trying to stick to our vision, so I think we can work this out through the consultation team process.

The successful organization is one in which the individual's goals and those of the organization are the same, and the successful leader always keeps that in mind.

KEY STRATEGIES IN THE DECISION-MAKING PROCESS

Inherent in the decision-making process are several key strategies that will be explored in depth. These strategies are basic to the process of change and provide a shift in paradigm relative to how school personnel view decision making. This shift in thinking goes from a very traditional view, where stakeholders (those with a vested interest in education) merely provide input to the person or persons with ultimate responsibility, to the more recent trends toward shared decision making.

Needs Assessment

A commonly accepted first step in a decision-making process is the compilation of data, facts, and materials that lay out the existing situation and generate central questions for reflection and action. For example: Why do we want to change? How are certain groups of students performing relative to the general population? Are these measures accurate? Do linguistically diverse students and their parents feel connected to the school? What do the results of attendance records, surveys, and so forth, demonstrate?

A comprehensive needs assessment is required in order to take the next step of establishing a vision. Although the focus of strategic planning may be on decisions regarding programs for particular groups such as linguistically diverse students, all of the steps must actively involve the entire school community. Student outcomes and expectations are developed so that no group of students is marginalized and high standards of performance are set for all. This is basic to having a decision-making process that affects the whole school, not just bilingual or ESL programs. Only then can all students be seen as equal on a developmental continuum, and as being the responsibility of the total staff.

A comprehensive view of student assets and needs requires a wide variety of data. The kind of data that staff must generate to accommodate this perspective should reflect the actual work of students and includes written and oral samples, projects, exhibitions, and observational records. In order for staff to gain a true picture of how the school is performing in terms of student achievement, these data must be generated for all students (see Chapter 7). In addition to student performance data, information for the needs assessment should include what all stakeholders—staff, parents, and the nonschool community—expect for students, as well as what they see as their role in the school. Other indicators of the current situation include such data as attendance figures, dropout rate, tracking information, and satisfaction surveys.

Establishing a Vision

A vision is a statement that reflects the dream a school holds for its students. It gives direction and is all-encompassing. It should be based on sound principles of learning and express the foundation and direction of the entire program. If the vision is comprehensive, it will set the stage for all the school's goals. Throughout the development of the vision for a school with linguistically diverse students, the Basic Premises become the guide, and help generate such questions as: How do linguistically diverse students fit into the general scheme of curriculum, assessment, and noncurricular activities? What does a developmental process imply for the inclusion or separation of special-needs students? How is the staff organized to support first and second language instruction? Although a vision reflects a dream, by basing it on sound principles of learning, it is attainable.

A common error made in education is for schools to work out a vision without addressing the assumptions or belief systems held by staff members, or failing to fully consider the implications of stated beliefs. For example, vision statements often include the belief that "all students can learn." To effect successful change, it is important to understand what people believe this statement means, and to determine whether it is a shared meaning. It is also important to understand how this belief plays out in day-to-day school interactions.

In order for staff to articulate a clear vision that all can commit to, time must be set aside for an open and continuous dialogue about what all staff (not just teachers) believe about students, schooling, and the social issues surrounding schools. Discussions regarding assumptions held about students who speak a language or languages other than English should include questions such as the following: Do we believe *all* students can learn and that they can learn to high standards? Does this mean that we have the same expectations in all areas of the curriculum for linguistically diverse students as we do for native English-speaking students? What are our beliefs about the English-only position as a political and social issue? How does this affect our programs? What are our assumptions about undocumented immigrants? Do these immigrant parents have the same educational expectations for their children as any other parents? Do these children have the same rights as citizens to receive an education? These and many more beliefs must be thoroughly explored. An open and nonthreatening discussion of these issues can often allow people to see their own beliefs in a different light, and to test them against those of others. Major or minor shifts in thinking can occur, particularly when staff members don't see themselves "out on a limb," but are part of a collaborative process. Risk-taking becomes less risky.

The following example provides insight into some relevant issues that may arise during the process of establishing a vision. Staff, both certificated and paraprofessional, are exploring issues as they begin developing a vision statement. After they have thought through their vision, their plan is to create an entirely new program. Their school includes large numbers of linguistically diverse students.

Establishing a Vision

LEADER (L) [at chart]: We had some discussion last time about why we want to change our program and decided we were ready to develop our vision statement. Any ideas? I'll write them all down, then we can begin to reorganize them into a coherent statement.

TEACHER (T) 1: Well, I'm sure we want to say that we believe all children can learn.

T2: But before we say that, don't we need to know what that means?

T3: What about those students who come in at the fourth to sixth grades—they don't speak English and they often haven't had much schooling?

T4: Well they can still learn.

PARAPROFESSIONAL (PP) 1: We should have high expectations for all students.

T3: Well, I sure don't want to be held accountable for those students I was talking about.

T5: When will students be moving into English? It had better be quick if we are setting high expectations in English.

PP2: Frankly, I don't think the bilingual program has been very suc-
      cessful—besides these kids are going to need to function in English
      in the real world.
L: We are here because we realize our program needs to change, but
    what does that say about primary language development and our
    expectations?
T1: I thought we covered that ground. I mean, isn't there a consensus
     here that primary language development is necessary for high-level
     English proficiency?

The above dialogue demonstrates that people can come together with
a strong commitment to change and ready to state a vision for that change,
but as personal beliefs are revealed it becomes apparent that individual
perceptions are quite different about what such statements signify. For
example, several teachers apparently believed all children could learn
but the specifics of expectation levels and issues such as accountability,
age, primary language instruction, and time frame for transition to English
became roadblocks to building a consensus.

Once an open and thorough examination of belief systems has been
achieved, the building of a vision can begin. But coming up with a statement is not the final step. Take, for example, the following vision a staff
developed for their middle school of 700 students, 50% of whom are linguistically diverse and who speak three languages other than English.

The staff and parents of SS school will provide a developmentally appropriate curriculum in which all students will achieve to their maximum potential. We will ensure that all linguistically diverse students
achieve high levels of bilingualism and that opportunities will be available throughout the three years of middle school for native English-
speaking students to develop proficiency in Spanish.

Now, reread the vision statement, considering the following questions:

1. Is the vision statement comprehensive?
2. Does it address the needs of all students? How?
3. What are the implications for program design?
4. What does providing a developmentally appropriate curriculum
for all students require in terms of reorganizing service delivery, staffing,
curriculum?
5. What provisions are made for language groups other than Spanish?
6. What are the implications for class assignment of students given
the goal of developing full bilingualism for Spanish-speaking students?
Spanish proficiency for English-speaking students?

7. Are there any considerations regarding texts and materials?

8. What are the implications that students will perform academically to their maximum potential have for grouping, tracking, remediation, and labeling of students?

As is obvious, there are many aspects and many ramifications to creating a sound vision that holds true for all students in a school.

Strategic Planning

Answering questions such as the ones posed above allows change to proceed. During the next stage, known as strategic planning, the program and curricular goals are developed, as is the design of the overall program. A solid strategic-planning process might take several months, with several small groups working simultaneously to come up with suggestions for a plan.

Several process skills are important in strategic planning in order to ensure the ongoing communication needed to build a cohesive staff. A necessary step on the road to realizing a solid vision is *brainstorming*. This is a technique that allows all participants to get the message that all ideas are of value. Brainstorming provides the opportunity for a free flow of information and ideas. However, this is not a "gripe" session or a mere oral interchange. All dialogue forms the basis for potential decisions. No suggestion can be rejected out of hand, and every idea is recorded on paper and posted for ongoing review and continued discussion.

Also critical to the entire process is the strategy of *consensus building*. This is a process by which decisions are made through mutual agreement and compromise (consensus), not through voting. It is essential that staff learn to clearly differentiate between the two. To vote means that potentially 51% agree on a decision but 49% remain opposed. This indicates that nearly half the staff would be in opposition to changes they might feel were imposed on them by a slim majority. The usual result is that changes fail due to lack of support and buy-in.

In the process of strategic planning, as brainstorming evolves into the task of developing program goals and design, all transcriptions from small-group work are consolidated. The initial overlap of decisions becomes the first step in consensus building. As the process continues with the recording of ideas, the staff comes to understand that compromise around ideas *is* the consensus. In this consensus-based model, all members of an organization learn to make decisions based on a vision, for the good of all, not just for one's friends or group. Arriving at consensus demonstrates professionalism and a commitment to predetermined student needs and goals.

Throughout this process it is also important to understand various dimensions of *group dynamics*. Constant grouping and regrouping of decision makers is a process that promotes changing group dynamics. As part of this process, ineffective leaders are often neutralized and new and productive leaders emerge, and alliances and coalitions are formed across concerns. Initially, groups can be assigned and reassigned so that the ideas of all individuals are validated across various settings. Later, as more ownership is taken for the vision, individuals will begin to group themselves by tasks, curricular areas, or level designations. The brief dialogue that follows illustrates the consensus-building process.

Building Consensus

The staff of a school with a majority of linguistically diverse students speaking several different languages has spent much time working out a vision that promotes high expectations for all students. Primary language development is possible only for some language groups, and the staff has made a commitment to a comprehensive English language program for all students. Four different groups of staff members are working on program design plans and recording these plans on chart paper. The transcriptions are then consolidated. Staff are now reviewing the consensus of ideas. The chart reflects the following list: (1) a sheltered English program; (2) multi-age groupings K–6; (3) staff agreement to teach these classes; (4) primary language aides (presently tutoring in individual classrooms) formed into a primary language cadre under the supervision of a resource teacher to offer primary language reinforcement on a scheduled basis.

TEACHER (T) 1: Well, I agree with the idea of providing sheltered English classes, but I don't want to teach one.

T2: Neither do I.

T3: OK everyone. We decided we'd do this—some people are going to have to teach these classes.

LEADER (L): Let's define consensus. We've agreed on a program. How do we balance our own personal desires with our goals?

T4: How about a survey? Everyone gets a first, second, and third choice. Then we'll all look at what the results are and decide what the assignments will be. People may not get their first choice this time.

T1: Well I guess that's fair. I'll teach a sheltered class if it comes to that but I just don't feel I have the skills.

L: What can we do to support people who need training? [Teachers 5, 6, 7 share ideas for several minutes.] Do we have a consensus then about the sheltered program? [There is general agreement among the staff.]

T2: I did not vote for this and I don't think I should have to change my assignment.

L: You may not have to, but if that becomes necessary you may need to compromise and go along with what the group has decided.

T2: OK, if I end up with a sheltered class I'm going to need help.

Leadership

In a shared decision-making process based on building consensus, the traditional role of the leader as the ultimate authority obviously must shift. Leadership remains a critical element within this decision-making model; however, the potential for taking leadership goes far beyond an individual, extending throughout the system, thereby fostering greater participation. The role of the formal leader is to continuously model participatory management skills, facilitate team building and conflict resolution, and continuously define consensus. However, leadership within a schoolwide decision-making process is not confined to the formal leader, but should be nurtured in as many people as possible. As leadership expands, the potential for support, assistance, and training increases dramatically.

In the shift from the top-down manager to the role of instructional leader in a shared decision-making process, many school principals have begun to fear that they will be reduced to mere facilitators. Much of the thinking about changes in the definition of leadership remains at the level of "power shifts" rather than at the level of collaboration with a focus on students and learning. True leaders in a school become effective through influence rather than through control and they must have the confidence to set high expectations and continuously uphold the vision. A firm grasp of curricular issues, such as those reflected in the Basic Premises, is also very important. In the beginning, the formal leader is the "keeper of the dream." As more and more ownership is taken, many more leaders emerge, and ultimately most staff will be able to clearly and strongly support and articulate the vision.

Conflict Resolution

Conflict is a fact of life and conflict resolution is central to the decision-making process when true and important change is occurring. For change to be successful, some preparation for the psychology of change must take place. Staff members who have traditionally functioned in a very compartmentalized, top-down environment will be asked to *express themselves*, *share ideas and time*, and *often subordinate* their own personal goals to the goals of the team. This can cause tension that results in conflict.

The discussion of conflict resolution also involves the governance structure of schools. In any shared decision-making process, a system for how decisions will be made and guidelines for participation and for how conflicts will be resolved are required. This is the essence of what is called governance. All staff, both certificated and paraprofessional, as well as parents and interested community members, must have access to both *formal and informal means for solving problems*. It is important that resolution of these *conflicts be linked to the vision* that has been created. That is not to say that conflicts revolving around the use of the copy machines, for example, won't arise or cannot be dealt with because there is no perceived direct link to the vision. Rather, it is understood that *conflicts must be dealt with at all levels*, but their resolution should not interfere with or refocus the staff away from its more important overall task of improving instruction.

A pitfall to creating a new governance structure is that often the development of such structures becomes the central focus of change efforts, overshadowing more serious instructional and curricular change. When the process of *change remains focused on students and learning*, however, the governance structure will evolve from students' needs, and derive its existence from the vision. Rather than driving the process, it becomes a support.

As reflected above, planning and implementing programs for linguistically diverse students require a rethinking of the usual ways of doing business in schools. Substantive change in instruction for linguistically diverse students can be accomplished only when it is addressed as a total school responsibility. It may seem to be an overwhelming process, but it must be viewed as one that occurs over time and continuously evolves. Given that the leadership and most school/community members hold true to the vision, the process of consensus building and ownership for the vision becomes more and more manageable. The decision-making process reflected in this chapter is not an all-or-nothing enterprise. It may begin with one staff member seeking out and linking up with one other colleague. The discussions and consensus between these two colleagues can spread to others if these educators have a commitment to change and are guided by a strong framework such as the one presented by the Basic Premises.

FITTING THE PARTS TOGETHER

The decision-making process that forms the basis of the book is part of a comprehensive framework that guides program planning for the education of linguistically diverse students. It is constituted of four critical elements: a vision for schoolwide reform, the Basic Premises for first and second language instruction, key areas for reform, and tools for the decision-making process.

The important interrelationships between the critical elements can perhaps best be understood using the analogy of a building. The *vision* for schoolwide reform forms the frame of the building, the structure that supports the entire building. The focus of the vision is the achievement of all students. All stakeholders—teachers, parents, classified staff, and the entire school community—will be included in this vision. All aspects of the organization are examined in the quest to fulfill the vision.

The *Basic Premises* for first and second language instruction are the foundation for the building. These pedagogical principles are the non-negotiable underpinnings of programs for linguistically diverse students. As we have discussed in the previous section, the quest for excellence that makes up the vision depends on having a strong foundation in teaching and learning, one that is grounded in research and practical wisdom related directly to second language acquisition and bilingualism.

The *key areas for reform* are the main walls within the structure. They include areas to which reform must be targeted if the frame is to be more than an empty shell. These areas include teaching and learning, organization, assessment, and processes for decision making. Changing any one area alone will not effect the needed changes. It is only working to re-form all areas in concert that provides the inner walls necessary to make the building livable.

The *decision-making process* itself holds the structure together, and serves as the glue or nails. No reform effort, even one that is grounded in powerful beliefs and vision, can sustain itself without a decision-making process that has ongoing action as its operative phrase. Ongoing action implies a system of activity that is consistently driven by the vision. It incorporates the pedagogical principles and comprises all of the practices that are critical to the reform. This results in day-to-day actions that follow a process for making decisions that all members of the organization can identify with and use.

This building analogy highlights the critical relationship these factors have to one another. A building with a serious weakness in any of the elements of its design may stand erect initially, but with time will deteriorate to a point where it is finally unrecognizable. Similarly, an educational reform process may appear initially to be an inspiring innovation, but will be unable to sustain itself if all of the factors discussed above are not operating in concert. In many schools with a large number of linguistically diverse students, staff members decide to undertake a comprehensive reform effort. They often adopt a vision that appears to be comprehensive, inclusive, and based on the belief that all students can reach high levels of performance, even though they do not ground their vision on any principles pertaining to linguistically diverse students. They assume that the innovations they have embraced will apply to all students. The staff and community may indeed have examined all of the key practices and have managed to incorporate major changes in these practices. But, because premises for bilingual learners have not been incorporated into the design, many linguistically diverse students will not be successful. This, in turn, has the effect of discouraging the innovators, since the success of the reform is highly dependent on the high achievement of students at specified benchmarks. In all of the planning and actual implementation, however, the stakeholders have failed to include any specific decision-making strategies that will aide them on a day-to-day basis to ensure the staying power of the reform. What will happen here as they attempt to sustain their efforts?

Part II, Premises in Practice, examines the five critical areas in which decision making will occur: primary language development, second language development, curriculum and content development, assessment, and community outreach. The strategies that will be developed in the following chapters not only focus on the improvement of instruction within existing staffing patterns and institutional structures but, more importantly, present guidelines for the rethinking of staffing patterns and program structures that can lead to better organization and use of resources. A decision-making framework based on a sound educational understanding of first and second language acquisition and interaction holds the key to successful planning for the academic success of linguistically diverse learners.

PART II

Premises in Practice

CHAPTER 4

Primary Language Development

Key Premises to Consider

• *Premise 1—Active Learning.* Knowledge is best acquired when learners actively participate in meaningful activities that are constructive in nature and appropriate to their level of development.

• *Premise 2—The primary language foundation.* The more comprehensive the use of the primary language, the greater the potential for linguistically diverse students to be academically successful. There are always ways to nurture the primary language regardless of school resources.

• *Premise 3—The quality of primary language use.* There is a difference between a token use of the primary language in instruction and its full development as a foundation for thinking and learning.

• *Premise 6—First and second language environments.* Bilingual academic proficiency requires that clear, distinct, and meaning-enriched contexts for each language be created during instructional time.

This chapter examines some of the major issues surrounding the importance and use of the primary language in the instruction of linguistically diverse students. Where primary language support is available, decision making for the use of first language resources must be carefully planned. Where little or no primary language instruction is possible at school, the use of specific second language methods can help students access information and concepts. For the variety of reasons discussed throughout the book, programs in which substantial periods of time can be provided in the primary language, if done well, create the best foundation for academic learning.

Major issues surrounding the education of linguistically diverse students in school revolve around whether they should be afforded the opportunity to receive native language instruction and, if so, how the students' two languages should be used in instruction, and for how long. The first major decision in program planning for linguistically diverse students obviously is whether the primary language will be used in instruction. How this decision is reached, how the primary language is perceived, and the reasons and understandings accompanying this decision will make the difference between a program in which the primary language is developed as a strong language foundation leading to academic success and one in which it is used merely as a token. This language-use decision sets the stage for all the other decisions that are critical in the direction and tone of programs.

Decision Making: Ask Yourself

Will the primary language be used in instruction? If so, how?
Who should receive primary language instruction?
How will the primary language be used to greatest advantage?
What Category of program can be offered?
How can the curriculum and linguistic resources be organized most
    effectively?
How will quality be assured?

PERSPECTIVES ON PRIMARY LANGUAGE DEVELOPMENT

As discussed in Chapters 1 and 2, language plays a vital role in the development and socialization of all humans. Its role in learning is particularly important because language is integral to our dialogue for thinking, problem solving, and understanding (Mead, 1977; Vygotsky, 1978). It not only contributes to the development of thought and mind, but is also an important factor in more abstract levels of thinking. Reflecting on the critical role of language, and how thought and words are related, Vygotsky states: "A word devoid of thought is a dead thing, and a thought unembodied in words remains a shadow. The connection between them, however, is not a pre-formed and constant one. It emerges in the course of development and itself evolves" (1978, p. 23). In school—a highly verbal environment—interference in the process of language acquisition can have adverse effects on students' academic progress.

As they enter school, all children (except those who have experienced extreme circumstances of deprivation) bring with them cognitive, linguistic, and social knowledge. This includes developed concepts and skills, ways of looking at the world, and a sense of self. For example, by the age of six, most children have the basic phonological, syntactic, and semantic skills acquired by most native speakers (Saville-Troike, 1979). They have also developed the basic foundation of language, with a minimum of 17,250 hours of listening to their native language and a significant number of hours verbalizing that language (Asher, 1982). The concepts and skills children bring are encoded in the language of the home, and embedded within their culture.

Any instructional decision-making process for linguistically diverse students must take into account these basic facts of development. Using one's primary language is the natural process available to all majority monolingual English speakers in this country. For non–English speakers, disregarding such a process creates stumbling blocks and hurdles that can inhibit learning.

To put this in concrete terms, let's say we were temporarily living abroad in China. For most of us, having our monolingual English-speaking children begin initial schooling, including literacy instruction in Chinese, instead of in English, would probably not be considered either acceptable or advisable. Why is this so?

Well, we could argue that our children would not be able to understand the content of instruction, making learning move more slowly and inhibiting their ability to develop academic skills fully. The language and skills the children had learned at home would not easily transfer to school. For example, 6-year-olds would not have access to the knowledge acquired in their 10s of thousands of hours of listening or their oral fluency acquired in the thousands of hours practice in speaking in their primary language, in a Chinese-only classroom. In fact, their primary language skills might even be ignored by their teachers.

It would seem not only unfair but unsound if, in addition to asking our children to begin all their learning in Chinese, the Chinese teachers taught them as if they were native speakers of Chinese (that is, assuming the same level of background and experience in the language as they do for native speakers). We would probably consider it unjust if the teachers asked our children to compete at the same level as native Chinese speakers, and judged their competence as learners only from a native Chinese language perspective.

Now, if we were confident that we could fully meet our children's English language and academic instructional needs, we might feel that the extra effort on their part would be worth the effort to learn Chinese. But, if we felt that there was a danger that our children would lose their English proficiency, we probably wouldn't risk it. If we had a choice between an all-Chinese language school and an English-language school, then, it is likely that we would choose the latter, eliminating many of the problems of basic understanding and allowing our children to make direct use of the language and thinking tools they had been developing at home. If we, ourselves, spoke little or no Chinese, an all-English environment would also allow us to participate fully in our children's school experiences and learning.

Let's say, however, that we do not have the option of an English-language school for our children, and that we will never be able to return to live in an English-speaking country. What would we want with regard to the education of our children? What would make sense to us? We would probably hope that the methods used for native Chinese speakers would be adjusted for our English-speaking children to ensure that understanding was occurring; that attention was paid to teaching our children to develop the ability to converse and express their ideas in Chinese; that our children be allowed time to work in small groups where they could practice and develop Chinese skills without continually having to compete for the "floor" with Chinese speakers; and that if our children's competence and abilities were being assessed, and judgments were being made about their cognitive and academic potential, the fact that they were in the process of developing language skills in Chinese would be taken into account. Finally we would be very appreciative if the Chinese teachers supported our home and family life with our children and found ways in which we could participate in school learning with our children.

Given these issues, would we think that our children needed these "special" considerations and approaches because they had deficits? Would we consider our children ready to compete on an equal footing with native Chinese speakers in school in 2 years? in 4? in 6? How would we feel if teachers and school officials tried to discourage us from speaking to our children in English, the language in which we were fluent? How would we feel if we were offered the possibility of some instruction in English? How might we hope this instruction would be handled?

As this example illustrates, second language speakers of English don't need primary language instruction because there is something wrong with them. They need it because it provides them the same basic, normal development provided to English-speaking youngsters in English-speaking schools. And, as second language learners they need second language development strategies. Yet bilingual programs that allow full access to cognitive and linguistic development in the first language are considered radical.

Accounting for the Primary Language

Unfortunately, even when educators understand and acknowledge the importance of primary language development, the debate about who should get primary language instruction and for how long continues. Often it is only those students who are clearly monolingual speakers of a language other than English who are considered candidates for primary language instruction. These students, of course, are the most obvious choice. But many other students live in bilingual worlds, and in homes where

English is not the primary language of communication. Although they may have more facility in English than monolingual students, English may not be the language in which they understand most concepts, or in which they relate to new ideas based on their foundation of sounds and meaning. Simple oral fluency in English is not a reliable indicator of the depth of understanding students possess (Cummins, 1986).

In order to make appropriate decisions about the provision of primary language instruction to any student, several important questions must be asked and answered. In which language did initial learning and development take place? What is a student's level of language proficiency across different dimensions of language use (interpersonal vs. academic) in each language? What are a student's schooling and literacy experiences? What is the student's age? What need do students have to develop bilingualism in order to live in their bilingual world?

Students' first language dominance and proficiency are foremost in determining the "who" and "how long" of primary language instruction, but program decisions must also take into account how a primary language program can be arranged to provide maximum benefit to students. These considerations, then, involve where students are beginning and what Category of program the school can offer.

ISSUES ACROSS PROGRAM CATEGORIES

The choice of program category affects all decision making and planning in the primary language. It impacts the strength and soundness of the foundation for academic learning, the organization and allocation of teachers and resources, the nature of transitions to formal English reading, and, where required, the configuration of all English instruction. There are several elements of primary language instruction, however, that hold true across *all* categories: (1) the importance of the first language for all students—across all ages and grade levels; (2) the need for oral language development, across content and over time; (3) a focus on meaning-centered literacy; (4) the constant need to monitor program quality; and (5) the importance of program coherence and coordination.

Primary Language Across the Grades

Although the primary language is important regardless of age, it interacts with the age of students (Lindfors, 1987; McLaughlin, 1984; Wong-Fillmore & Valadez, 1985). At each stage of schooling, the primary language plays a particular role. At the *preschool* level, developing control of language is a major task of early childhood. It is a time when children are expanding their ability to relate to others outside of their immediate family and are beginning to use their language to get their way, explore thoughts and ideas, and make themselves understood. This is a particularly critical period in which children begin to develop the habits of school learning and interaction. At the preschool level, full primary language programs have demonstrated their importance in giving children a strong head start toward literacy and learning by opening the world of language and thinking to them (Campos & Keatinge, 1984; Cummins, 1989; Roberson, personal communication, 1995). Unfortunately, because of the perception that young children learn language faster than students of other ages (Collier, 1987), many preschool programs are mistakenly organized in English. Kindergarten teachers also face many of the same issues with regard to initial literacy instruction. It is very important to remember that children have a foundation of knowledge about language and thinking that is ready to burst forth at this stage of development. Because it is encoded in the child's primary language, this is a particularly critical time to maintain and reinforce primary language for this burgeoning conceptual development.

In the *primary grades*, children's oral language and emergent literacy knowledge is used to move them into a more formal visual-symbol system for communication. Through this system, children are encouraged to explore their own ideas as well as the ideas of others. At this stage, the first language provides the semantic, syntactic, and phonological system that is the basis for the movement to formal reading and writing. The opportunities students experience in beginning to read will have a lasting impact on their view of themselves as literate individuals.

The tasks of literacy begin to change at the third and fourth grades, reflecting a move away from exploring the nature of reading toward using reading and writing as the primary tools for academic learning. The type, context, and nature of literacy tasks shifts from reading and writing narrative (story) text that reflects familiar and contextualized topics to expository (informational) text that is further and further removed from students' immediate experience, and that is increasingly decontextualized. For students who are dominant in their native language, access to a greater depth of literacy understanding and sophistication can be the benefit of primary language use. Because the shift in literacy tasks discussed above coincides with decreased opportunities for oral language development, more decontextualized levels of English instruction usually do not provide the support second language learners need to fully understand everything they are required to read.

Unfortunately, many students whose school content and language experiences have been narrow are judged not to be able to benefit from primary language support. Instead of recognizing the likelihood of their having gaps in a school vocabulary and knowledge base (Miramontes, 1987, 1994), they are often thought to have limited capacity to understand concepts in the primary language (Hansegard in Skutnabb-Kangas, 1981). This leaves many such students without the opportunities they need to fully access and utilize the new material they are expected to learn.

At the *intermediate and high school levels*—the periods between 4th–8th grades and 9th–12th—students' previous background literacy experiences, their exposure to English, and the sociopolitical context of languages take on even more critical roles in planning for academic success. Although older students are engaged in many of the same types of literacy activities as younger students, the level of sophistication, the degree of decontextualization, and the demand for expression of more complex thoughts and ideas constantly increase. In programs where bilingualism and biliteracy are the goals, continued development in both languages extends students' range and proficiency (see Chapter 6).

Not all programs can offer students the full primary language access accorded native English speakers. Where primary language instruction is limited, factors such as students' previous schooling experiences, literacy experiences in their first language, and their exposure to and proficiency in English must all be taken into account in developing programs. With older students, the interaction of these three factors guides program planning. For example, for students with strong primary language literacy skills and a strong schooling background, the primary language foundation has already been established. With primary language reinforcement (Category III) and a strong English second language development program, they are usually on the road to success. On the other hand, for students who, though older, are not literate in any language, the basic principles of beginning literacy apply. Where primary language literacy is not feasible, these students need an intense second language oral and literacy program with primary language reinforcement.

Issues of Language Loss. Some of the most difficult decisions in program planning arise where students' language dominance is mixed, that is, where they have some difficulty expressing themselves fully in each of their languages. For these students a more careful evaluation of their strengths in both languages is critical to fully utilizing their linguistic resources to support learning. For some of them, the possibility of language loss will be an important factor to consider when making determinations about appropriate instructional programs, as well as their potential for recapturing what has been lost. The following example demonstrates the complexity of these linguistic interactions.

Losing an Asset

For Joaquin the primary language has become primarily receptive. Although his parents speak only Spanish at home and he also hears it all around him in the community, Joaquin has been schooled only in English. He is an alert, active, and engaging youngster. But as demonstrated below, he is losing his abilities in the primary language and is no longer proficient.

> Viva cinco personas en una casa y su papá sa fue pa'trabajo . . . Su nombres fueron José y Rosa, An then . . . Y luuego, lego estaban durmindo . . . Y lego, fui a ver y fue la gato de nosotros. It was the cat. [Five people live in a house and their father went to work. Their names are Jose and Rosa, and then, and then, then they were sleeping . . . and then s/he went to see and it was the cat of ours].

Joaquin's grammatical structures are confused. He attempts to borrow words from English but returns to Spanish to continue his story, a story that seems garbled and disconnected. Although he also has some difficulty relating his thoughts in English, he prefers to use it. Joaquin has a store of knowledge in Spanish that is no longer as readily available to him, and the potential for developing full bilingualism that he has not had the opportunity to develop. Because in school he has been taught mainly as a native English speaker rather than a second language learner, he has also missed the opportunities needed to become fully fluent and proficient in English.

When language loss has occurred, planning for primary language support must be more carefully considered. For example, oral language development in the first language should be a major focus, since there will necessarily be gaps in students' vocabulary and in their ability to express themselves in content areas in a language they have not used for school learning. Nevertheless, carefully planned opportunities to engage in the use of the primary language can help students use all of their resources more effectively, regain their bilingualism, reconnect with families, and be able to more fully participate in their bilingual communities. Cases where a clear dominance cannot be determined cause great ambivalence about program planning. Where program structure is haphazard and assessment criteria are not clearly defined, many of these students are shuffled back and forth between languages. Balancing languages within the environment and understanding the next stages of development for these students in each language is the only way to sort through student needs in order to offer them a strong program.

Oral Language Development

What we know about teaching and learning indicates that a strong instructional focus on oral language is essential to developing a strong foundation for literacy development (Dudley-Marling & Searle, 1991; Smith, 1982; Vygotsky, 1962). A first step in literacy development and an important step in concept development across content areas is helping students extend and elaborate the language they bring from home in order to connect home language and experience to school language and learning. Oral language is an important vehicle for making these connections. The range of linguistic and experiential variability in student populations adds to the importance of creating a strong oral language component. As numerous studies indicate (Commins & Miramontes, 1989; Miramontes, 1990b, 1994; Zentalla, 1988), variations in bilingual students' speech patterns and proficiency in either or both languages are not unexpected occurrences. Because of the range of language contexts that bilingual students must handle across two languages, it is also not uncommon for students to be perceived as deficient in at least one area across their linguistic terrain. A more useful alternative, nondeficit, proactive view is to see these students as proficient in several areas across both languages, and to work to fill in gaps by engaging students in exploring and thinking about new concepts and ideas orally in the primary language.

In program planning it is important to consider the wide variety of tasks students are asked to perform in school and what is required to be thought of as successful. Students are expected to be able to talk about a wide range of topics, learn how to identify and present problems and seek solutions, give oral arguments for their positions, develop and defend points of view, and communicate across a wide range of situations, purposes, and people. Opportunities for students to learn about, explore, and discuss new ideas, analyze information, and support their positions orally can be invaluable in supporting thinking, reading, and writing. When most native English-speaking students engage in these activities, the link with their primary language happens automatically as part of the curriculum. For linguistically diverse students this same opportunity occurs only when the primary language is used as the medium of instruction.

Meaning-Centered Literacy

Becoming proficient readers is one of the most daunting tasks many students will ever face in school. Deciding how to help them seems to be one of the most daunting instructional tasks teachers face as well. For several decades a "great debate" has raged as to how to teach reading (Chall, 1989; Goodman, 1986). In essence, it revolves around whether students first need to learn the parts of reading (alphabet, phonetic elements, etc.) before they can truly engage in reading for meaning, or whether students should begin with a whole text, focus on its meaning, and learn the "parts" as they are needed to pursue meaning. Whether one ascribes to the parts-to-whole or the whole-to-parts position, each assumes and depends on a background of student cognitive and linguistic experience as a prerequisite to successful instruction. In order to make sound decisions about literacy instruction, then, it is important to understand what is assumed about students' development from each perspective.

A parts-to-whole perspective assumes that students' phonological, morphological, and semantic experience with language provides the basis for sounding out new words, a process that challenges even many native speakers of a language who have 6 or 7 years of prior experiences with language. Unfortunately, linguistically diverse students are usually required to begin to read in a language whose sounds they may not hear, whose words they may have difficulty pronouncing, and whose vocabulary is unfamiliar to them.

A whole-to-parts perspective assumes that students have been using, experimenting, and playing with reading and writing from an early age. This exploration of reading and writing draws on the purposes and sounds that surround them. As literacy emerges, children are acquiring the skills and abilities to encode their language into symbols. This background of sounds, structure, and meaning of a language is what children bring to the new learning they experience in school. When teachers encourage children to try invented spelling, for example, they are assuming that children can understand, express and pronounce the ideas they are trying to share, and then can "sound out" the words they are trying to write.

Educators approaching reading from both perspectives often ignore the implications of these assumptions with regard to the close relationship between literacy and the primary language in which students have been exploring and expressing their ideas—their thinking language. For students new to English, the school and home languages are not equivalent in serving as tools for thinking and school learning, or for building a strong literacy foundation. Students' level of language proficiency and flexibility delimits the level of sophistication with which they can engage text. In the first language, students have full access to background learnings. Second language reading limits students to functioning at the level of basic expression, vocabulary, and understanding they are acquiring. Practices such as concurrent beginning literacy instruction, students choosing the instructional language in which to read and write, and changing the instructional language from one day to the next divert students' energies from extending and refining their literacy abilities. Given the sociopolitical context, which tends to diminish the importance of languages other than English, the primary language loses out and the foundation is eroded.

Unlike native English speakers, students who live in bilingual worlds have three tasks with regard to literacy development, a triple transfer task. The first literacy task, which they share with all other children, involves learning to manipulate symbols as a way of communicating their ideas, that is, to transfer their ideas to text. This requires learning to encode and decode ideas in print, and is based on extending their existing background experiences, home learning, language, and thought.

The second task for bilingual students is to learn to transfer their ideas orally from their first language to their second, learning to communicate them fluently in the second language. This means, among other things, that they have to learn a second phonetic, syntactic, and semantic system as well as the sociolinguistic parameters of its use.

The third task is to learn to transfer their thinking and literacy skills from their first language to their second. This requires a strong background in the vocabulary and structure of the second language, which can, in turn, support learning a second grapho-phonic cueing system. This unique triple transfer need requires the careful thought and planning for instruction discussed below.

A Quality Environment for Primary Language Literacy

Many of the issues addressed in this section, although specific to Category I and II programs, directly relate to successful literacy development in general. Additional issues related to Categories III and IV (reinforcement and the home–school connection) are discussed in the final section of the chapter.

Program Quality. Of course the use of the primary language in and of itself does not automatically ensure good academic progress. As in the school experiences of all children, the quality of instructional planning, teacher competence, program coherence, and the orientation of the curriculum play major roles. An added dimension of critical importance for children who live in bilingual worlds, however, is *how*, *where*, and *for what pur-*

poses each language is used. In bilingual programs, therefore, quality is defined and must be assessed along three dimensions: (1) in terms of good instructional practice and adherence to the basic elements of first and second language instruction—the Basic Premises; (2) in relation to the planning for the use of the two languages—the basic factor that differentiates bilingual education from monolingual education; and (3) in terms of teacher models. These same dimensions apply to Category III and IV programs where little, if any primary language is used (see Chapter 5).

The quality of the linguistic environment and the richness of the opportunities provided for students will ultimately be the measure of their success. As Paolo Freire (1970; 1985) suggests, reading is a political act, and teachers wield a great deal of power over students and the role literacy will eventually play in their lives. This power is expressed in the choices they make and the limitations they place on the types of texts with which students' will interact. The types and quality of materials made available to students, the language in which those materials are presented, and the types of opportunities students have to read them will reflect to students what their relationship is to the literate world. For this reason, the engagement of students in a wide variety of literacy activities in which they have choices, feel comfortable in exploring print, feel like authors, and see books as good places to gain information is basic (Barrera, 1992; Edelsky, Altwerger, & Flores, 1983; Thonis, 1970; Tinajero & Ada, 1993; Perez & Torres-Guzman, 1996). Students also need to see themselves reflected in the texts, thoughts, and ideas they encounter.

Equally important for students beginning literacy in their first language is the message that their primary language is an important and perfectly valid language for literacy. Literacy development is undermined in bilingual classrooms that do not provide a strong environment where the primary language has equal, inviolate time, space, and emphasis, or where there is constant competition between languages (Escamilla & Medina, 1993). School and teacher attitudes toward the primary language are directly communicated by the opportunities afforded students to explore, develop, and expand this language fully. When English is given *de facto* dominance, it says to students that their primary language is not important or of value. The following reflects a common scenario in bilingual settings today.

Sending Mixed Messages

Ms. Rodriguez has a self-contained first-grade class where two hours every morning are devoted to literacy development. Over half of Ms. Rodriguez's students are limited-English-proficient Spanish speakers.

Although Ms. Rodriguez meets with small groups of students for Spanish reading instruction, children are allowed to read and write in whichever language they choose. English speakers very rarely dabble in Spanish reading and writing, but Spanish speakers often choose to do their work in English. Ms. Rodriguez is always pleased when her students begin to pick up English books to read, feeling that this means they are moving quickly toward the eventual goal of being good English readers.

In environments such as the one described above, students quickly get the message that what's really important about reading is reading in English. They may also be led to believe that unless they are fully proficient as readers of English, they really can't be proficient readers at all. Such messages can greatly affect their perceptions of themselves as literate individuals, and their interest in developing the strong primary language literacy foundation that will eventually support their second language reading.

Another common issue is a clear understanding of what constitutes a strong literacy foundation in the primary language, as illustrated in the following example.

Is Interest Competence?

Rosa is a first-grade student. She is in a classroom with both English and Spanish speakers. Although she is receiving reading instruction in Spanish, much of the rest of her school day is conducted in English. Rosa often expresses the desire to read in English like the other kids, and during free reading time often picks up an English reading book. Because of her interest in English literacy, her teacher feels she is ready for formal English reading and is thinking of moving her to an English reading group.

In drawing her conclusion, the teacher is not making the distinction between informal English reading opportunities and formal reading instruction in English. If she allows Rosa to choose to read only in English or to switch back and forth during this formative period of literacy development, she will be inhibiting Rosa's opportunities to fully develop the strong primary language literacy foundation she will need to succeed at the more sophisticated uses of literacy in general, and in decontextualized English print in particular. Picking up an English reading book is not an indication that the appropriate level of primary language literacy development to support *successful* development and competence in the reading of a second language has been attained. The question of "readiness" cannot be decided solely on students' interest (see Chapter 7).

Unfortunately, this is a not uncommon occurrence, and its debilitating effect on a strong primary language literacy foundation is poorly understood. When students are experiencing difficulties in learning, determining a true need for services such as special education is severely compromised by a lack of appropriate understanding regarding students' background knowledge and by inappropriate instructional planning (Baca & DeValenzuela, 1994; Cloud, 1994; Howe & Miramontes, 1992; Miramontes; 1990a). Issues that are raised in relation to the weakness of this haphazard approach to literacy development are captured by the following questions: How are students' practice and experience with literacy limited by their second language? What first language opportunities for extending literacy are being missed? How do these classrooms meet students' need for conceptual development? What messages are sent about the relative importance of each language? How can the time in this classroom be reorganized to increase the effectiveness of the literacy instruction? If the promise held by developing a strong foundation in primary language literacy is to be realized, teachers themselves must be convinced that literacy development in the primary language will eventually lead to English reading proficiency, and that the time invested is worth it. Using primary language literacy merely as a means to get to second language literacy devalues the process and weakens the foundation.

Even for those teachers who are trying to provide a strong program, the traditional one-teacher, one-class structure of schools exacerbates the difficulties of planning for instruction. It is very hard to build a strong primary language foundation in a self-contained situation where one teacher is responsible for all curriculum in both languages. Ms. Rodriguez could, however, group students by primary language during this time, setting up different sections in her classroom where resources for a particular language are grouped, and where children are surrounded by that language as they work. Other times and settings during the day could be structured for students to interact across languages. A better solution is for Ms. Rodriguez to team with another teacher, so each one could concentrate on one language. In this way, there is more opportunity to establish the strong primary language literacy environment that is needed.

As in the example above, research (Legaretta, 1977; Milk, Mercado, & Sapiens, 1992) and informal observations in districts across the country clearly indicate the dominance of English in bilingual classrooms and the weakness of primary language environments for literacy. In some cases it occurs because teachers who are more dominant, proficient, and comfortable in English are unable to use the primary language effectively and exclusively in instruction. But even when teachers are fully bilingual or native speakers of the other language, English predominates. Given both the external pressure for English to dominate in our schools and the fact that most bilingual teachers are more comfortable teaching in English, a very special and specific effort to balance the influence of English in bilingual programs is critical in order to allow literacy and concept development to flourish. Teachers must take conscious steps to counterbalance these pressures if they are to be successful in fostering a strong foundation for literacy in the primary language.

In setting up classrooms for linguistically diverse students, the need to provide an abundantly rich language environment in each of the languages in which students are intended to gain fluency and proficiency should be a major focus. Often ignored, however, is the basic proposition that in order for students to become proficient, fluent, and fluid in literacy in a particular language they need extended, enhanced interaction with text and print in that language, within a text-rich environment that is targeted to that language. Without such planning and attention to language use it is little wonder that students in many primary language programs leave these programs with narrow, literal reading skills. Unfortunately, as many teachers in upper grades discover, such basic skills only partially contribute to the strong literacy foundation necessary for successful second language reading.

Language Planning for a Strong Literacy Environment. Rich non–English environments do not occur naturally in schools. Rather, they must be created and nurtured. This idea of creating and purposefully maintaining specific environments seems to be uncomfortable for many educators. In many bilingual classrooms, for example, there is a general aversion to deliberate planning for which language to use. Arguments against planning distinct environments for each language are made citing students' innate curiosity and the common use of two languages in the daily discourse of bilingual communities. Some teachers point to students' interest in English and their "ability" to read in either language as reasons for not creating distinct environments. Others argue that it is "normal" for bilinguals to use their two languages interchangeably for communication. The reaction is generally to suggest that any manipulation of factors in an environment, such as setting aside times for the use of a particular language, infringes on the idea of "free choice" and students' "natural"' use of language. But, in fact, purposeful planning for language use is not different from our preparation and planning for other areas of the curriculum.

For example, when good teachers set about creating an optimal environment for literacy development, they spend a great deal of time carefully planning their classroom environments to assure plentiful choices for students. They select reading materials representing a wide range of genres and topics across a wide range of ability. They set up their classrooms to be comfortable and inviting places for students to read and write, making reading and writing materials readily accessible to students and providing many "teasers" or prompts that will help motivate children to engage with print. They do not use only the books, furniture, and fixtures generally available in schools, but rather manipulate the environment to create a particular desired effect that their students will experience, and within which they will operate. They do this to ensure that students are provided with the particular types of opportunities they believe will best provide for literacy development.

In a monolingual setting all of this is fairly straightforward. All of the materials are in English; English is supported throughout the environment; books, articles, magazines, and so forth all contribute to giving students multiple opportunities to explore and extend their language skills—in the targeted language. Successful, flexible readers of their primary language is the goal these teachers are seeking. What, then, do this goal and the careful planning of the environment created to reach this goal imply for the literacy instruction of children from other primary language groups? They mean that purposeful planning for a rich environment in the foundation reading language is critical to developing strong literacy skills.

While the exploration of ideas, the opportunity to take on the persona of author, the ability to take command of words and their meanings, and the development of reading and writing fluency should be at the heart of all literacy programs, the language in which students participate in these activities is also critical. The general failure in classrooms to take equal care with regard to the non-English environment is the essence of a major contradiction between what many people believe is good teaching and how they hold to those principles and purposes for linguistically diverse students. At the heart of creating clear contexts for languages in the literacy environment are the issues of priorities, the quality of accomplishments, and the sustainability of these accomplishments over time. Depth of understanding and skill comes only through quality interactions with the task one is attempting to master.

As described in Chapter 6, learning content across two languages also requires particular planning strategies. This language planning is important across age and grade levels. Instructional adaptations to meet particular student needs must also account for the use of language.

Program Coherence and Coordination

Across all dimensions, teachers must work together to create strong programs (premise 12). Very important to this process in Categories I, II, and III are the quality and breadth of the teacher's linguistic competence. Fluently bilingual teachers are scarce in this country (Milk et al., 1992; U.S. Department of Education, 1990). Because the language teachers use and the language they model serve as the major determiners of what students will use (Ramirez & Merino, 1990), staffing with bilingual personnel requires careful and deliberate planning to maximize the use of this scarce teacher resource. Just as students come to school with a wide range of cultural and linguistic experiences, so do teachers; therefore, staffing of programs must be based on the consideration of teachers' areas of strength, and not solely on their preference for grade level or language.

A key to successful program development is a schoolwide organizational plan that fully utilizes individual teachers' skills to help students develop primary language proficiency. One of the most useful and productive ways of planning for dual language instruction is to create teams of teachers, each with responsibility for instructing in one of the two languages. By working together, these teams can more efficiently provide services for more students, in a stronger environment than can any one teacher trying to meet the needs of all students, alone. As will be discussed more fully in Chapter 6, a balance of language environments for first and second language development as well as for cross-cultural settings can be organized with careful planning.

At the secondary level, planning for strong first and second language programs also requires a high level of coordination. Secondary schools that offer primary language classes in the content areas often offer ESL classes that are language- rather than content-based. Consequently, students may lack the English vocabulary necessary to understand a chemistry class in English, for example, although they can handle the subject matter effectively in their primary language. The departmentalization of junior and senior high school programs— ESL, bilingual, and the discipline areas—makes coordination more difficult. Although this is at times a formidable obstacle, it can be overcome by creating interdisciplinary teams of teachers who coordinate the topics of their instruction. Working together, primary language, ESL, and English-only discipline teachers can work out a program that balances students' need for understanding concepts, language arts development (primary language), second language learning, and English content instruction. For example, the student might receive a primary language arts class and a sheltered biology class, and the ESL lesson might be organized to help students learn to interact with the language of biology and with science discourse and strategies.

ISSUES UNIQUE TO EACH PROGRAM CATEGORY

Category I: Full Primary Language Foundation

A Category I program offers students the opportunity to fully develop primary language literacy as well as subject area knowledge across all content areas. As discussed above, the firm foundation in both Categories I and II can be created only with deliberate attention to careful planning for language use, providing strong oral language development, engaging students in a wide range of literacy activities, and enriching the first language environment. Because of development over time, the amount of instruction using each language is balanced differently depending on age and proficiency.

The balance between first and second languages shifts gradually across grades. At the beginning levels of literacy (K–1), maximum time in the primary language is important to extend and develop the oral language and concepts that will support literacy development. In the first language children are interacting with print, learning to express their ideas orally and in writing. They are reading and sharing the ideas others have written, learning skills that help them gain meaning, and participating in reading a wide variety of genres. In the second language they are busy becoming proficient in speaking this language in a wide variety of contexts, becoming comfortable in spontaneous situations, understanding more sophisticated materials and ideas, expanding their vocabulary, expanding their ability to present and argue positions, and talking across a wide variety of settings (Chapter 5).

At second and third grade, primary language literacy is expanding. Students are using reading for a wider variety of purposes. There is increased emphasis on content knowledge and the use of reading and writing to support it. Children are more aware of text in their second language, and are beginning to have more informal experiences with literacy. Listening and discussion of stories and information now begins to extend to more formal contacts with English print, such as group writing of stories. Modified Language Experience Approach (LEA) activities such as those described in Chapter 5 are an effective way of helping students become comfortable with English print. This movement from informal to formal

English literacy will depend on individual students' degree of proficiency in primary language literacy and second language development.

At the intermediate grades, very specific planning for the distribution of curriculum over the languages is necessary for programs where the eventual goal is full bilingualism. Here the use of languages reaches a 50–50 balance. In programs where an early transition is made into all-English, establishing sound criteria for this transition and planning for this period are critical. Transition periods as described in Premise 7 are vital to both types of programs. At the secondary level, balancing the sometimes competing needs of learning content and learning a second language requires coordination in planning a student's overall program.

Perhaps one of the most difficult decisions regarding the interaction between first and second language reading concerns students who are having difficulty in primary language literacy but may need to read in English. In a continuous progress assessment as described in Chapter 7, knowledge of such students' difficulties would have been recognized by teachers for some time. Adaptations to reading instruction would have been tried with constant monitoring. The question of whether there might be something inhibiting the students' performance (for example, a learning disability) could be determined with this careful monitoring of students' performance over time. However, in some cases, it is simply that students are working up to capacity, a capacity that is different from that of other members of their classes. In such cases, the student may become a bilingual reader, but with limited proficiency in both languages. The key to such decisions is gathering authentic, performance-based information that demonstrates the range of abilities the student possesses. Denying primary language instruction to such students is shortsighted and assumes that they will be able to perform better in an unfamiliar language. Perhaps more than other students, these students need a high level of support, communication, and connection to family. Supporting these students' bilingualism should be a high priority.

Transition to English Literacy. The specific criteria for the transition into formal English reading are described in the chapter on assessment. In general, these criteria reflect the skills of a strong and flexible reader— that is, a reader who is familiar and comfortable with a range of genres, who can read for a variety of purposes, and who can also use writing along a range of functions. This type of flexibility is beginning to be demonstrated by primary readers with 3½ to 4 years of literacy experience in school. Older students with prior literacy experiences in the primary language may reach this foundational level of reading more quickly.

Category II: Primary Language Support—Literacy Only

A Category II program allows students to develop primary language literacy, but resources are not sufficient to include extensive content instruction in the primary language. Although a limitation is that students do not have access to the full range of concepts across the academic curriculum, the strength is that students do have the opportunity to develop a strong literacy foundation in their primary language. Literacy development in a Category II program must be linked to a strong content-area focus. This allows students to encounter and expand ideas from the content areas in their reading, and supports content-area instruction in the second language. In planning for instruction, it must be remembered that students' exposure to their first language and to experiences that will enrich literacy, such as working with the vocabulary for science, social studies, and math, will be more limited. Because all other areas of the curriculum are to be delivered in English, a strong second language program that balances language and concept development is necessary. Careful planning is also necessary to avoid inappropriate literacy demands in the content areas. In addition, because students are not learning about all content areas in their first language, it is important to make this information comprehensible.

Transition to English Literacy. The criteria for the movement into formal English reading are the same as for Category I. This basic foundational level of reading and broad exposure to content knowledge will be the key to helping students pass effectively through the transition period prepared to enter an all-English reading program and be successful. As described in Category I, these criteria are based on the proficiencies of a reader who is familiar and comfortable with a range of genres, who can read for a variety of purposes, and who can also use writing for a range of functions. As with Category I, this type of flexibility is often most readily demonstrated by primary grade readers with 3½ to 4 years of literacy experience in school, and more quickly for older students.

Category III: Primary Language Content Reinforcement—No Literacy

Our discussion thus far has focused on the implementation of bilingual programs with full primary language literacy opportunities. As reflected in the basic premises, however, even though its place in the school curriculum cannot always be in the mode of full implementation, the primary language will always be useful and play a vital role in the development of learning for linguistically diverse students.

However, with significantly limited resources in terms of primary language personnel, the question of how, fundamentally, the primary language can support the thinking life of the student arises. That is, where basically is the primary language most necessary, or where can the use of the primary language reap the greatest benefit? As discussed, the primary language is a key to linking prior knowledge and experience to big ideas and concepts. These ideas and concepts tend to be abstract in nature, tied to such questions as why, what if, how, and so forth, and require a good deal of language to be explored. As an example, imagine yourself being asked to discuss such topics as what a friend is, what love is, or why there are wars in a second language. A Category III program provides students opportunities to learn and to work with the important concepts of the academic curriculum in their primary language. In order to offer a Category III program, schools must commit to daily instructional and planning time, as well as provide resources for concept development in the primary language.

To help understand the challenge for students across a variety of levels, think about a situation in which you might be asked to listen to a lecture in a second language. Even when the information is familiar, hearing it in an unfamiliar language undoubtedly restricts, if not totally inhibits, your ability to think about the information and to incorporate it easily into your existing knowledge base. It is even more difficult if you are expected to do something active with the information, for example, if you are asked to give a talk or a lecture, or to argue a point. This takes more than the ability to listen or read and understand. It requires flexibility with the ideas and oral proficiency. The task is even more difficult if you are also expected to read and write information in a lucid and comprehensible fashion, within the conventions of that language. This example points out the complexity of the tasks students face in dealing with academic content and literacy, the wide range of skills demanded, and the level of proficiency required in their second language.

Helping students move beyond the concrete conceptualizations and understandings of a topic, necessitated by their second language proficiency, is the most basic role the primary language can play. A major benefit of offering students a Category III program is that the periods of time provided for primary language reinforcement create a basic framework for this extended understanding and open the door to students' full range of language and thinking abilities. This can be accomplished by allowing time for students to discuss topics with a more knowledgeable other in their primary language. Such a program necessitates a well-organized plan for a daily hour of primary language content learning. An understanding of how students use language in their homes and communities, and how they feel about the use of their primary language, is very important to providing them with appropriate and useful concept instruction.

Social studies is usually the best choice for such lessons because it incorporates a wide range of concepts and ideas. Lessons for these sessions do not include primary language reading. Rather, they are focused on the elaboration of abstract conceptual knowledge. Instruction is based primarily on oral discussion and reading aloud to students. Lessons should focus on understanding the interrelationships between new content knowledge, previous content knowledge, and previous experience. Discussions can be enhanced by reading literature, newspapers, and so forth, to students in their native language. Stimulating ideas; enhancing students' ability to question, reason, discuss, and debate; securing a knowledge base; and stretching thinking into higher levels are the principal purposes and strengths of providing at least this level of primary language support. Specific strategies for this category are discussed in greater detail in Chapter 6. The possibilities offered by a Category III program include supporting families' engagement in school learning.

Given limited school resources, an important strategy can be to organize students in cross-grade groupings. Where paraprofessionals or other staff are an important part of providing such services, their instruction must be directly coordinated and supervised by certificated teachers. Professional development is very important. Paraprofessionals must clearly understand and support the goals of instruction. This is not reading or review time, but a time for developing and extending students' thinking as broadly as possible about the content. It is a time to examine the topic, extend ideas, and relate new information to prior experiences and known concepts. The primary language must be used exclusively and without translation. Providing training on questioning strategies, clarifying the purpose as concept elaboration and not literacy instruction, setting aside planning time to familiarize staff with the basic content, concepts, and goals, are all essential to making these sessions successful. As with Category IV discussed below, parents' role in the home becomes increasingly important in supporting the conceptual foundation students need to assure academic success. Second language curriculum must also reflect themes of the regular content instructional program so that topics covered will be reinforced in each language.

Transition to English Literacy. For students in Category III programs, English literacy begins immediately. As described in Chapter 5, the Modified Language Experience Approach is an effective way to help students move into print. A major decision point for students in both Categories

III and IV is determining when they are ready to successfully function *without support* in all-English instruction. Sheltered instruction, literacy approaches, and support structures for second language learners are addressed in the following chapter, along with criteria for transition periods.

Category IV—All-English

In a Category IV program, there is no consistent daily instruction in the primary language. A lack of instruction in the primary language, however, does not mean that the primary language is no longer important to students' academic development. When sufficient school resources are not available to develop the primary language on a regular basis, teachers in Category IV programs must seek ways to tap into students' conceptual base in the primary language and validate students' home language in the school environment. This type of support may be possible only on a very limited level, say once or twice a week for 15–30 minutes, but even minimal opportunities to discuss topics in their primary language can be very helpful to most students.

Community members who are themselves literate and knowledgeable can be an invaluable resource in providing primary language opportunities. They can help build connections between home, community, and school learning. When establishing such a support structure, it is very important to work with volunteers to help them understand the purpose and goals of the sessions. Many of them may not fully understand how important the primary language can be in the overall curriculum, and how they can help students extend ideas, practice discussion of important ideas, make connections between previous knowledge and new knowledge, and tap into their bilingualism.

Perhaps the most important thing school personnel in a Category IV program can do to support student learning and to support families is to validate child-parent learning in the home language. Although this is an important strategy for any category, when there is no primary language support in the school it is even more critical to attend to encouraging parent-student communication in the language most comfortable to the parents, regardless of whether they are literate or not. Unfortunately, teachers (and parents) have been heard to say that they think it will do more harm than good for parents to speak with their children and help them with their schoolwork in a language other than English. To discourage parents from interacting fully with their children in whatever capacity they are able limits children's cognitive and linguistic resources, and can work to undermine parents' authority, creating chasms in families.

There are many concepts, ideas, skills, know-how, and values that parents facilitate and impart to their children (Moll, 1990a,b). Keeping lines of clear and significant conversation open between parents and children is critical if parents are to be given a chance to participate in their child's schooling.

The most important message parents can hear from teachers, especially English teachers, is that their role in the home is to maintain and extend the family's primary language. This is the answer to the question of the best way to maximize the resources in this setting. Thinking back to the example at the beginning of this chapter of living in China, imagine how much or how little you could communicate to your child if you were restricted to using only your minimal command of Chinese—even for such a task as teaching them to prepare a meal. Clearly, limited-English-speaking parents, regardless of their literacy levels, can contribute more fully in their primary language.

In addition to promoting and supporting parent–child interaction in the home language, a schoolwide plan must be developed that coordinates efforts to optimize instruction for second language learners. This requires that classroom teachers organize English environments to provide access to concepts, providing information and learning that is comprehensible to students and opportunities for students to fully participate in instruction. A strong, well-organized curriculum in English as a second language that includes literacy development is also necessary. This second language curriculum should be closely tied to themes of content instruction, using appropriate second language instructional approaches described in Chapter 5.

Decision Making on Your Own

1. Questions that highlight major issues regarding the primary language include: Is the primary language used in instruction? If so, how? Who receives primary language instruction? Is the primary language being used to greatest advantage? What level of program could be offered? How can the curriculum and linguistic resources be organized more effectively? How is program quality assured?

In order to answer these questions about your setting you need to gather the following information: numbers of students in each primary language group; how the primary language is currently used in the school; whether languages have clear and separate contexts for instruction; teacher proficiency in students' primary language(s); textbooks and materials available; additional community resources, political climate, and so forth.

2. Think about the Basic Premises and major elements presented in this chapter on primary language. Generate a list of additional questions that will help you to decide how best to serve students in your setting or school.

3. Compare your list of questions with those of a colleague and refine your list. Have you considered all the major issues?

4. Form a small group and brainstorm the optimal primary language practices possible in your setting. Use the Basic Premises highlighted in this chapter to weigh your decisions.

5. List two or three changes that might have to be made.

6. What are the implications of your decisions for other areas, for example, in curriculum, community involvement, or assessment practices?

7. Use these data to begin a school profile.

CHAPTER 5

Second Language Development

Key Premises to Consider

• *Premise 1—Active Learning.* Knowledge is best acquired when learners actively participate in meaningful activities that are constructive in nature and appropriate to their level of development.

• *Premise 4—Strategies for second language development.* Second language development creates an added dimension to instructional decision making. Instruction must reflect specific strategies designed to meet the needs of second language learners.

• *Premise 5—Contexts for second language development.* Second language instruction must be organized to provide students the time, experiences, and opportunities they need to fully develop language proficiency. This requires a range of social and academic contexts in which both language and content are emphasized.

• *Premise 6—First and second language environments.* Bilingual academic proficiency requires that clear, distinct, and meaning-enriched contexts for each language be created during instructional time.

• *Premise 7—Transitions and redesignations.* Decisions regarding transition to formal second language reading and redesignations that exit students from programs cannot be made arbitrarily.

Second language instruction is a key component of any bilingual education program, as well as a major part of a program for students who receive little or no support for the primary language in school. The determination of how second language instruction should be delivered will be based in great part on the level of primary language instruction that can be provided in your program.

A major theme of this book is that meeting the needs of second language learners is a schoolwide responsibility. Unfortunately, these needs are largely overlooked in most schools. Of those students eligible for services, approximately 33% actually receive them (Linguistic Minority Research Institute, 1994, p. 199). Where services are provided, second language learners are often served solely by the English as a second language or bilingual program, and it is assumed that students' needs are their exclusive responsibility. Assuring that reinforcement and sheltered instruction occur for students in their classroom is often ignored. The usual pattern for second language instruction in elementary schools is that for 2 years or so second language learners are pulled out from the main instructional environment (usually for 30–45 minutes, on a daily or weekly basis), and then return to their classrooms for the rest of the day. There is minimal coordination of their curriculum across settings, and little or no communication among their various teachers. This lack of coordination among services is compounded for students with exceptionalities who receive special education services almost always in English, and without second language methods regardless of language background.

Across grade levels, many "regular" or monolingual English track teachers do not see the need to modify their instruction for second language students. At middle and high school levels, departmentalization increases the tendency to view the needs of second language learners as someone else's problem. This attitude may be more understandable when there are just a few second language learners in a school. But regardless of number, if an equitable education is to be provided for all students, the question before the entire staff should be "How can we best organize ourselves and our resources to meet student needs?" This implies a careful analysis of the resources and expertise within the building based on a thorough understanding of the conditions that foster second language development. The only way this can be accomplished is through a school-wide decision-making strategy in which the needs of second language learners are everyone's concern.

Decision Making: Ask Yourself

Is time set aside every day for second language instruction?
What strategies do we need to employ to assure that instruction is understandable to second language learners?
How is instruction organized to allow students to gain both linguistic and academic competence in their second language?
How do students begin reading in their second language?
How can the students' knowledge of their first language be used to support the second?

PERSPECTIVES ON SECOND LANGUAGE ACQUISITION

A number of perspectives from current research in language acquisition undergird the proposals for how to create appropriate second language instructional environments as presented in this chapter. While there are many similarities between first and second language acquisition (Larsen-Freeman & Long, 1991; McLaughlin, 1984), the significant differences between them impact program planning.

Many factors contribute to successful second language development. Some of these factors are under the control or influence of teachers; others are not. How quickly students will become academically proficient in their second language is impacted by variables related to the context in which students must use the language, as well as by variables related to the psychology of the individual and how students feel about the language. These include the reasons for needing or wanting to acquire a second language, the intended length of residence in this country, and the possibilities for using one's second language in day-to-day life. Second language acquisition is also impacted by the nature of the program in which students find themselves, and how much access they have to conceptual development in the primary language.

Language Acquisition

Language is a natural function of human development (Brown, 1973; Slobin, 1979) and, except in very rare cases, people are continually surrounded by their native language and have constant opportunity to use it and to practice. There is a natural progression from simple to complex functions as most children move from primarily oral communication to becoming fully literate. Throughout the world most native speakers will, in all likelihood, use their primary language for the rest of their lives.

Like primary language acquisition, second language acquisition follows a broad developmental continuum (Larsen-Freeman & Long, 1991; Selinker, 1972; Slobin, 1979) in which learners progress through overlapping and interacting stages of development (Ellis, 1986). But, in contrast to first language acquisition, second language acquisition can begin at any age. Except for very young children, second language learners have already acquired all the functions of *language* in the larger sense—a tool for human communication—through the first language. They have learned to communicate ideas, mark their identity in society, and fulfill psychological needs (Smith, 1972). As second language learners they may have an awareness of the differences among languages, an awareness that older learners, especially, can utilize to facilitate their second language growth.

Central to the developmental perspective of second language acquisition is the concept of interlanguage (Selinker, 1972). Interlanguage is the expression of a second language learner's developmental process, and can be thought of as an individual's second language system at a given moment, reflecting changes in proficiency over time (McLaughlin, 1984). As second language development proceeds, the learner's expressed language is a continual approximation and reapproximation of the target language. By recognizing this developmental process, teachers can better understand and interpret students' performance, thus enabling them to analyze the nature of the errors students make.

As indicated previously, it takes a long time—5 to 7 years or more—to develop full academic proficiency in a second language (Collier, 1995; Cummins, 1986). Just how long it will take to become proficient will depend on a number of factors. These include age, native language literacy, aptitude for language learning, attitude, motivation, cognitive style, and adequacy of the instructional program. When services are provided in schools, the 2 years often funded for the support of second language development are simply not sufficient to allow students to fully develop their linguistic or academic potential. Because language skills develop over time, programs must accommodate students' changing needs as they progress from predominately oral interaction to more sophisticated literate and academic behaviors.

There is no single profile that can define the second language learner. Linguistically diverse students, K–12, arrive at school with a range of abilities in their first language, and at all stages and levels of development in their second. They may also arrive with exceptionalities or special needs that may or may not affect their second language development. In order to plan appropriate instruction, it is necessary to gather information about student experiences and about their level of schooling in both languages. For example, some students may arrive with extensive native language literacy, others none; some may enter with a sizable receptive vocabulary, but have little idea how to make use of what they know in face-to-face interactions.

The first and second language instruction of older students who have had significant literacy and schooling experiences in their own language requires different planning, for instance, than that necessary for students with little or no literacy or schooling experiences. The former group needs to learn to apply their existing literacy skills to a new code. The latter must not only learn the new language, but learn how to read and write as well, a process that will be greatly facilitated if it can occur in the student's primary language. The needs of students with mixed dominance who have varying patterns of strengths in their two languages may be overlooked because they display oral proficiency in English, but they, too, will need second language instruction geared to their proficiency level.

Language and Affect

As discussed in Chapters 2 and 4, first language acquisition is linked to the development of thought and identity. While first language development is part and parcel of the formation of an individual's core being, a second language can threaten that very identity and sense of self. An individual's age, aspects of personality (such as intro- or extraversion, and other psychological factors including culture shock and motivation also can impact the rate of acquisition (Ellis, 1986; Larsen-Freeman & Long, 1991; Wong-Fillmore, 1982).

To a great extent, the affective psychological factors that manifest themselves within the individual are linked to the learner's sense of security (Stevick, 1976). Second language speakers of English in schools face the dual task of acquiring a new linguistic system and learning academic content. Because of the overwhelming nature of the task, there is a tendency to feel inadequate at all stages of development even under the best of circumstances. Any additional stresses or negative influences can slow down and hinder the acquisition process, while feelings of uncertainty can undermine the learner's determination to succeed. These psychological factors have been described as acting as a kind of affective filter (Krashen, 1982) allowing or blocking input depending on the learner's attitude, motivation, and experience. The confidence to be able to speak freely in a second language develops over a long period of time. It grows partly in relationship to the opportunities students have had to become comfortable with their second language and to take risks in a variety of settings and levels of interaction.

Student attitudes are influenced by their circumstances and status in this country. Planning instruction for second language learners requires that teachers and schools consider these factors. Questions to be asked include: Are the students in our school war refugees, immigrants, the children of foreign graduate students, or a combination of all three? Do they have rural or urban backgrounds? How much schooling have they had? Are they here temporarily or permanently? Are they poor or affluent? Is their native language viewed as high or low status in this country?

Additive or Subtractive Bilingualism. A key issue is whether second language instruction is an attempt to replace a student's primary language with a second language or to add the second language to the individual's linguistic repertoire. In other words, are programs organized for additive or subtractive bilingualism (Cummins, 1989; Lambert & Tucker, 1972). For the variety of reasons discussed throughout this book, an additive rather than a subtractive perspective is critical to academic success. If students view the acquisition of their second language positively, there will probably be fewer affective or psychological barriers to learning. If students feel they are in a punitive setting, or view learning the second language as a threat to their sense of identity, they may actively resist second language instructional efforts.

Teachers can't easily change the psychological, social, and political factors that affect second language acquisition, so it makes sense for them to concentrate on the factors that *are* under their control such as the classroom environment, instructional organization and strategies, opportunities for practice, and a schoolwide commitment to appropriate instruction for second language learners. Within their classrooms, and across the school, teachers can create the range of settings and contexts in which second language learners will need to function in and outside of school. In addition, they can always seek ways to make reticent learners feel comfortable about speaking out in the classroom, and actively affirm the worth and dignity of each and every student.

ISSUES ACROSS PROGRAM CATEGORIES

The category of program offered will affect the final organization of the second language program. Specifically, it impacts the extent to which students can rely on their primary language for continued conceptual development as they learn their second language, how much time is devoted to second language instruction, and the balance between time devoted to content and time devoted to structure. There are many elements of second language instruction, however, that are critical regardless of program category. These include planned daily instruction; attention to the second language environment; balancing program components; integrated curriculum and thematic units; oral language development; the use of learning strategies; and the teaching of other second languages. A more detailed discussion follows.

Planned Daily Instruction

Becoming proficient in a second language is a tremendous undertaking. Given the complexity of the task, second language learners need planned daily instruction designed to promote second language acquisition. Regardless of program type, a specified time for second language instruction is needed so that the environment can be consciously organized to be understandable and accessible to second language learners and to involve them actively in using their second language. The amount of time for second language instruction can vary from a 30-minute period to several hours a day, depending on students' age and the level of primary language support available. It should not be assumed that providing for ESL development is automatically a pull-out activity. Even though targeted time may have to be provided outside of the general education classroom, strategies for grouping and regrouping students within the classroom itself also need careful attention.

Even when the regular classroom is organized to maximize comprehension, a specified time for second language instruction is still necessary to allow second language learners the opportunity to talk and discuss without having to compete for the floor with fluent native speakers who can usually outperform them linguistically. While second language learners do need to spend instructional time interacting with native-speaking models, they also need time to fully participate at their own level of proficiency. They need opportunities to practice the structure of the language and the language of the content curriculum in a way that native speakers don't need. They also need to receive literacy instruction that is appropriate to their level of second language development. Without these opportunities, they will nearly always be overshadowed by their monolingual peers.

Unfortunately, many second language learners do not receive daily second language instruction. In some instances no resources are allocated to provide for second language instruction, because too many educators still assume that by just being in an all-English environment second language learners will have adequate opportunity to master the language. In other cases, teachers resist providing second language time, believing that it somehow unfairly segregates second language learners from their English-speaking peers.

Even in many bilingual programs there is no time of the day set aside specifically for second language development. Teachers may believe that a program that provides primary language instruction and in which students can hear both languages presents the conditions necessary to become proficient in English. These beliefs may result from the way teachers are prepared and the structural arrangement of their work. Bilingual and English as a second language teachers are separated not only from monolingual English instruction teachers, but from each other as well. Professional development is divided into different programs and departments, creating a false dichotomy between bilingual and second language programs, and implying not only that English as a second language instruction has no role in bilingual education, but that these two program areas are at odds with one another—a common myth that impacts program design. Although many teachers in bilingual programs overemphasize

English (Escamilla, 1992; Legaretta-Marcaida, 1981; Milk et al., 1992), others may consciously or unconsciously minimize their emphasis on English language development in an attempt to reject the dominance of English.

In addition, teachers who have embraced the movement toward more process approaches to instruction may believe that a print-rich environment and a meaning-based curriculum are sufficient to guarantee success for all students, overlooking the specific needs of second language learners. Second language instruction may not be provided if teachers believe that methodologies or approaches that have proven themselves to be successful with monolingual English students from the mainstream will automatically prove beneficial to second language learners, regardless of their previous literacy and educational experiences.

The Second Language Environment

Students need many opportunities to listen and verbalize in the second language. The teacher's role, then, is to organize the environment and mediate the instruction. If students are to make sense of their instruction, every aspect of classroom design, including the physical environment, the content covered, and strategies used for grouping and instructional delivery, must be considered. A successful second language teacher purposefully plans for different linguistic and cognitive settings with the aim of creating independent learners who can function in the disembedded, cognitively demanding environment that characterizes high-level academic work.

Teaching methods based on lecture and text do not tend to provide such an environment. As illustrated in the following example, there are many ways to craft instruction to maximize student access to its meaning. In this example, teachers A and B are both teaching a lesson about the three states of matter. They both teach science to middle-school classes composed of second language speakers of English.

Making Instruction Comprehensible

Teacher A arrives at class with lecture notes in hand. She writes on the board "Three States of Matter: Solid, Liquid, Gas." After her 20-minute oral presentation, students are directed to read a portion of their science book and to answer the questions at the end of the section. As students work, she circulates among them and answers questions individually when hands are raised.

Teacher B also arrives at class with lecture notes. In addition, she carries a box full of equipment, including many bowls, a small hot plate, and a bag of ice cubes. Teacher B also writes "Three States of Matter: Solid, Liquid, Gas" on the board. But underneath each word she adds a drawing to represent each concept and illustrate the molecular structure. As Teacher B lectures she in turn melts ice, boils water, and, under the drawings on the board, writes ice, water, and steam. Students in class B are also assigned a portion of the text to read. But instead of answering the questions in the text, they are asked to work in pairs to write down comprehension questions for their peers to answer about the passage. As students begin to read the text, Teacher B sits down with a group of four beginning ESL students to review the main ideas, prepare the students to participate in the next day's lesson, and show them that they are to copy and label the drawings of the three molecular structures into their science journals.

Strategies that assist in making instruction more understandable include simplifying but not artificially restricting language structures (shorter sentences, use of unambiguous terminology); contextualizing both oral and written texts with pictures, charts, diagrams, and realia; providing for repeated access to ideas and vocabulary; and creating interaction structures that allow for both comprehension and the need to act on and talk about content. Whereas Teacher A relies solely on lecture (words) and text to provide meaning, Teacher B has incorporated drawings, visuals, demonstrations, and collaborative interaction into the lesson. Meaning-based lessons like Teacher B's that are designed to maximize comprehensibility can provide for a range of language learning needs. They allow beginning students to identify key vocabulary, while more advanced students may be able to respond orally or in writing to more complex concepts related to the content. While many of Teacher B's actions were intended to provide for the needs of second language learners, it is clear in a class composed of both second language learners and monolingual English students that everyone in the class benefits from the increased comprehensibility of the lesson.

Maintaining the Integrity of the Environment. Simply submerging second language learners in their new language is a poor practice (Krashen, 1985). At the same time, it is also true that learning to speak another language is not easy, and fluency is not accomplished without deliberate interaction in the target language. Therefore, during second language instruction, a monolingual environment should be maintained in order to create a context in which students must concentrate on understanding and communicating in that language (Premise 6). Just as students must exert effort to interact entirely in their second language, their teachers must exert effort to present materials in a manner that is understandable and accessible to students. In this way, both student and teacher are engaged in an interactive task of creating meaning in order to further language development. For teachers, this means sustaining a frame of mind that views each moment of instructional time as an opportunity to mediate learning by expanding vocabulary, providing concrete examples, and giving explanations (Tharp & Gallimore, 1990). Every strategy possible should be employed to assure that learners can understand and make use of the information in the lesson.

Maintaining a monolingual environment during second language learning time does not diminish the value of the primary language, nor does it preclude its use in the *overall* instructional environment. It simply means that teachers must provide a time and a context where students have to rely solely on their second language to accomplish the goals of the lesson or activity. What is important is to develop a balance of language use distributed across the curriculum and over time. In this way students can use their primary language to maximize conceptual development while making the most of second language time to progress in their second language. This balance also assures that the primary language is not used as a token, through rapid translations, but has its own integrity as a vehicle for conceptual development (Premise 3).

A stumbling-block to creating such environments in schools is the natural tendency for students to use their primary language in all-English situations as a way of acquiring meaning, asking questions, and confirming comprehension. This is to be expected since most of us revert to what we know when confronted by a difficult task. It is possible to encourage the exclusive use of English during second language time, however, by supporting and modeling the use of English and by commending students for attempts made to communicate. When teachers are consistent in sticking to the language of instruction, over time students do respond positively and will increasingly participate using the target language.

Balancing Program Components

Designing an appropriate instructional program for second language learners is a complicated process. As well as acquiring knowledge about science, social studies, math, and so forth, students need to gain the knowledge of form, structure, and style that is already possessed by native speakers. Second language curricula must include the full range of expression that students will be accountable for in school. In very basic terms, students must learn about something, be able to talk about it clearly (ask, answer, and discuss), and be able to read and write about it. Eventually, they must be able to do this within the conventions of standard English.

Because of students' continual growth and change in second language proficiency, the curriculum must be sensitive to, and articulated across, developmental phases. Every level of increasing abstraction demands increasingly sophisticated language skills, and instruction in every area of the curriculum must reflect a commensurate change in the content and cognitive demand required by these changes over time. The cognitive and linguistic demands on students are also constantly shifting across *oral language, reading, writing*, and *content development*. Therefore, in order to extend students' language abilities, carefully orchestrated opportunities in each of these areas will have to be a regular part of daily instruction.

Instruction across these areas will require particular attention to a range of linguistic elements. Because of their lack of familiarity with the language, for example, as part of their oral language, reading, and content instruction, new English learners need specific attention to the formal aspects of language. This does not imply that grammatical structures must be the organizing framework for the curriculum, but rather that they should be accounted for in program planning. In trying to determine how to balance the technical aspects of language use with the academic needs of learners, it is useful to think of creating an overall curriculum with changing priorities. Imagine a camera lens that is focused on a group of people in the mountains. At one moment the lens zooms in on the people in the foreground with the mountains providing a beautiful backdrop. The lens then zooms out to focus on the mountain peaks but the people remain in the picture providing perspective and scale. This same idea applies to the second language curriculum. While both language proficiency and content meaning are always in the picture, the emphasis of particular lessons will shift. The Concept Development Strategy discussed in the next chapter is one way to begin to balance these shifting priorities.

As with the development of all appropriate curriculum, decisions must be made about the topics to cover, how to provide for both language and content learning, and how to devise the settings that will develop the range of abilities that are necessary for success in school (Enright & McCloskey, 1988; Gibbons, 1993). Oral language development must account for both the structure of the language and the specific ways of talking about content. Reading and writing development necessitates building a foundation of vocabulary and knowledge about which to read and write, as well as learning the conventions of English literacy. Content lessons will always have oral and written aspects that require knowledge of these conventions. Although the three areas—oral language, literacy, and content—overlap, if lessons are not designed with a clear idea about the primary focus of any particular instructional activity and how to balance lessons across all three, aspects are likely to be shortchanged. For example, if the primary concern is literacy skills, the content may be treated as incidental. If content and oral language are attempted together, content may predominate and opportunities to extend students' ability to articulate their ideas fall by the wayside.

Integrated Curriculum and Thematic Units

Second language learners have the greatest success in environments where they can meet new language and concepts repeatedly across the instructional day. The more students can hear and see familiar content, ideas, and vocabulary, the more quickly they will be able to comprehend, assimilate, and produce their new language. Therefore, their second language curriculum should not be created in isolation, but should be based on the content of the "regular" instructional program, that is, the core curriculum for the students' age or grade level.

An integrated curriculum, centered around thematic units that encompass all the content areas, is ideal, since it allows students to meet concepts and vocabulary in a variety of settings and contexts (Enright & McCloskey, 1988). Learning about a smaller range of topics in depth rather than trying to cover too many topics superficially increases the chances that input will be understandable, that students will begin to build the kind of schema or internal framework needed for academic success, and that they will begin to incorporate their second language more fully into this schema. Too often, teachers get caught up in trying to get through all the chapters in a textbook or items in a course syllabus. This results in students' knowing very little about a lot of topics. In contrast, when students are allowed to study a topic in depth, they can practice using language at many levels of abstraction and develop academic skills they can then transfer to new topics and ideas. This process can be facilitated by including a deliberate focus on cognitive learning strategies (Chamot & O'Malley, 1994; Herzog, 1995; Oxford, 1990), discussed further in a section below.

Where second language and content-area instruction are the responsibility of different teachers, the creation of an integrated curriculum and the development of content-based instructional materials for language teaching require cooperation and collaboration. While it is not possible to completely revamp a school's curriculum overnight, it is possible for teachers to begin coordinating curriculum with simple and small collaborations regarding a single lesson or a portion of a unit. The kind of collegial collaboration needed to sustain this coordination of curriculum requires frequent, regularly scheduled opportunities for schoolwide planning.

Focusing Instruction. A distinction between a content focus and a language focus has been discussed by Snow, Met, and Genesee (1989). This distinction identifies *language-sensitive content lessons* as different from *content-enriched language lessons*. Language sensitive content lessons are at the core of what is known as "sheltered" teaching or Specially Designed Academic Instruction in English (SDAIE) (Sobul, 1996). The goal of content-focused instruction is to enable students to understand the basic concepts presented in the core areas of math, science, and social studies. In devising instruction it is necessary to find ways to make the content lessons comprehensible to second language learners as well as to provide them with opportunities to actively use the content language they are learning. Features that characterize such an approach include the identification of key concepts and vocabulary in a particular content area or lesson, hands-on interactive activities, visual support (pictures, posters, charts, maps, videos), models, advance organizers, and repetition of concepts across activities and lessons (Gordon & Tobias, 1993). The focus of such lessons is the content itself, and the second language is the medium through which the content is learned. There is minimum use of lecture, and text materials about the topic are provided at a range of reading levels to accommodate the varying language levels of the students. Grammatical accuracy and increasing communicative competence are not the driving forces behind lesson organization. These lessons are described in Chapter 6 as Concept Comprehension Lessons for Categories III and IV (in Categories I and II, these are primary language lessons).

A content-enriched (or content-based) language lesson is a language-focused lesson that utilizes the main ideas and vocabulary of content instruction to sharpen the range of students' linguistic and sociolinguistic skills. These lessons are at the core of what is called content-based ESL, and reflect both spontaneous and scaffolded opportunities for students to develop language. Content-enriched language lessons may be either oral language or reading and writing lessons.

Oral Language Development

Because sharing the ideas they have learned, asking good questions, and seeking and sharing information are all skills students need to develop, oral language plays a critical role in students' overall academic progress. Within the area of oral language, opportunities for both spontaneous language expression and scaffolded oral expression are important.

Spontaneous language lessons use concepts from the content areas to help students gain facility in talking about the main ideas and the interrelations among major themes. Unlike scaffolded lessons, they rely on the language students already know and are able to use. The Integrated Group Lessons described in the next chapter provide an excellent setting for this type of language expression. At the beginning these lessons are more focused on listening, gradually extending over time to encompass more sophisticated verbal expression.

Scaffolded oral expression lessons, on the other hand, provide students the time to practice the uses of English—to say the words, to try out new vocabulary, and to work on expressing their ideas in a safe setting. An important aspect of oral language development lessons is instruction in the technical aspects of language use. Situated within the context of the larger content themes, such instruction focuses on vocabulary development, opportunities to hear and to use basic sentence structures and grammatical conventions, and opportunities to gain practice in using appropriate interaction styles. This kind of practice prepares students for the kind of formal oral language use described by Barnes (1990) as presentational talk, which is often the basis on which student work is evaluated.

Communicative competence (being able to get your message across) is the driving force behind oral language development, and both types of lessons, spontaneous and scaffolded, are necessary as a regular part of a second language program. Unfortunately, once students have made the initial shift to second language literacy, oral language development is usually dropped. Yet, as ideas become more and more complex, learning to use the vocabulary of those ideas and to express them clearly becomes increasingly important. A strong foundation in oral language is also a key to successful reading and writing (something that though also true for native English speakers is all too often missing from the curriculum).

Another useful idea for organizing and integrating language and content teaching is the notion that language teaching objectives can be specified according to whether they are directed toward content-obligatory or content-compatible language (Snow, Met, & Genesee, 1989). Content-obligatory language includes the vocabulary and language structures that are key to understanding and expressing ideas related to content. For example, in order to discuss numbers in a math class, students need to know the names of the numbers as well as expressions like "is smaller than," "is bigger than," "is equal to." Students studying the rain forest might need to learn the names of the various layers of the forest as well as details about the latitude and longitude of the tropics, information on plants, and the habitats of endangered species.

Content-compatible language includes the vocabulary and structures that complement these ideas and can be utilized for additional practice in language lessons focused on form rather than content. In the numbers example, an extension would be not only to practice the names of the numbers through counting activities, calendar work, or games, but to include work on comparatives and superlatives (big, bigger, biggest) across a range of adjectives and to teach the distinction between those that use er/est and more/most. In the rain forest example, in addition to learning the specific vocabulary, students might get practice in prepositions (above, below, in between) as well as general map reading skills, asking for directions, working with numbers, learning names of zoo animals and classification and questioning strategies. Gibbons (1993) suggests that lessons be planned around a framework that requires teachers to identify the topics, activities, language functions, language structures, and vocabulary to be covered in the lesson.

There are many good, in-depth examples both of how to create a content-based second language curriculum and how to create and adapt appropriate materials descriptions (Crandall, 1987; Enright & McCloskey, 1988; Met, 1994; Richard-Amato, 1996). In addition, publishers have responded to the need for content-based materials and increasing numbers of content-oriented books, including entire social studies and science series, have been created specifically for second language learners. While these series carry with them the problems inherent in all broad-based textbooks, they do represent a substantial addition to the resources available to teachers for instructional planning. In addition, some new ESL series have incorporated both content themes and learning strategies (see Chamot & O'Malley, 1994; Chamot, Cummins, O'Malley, Kessler, & Wong-Fillmore, 1996). As with all curriculum decisions, in choosing content-based ESL materials it is important to consider the topics covered, how students will be involved in the activities, and whether students will be engaged in activities that require or allow them to use higher-order thinking skills.

Literacy in the Second Language

No matter what category of services can be offered to students, at some point they will need to begin formal literacy instruction in their second language. Common to all program categories is the need for transition periods, the efficacy of situating literacy instruction within the overarching themes of content instruction, and achieving a balance between meaning and the technical aspects of reading and writing.

When and how to approach this formal English reading must be part of a school's overall plan for second language learners. This decision should be based on a variety of factors, including students' level of oral proficiency in English, their level of literacy in the primary language, and their level of access to instruction in the primary language. Criteria for these decisions are discussed in detail in Chapter 6. A deliberate process for deciding when students are ready for all-English instruction must be put in place. This process should be based on how much students can understand and use English for themselves. Without strong oral fluency or an adequate vocabulary base, students will find it difficult to make sense of the text they encounter.

The goal of literacy development is to help students become proficient readers and writers of English and able communicators of their ideas. This includes everything from reporting on a storybook read for pleasure to being able to use literacy skills to analyze the social forces that affect students' lives (Cummins, 1994; Freire, 1970, 1985; Shannon, 1990). Whether students are developing literacy in their primary language or not, initial reading should focus on meaning. The ideas students understand and can talk about in English are the most appropriate basis for instruction. Thematic units help to support beginning literacy instruction by increasing students' access to concepts and ideas across the school day. They also provide the impetus for the kind of group experiences that can form the basis for second language literacy development.

A whole language approach, although well suited for literacy development in the native language, can present some formidable challenges to second language readers and writers. The emphasis on individual reading selections and self-selected topics, for example, often makes it difficult for students to discuss their stories, because there is a relatively small common fund of vocabulary and ideas on which to ground meaningful discussions.

As an example, let's examine how the practice of "author's chair" poses special challenges for second language learners. Typically, during author's chair students read aloud drafts of work in progress to solicit feedback for revision. They can also use author's chair to share a finished product or a publishable piece with classmates. In order to participate successfully, students must learn the roles of both author and audience member. Authors must have written something that can be understood by classmates, know how to ask for help, and know how to record and make use of the feedback given to them. Audience members must be able to listen critically in order to provide positive feedback, as well as constructive criticism.

These roles are challenging for monolingual English speakers, and pose additional hurdles for second language learners. If students can't understand their peers' stories, they will not be able to provide appropriate feedback. Even if their understanding is sufficient, they may not have mastered enough English to give feedback or to express themselves in a way that is generally understandable to their peers. As a result, author's chair may unintentionally shut them off from participation instead of opening up avenues for self-expression. Finally, author's chair assumes a value on public display that may or may not be culturally appropriate for all children.

This is not to say that practices such as author's chair should be abandoned for second language learners. It simply means that teachers must recognize and attend to the additional support second language learners need in order to successfully participate. For example, oral language lessons could be developed for preparing second language learners for author's chair. Activities could include opportunities for role play in a safe setting, explicit instruction of needed vocabulary, and special attention to building common experiences for writing to increase comprehension. Another example of appropriate support is presented below.

Help or Hinderance

In a fifth-grade class composed of English, Spanish, and Vietnamese speakers, the current theme is "How we Interact with our World." As part of their work around this theme, students choose a topic to research on their own or in pairs and to share with the rest of the class. The teacher has brought dozens of books and resources to the classroom to assist students in their independent investigations. While this is not a bilingual classroom, the teacher found two books in Vietnamese and several resources in Spanish that students are free to use in their research. The final discussions, however, will be in English so that all the students can participate.

Although the teacher in this class is trying to support students by providing them with primary language resources, this approach is problematic for several reasons. It assumes that, on their own, students have the necessary skills to comprehend and interpret the information in their primary language well enough to make use of it. Further, once students have gotten the information in the primary language, they are expected to be able to translate these ideas into English without help, a very sophisticated skill for which they have received neither instruction nor guidance.

It is possible, with careful planning, however, to organize instruction to benefit from the availability of even limited resources in the primary language. For example, there could be regularly scheduled opportunities for students to discuss their ideas in the primary language with either school personnel or community members. Or such discussions might be organized in response to the availability of particular resources. It is important that such opportunities be carefully planned so that they do not turn into passive lectures by people unfamiliar with the context or goals of instruction. In any case, second language instruction would have to build on this knowledge. Students could then be guided in the transfer of these ideas by having focused opportunities to talk and write about the topic in English.

Language Experience Approach. Modified Language Experience Approach (LEA) is a strategy that can be used effectively with linguistically diverse students of all ages. Its strength lies in its integration of oral language, reading, writing, and content themes. LEA can be used to make the transition into English reading in Category I and II programs after students have developed a strong foundation in primary language literacy. It can also be the main approach to beginning literacy instruction in Categories III and IV. Adapted for second language learners, the essence of LEA is "What I can think about, I can talk about. What I can say, I can write (or someone can write for me). What I can write, I can read" (Gillet & Gentry, 1983; Van Allen & Allen, 1967). The major modification of the Language Experience Approach for second language learners focuses on the "What I can say." Although filled with ideas, many second language learners are not able to express their ideas fully in English. Therefore, oral language development that helps students become flexible and fluent in the expression of their ideas must play a much more prominent role in this process than is generally assumed for native speakers.

The basic format of the modified Language Experience Approach consists of several predictable steps revolving around language-sensitive content lessons. First, teachers organize specific activities or experiences based on class themes and students' interests. Following this activity the teacher engages students in an oral discussion of what happened. Scaffolded lessons support students in both discussions and spontaneous language during the activities. Oral discussion and scaffolded lessons are followed by a shared writing process in which students dictate their thoughts to the teacher, producing a group-generated chart or story that reflects the steps, impressions, and reactions to the experience. The chart created during the group writing becomes the basis for individualized reading experiences. The features of this modified Approach are (1) core ideas, (2) group experience, (3) scaffolded oral expression activities, (4) LEA group writing, (5) using key phrases and key vocabulary, and (6) development of independent work.

1. *Core ideas.* The activities that form the basis for the LEA should emerge from the core ideas and key concepts of the themes that comprise the academic curriculum. This helps to create coherence for students as it provides for exposure across contexts to the language, vocabulary, and structures they need to know. In this way vocabulary and ideas are learned in meaningful contexts and not in isolation.

2. *Group experience.* The group nature of the LEA experience is fundamental for several reasons. While all of the students will draw on their unique background experiences in relating to the instruction, no student is left out of the discussion of their common instructional activity. This gives each student an opportunity to participate equally, which is not always the case when we ask students to use their own experiences to write or think about an instructional topic. The oral discussions (spontaneous language opportunities) that are central to the experiences ensure that second language learners have opportunities to become familiar with, talk about, and use the vocabulary and concepts that comprise the experiences. These discussions can also draw from, or be the basis for, students' scaffolded oral expression lessons. Finally, by providing a group of students with common experiences, teachers can help to create a greater sense of community and cohesion among the students.

3. *Scaffolded oral expression activities* (modification). A major modification of the Language Experience Approach is the use of a scaffolded language lesson (see also Chapter 6). In these lessons students have the opportunity to use various forms of language in ways that help them to become comfortable and fluent in spontaneous discussions. In scaffolded language lessons particular linguistic elements are targeted, and students are engaged in interactions in which they have opportunities to use and practice these forms. Targeted language is drawn from the content and themes of the overall lesson, contextualizing the new linguistic learnings. These lessons can be very helpful before as well as after the group experience, preparing students to recognize and be able to use the words and discourse patterns of the activity.

4. *LEA group writing.* The group writing process is a critical step in the LEA. Charts and stories are created in which students can see their own thoughts and ideas in print as well as how to put them there. They allow students to see the vocabulary and key concepts of the unit in a context that is meaningful. The student-dictated charts are especially valuable

because they reflect language and structures appropriate to students' language proficiency levels.

The question always arises of whether teachers should write down students' "mistakes." It is important to remember that in a second language setting, the purpose of the M-LEA is not simply literacy development, but also to help students learn the forms and structures of the second language. This is not a dialectical issue, but a matter of providing students with accurate models and representations of the oral language they have been practicing. Providing effective oral language preparation and modeling before the writing phase is key to preparing students to orally compose text that closely approximates what will be written down. The scaffolded oral expression lessons can be particularly helpful in this regard.

The charts also provide a model of written language that students can use in their own writing. This is especially important in view of the current trend toward encouraging students to be creative and invent their own spelling, a task that may be well suited to native speakers but is particularly difficult for students who do not have either familiarity with or mastery of the sound system and vocabulary in English. In addition, the group stories provide reading material for students that is familiar and predictable. In this way content materials can be incorporated into reading instruction at levels that are appropriate to students' stage of development.

5. *Using key phrases and key vocabulary.* Once the group writing stage has been completed, students move on to create their own written word files or word banks. Key phrases and vocabulary needed to talk about the content in a meaningful way should be built into both the chart stories and students' own files. These words and phrases reinforce the core ideas and provide predictable patterns for students to use and recognize. They then become the tools that students can use as background information and resources for independent reading and writing.

6. *Development of independent work.* The final component of an LEA cycle is the student's independent reading, writing, and extending experiences. This may include personal journals, choices for free reading, and opportunities to explore the topics in other areas of the curriculum.

This cycle of organizing activities, talking about content, creating group stories, and engaging in independent work is one that is repeated throughout the instructional program. The predictable and recursive nature of the activities provides students multiple opportunities to use language in different ways.

Transition Periods. Transition periods mark a shift in the formal academic expectations for second language learners, and they redefine the relationships in instruction of one language to the other. Although transitions are marked by decision-making points, they are substantially more than a dot on a continuum. Rather than indicating the end of the second language program, for example, the introduction of formal English reading should initiate a period in which specialized strategies, alternative materials, and extensive mediation practices are incorporated into the second language program.

Four basic questions are critical to transition decisions: (1) When are students ready to begin a formal English reading program? (2) What are students bringing to the all-English reading process? (3) What do they need to become successful English readers? (4) When are students academically ready to successfully function in all-English instruction *without support*?

As the examples in Premise 7 demonstrate, second language students who have been exited from services are often left to their own devices to negotiate complex tasks and topics in English. By understanding and mediating the transition period, teachers can provide students the kinds of support they need to eventually succeed on their own. Because it is possible to predict many of the difficulties students will encounter and the errors they will make during these periods, it is possible to provide materials necessary to prepare students to deal successfully with more complex English tasks. For example, developing sufficient oral language to communicate their ideas clearly prior to "writing" a story about the implications of the Bill of Rights gives students a broader understanding, range of words, and ways to express their ideas.

The transition period for students who receive formal primary language literacy (Categories I and II), must include help for students to understand the differences and similarities between their first and second languages. Even though students making this transition are literate and can transfer most of the knowledge and skills they have acquired in reading and writing to the literacy tasks of their second language, they will need specific help in mastering the vocabulary and particular conventions of English, as well as in connecting new ideas to an already developed internal schema. They will also need to learn rhetorical structures in English and cultural schemata that may be different from reading in their first language (Escamilla & Medina, 1993). When and how transition periods will occur will be considered in each program category.

Learning Strategies

Learning strategies that encompass the tactics and methods that can be used to acquire, remember, and utilize information and knowledge provide students with a framework for approaching all academic tasks and can facilitate both their linguistic and academic development. Research indicates that all successful learners generally make use of a variety of specific strategies or techniques to enhance their learning. Drawing these strategies to students' attention and teaching them how to consciously incorporate them into their own study process provide an additional tool for academic success (Oxford, 1990; Rigney, 1978; Rubin, 1975).

Strategy use with second language learners provides them with a way to approach content in an organized and analytical fashion, and can be particularly useful for students in the intermediate and upper grades. The Cognitive Academic Language Learning Approach (CALLA) (Chamot & O'Malley, 1994) provides a comprehensive framework for understanding and implementing learning strategies in a content-based approach to language instruction. In CALLA three categories of strategies are distinguished: metacognitive strategies or global skills that involve higher-order thought processes in planning for, and ongoing monitoring of, learning; cognitive strategies that involve learners in the particular task at hand; and social/affective strategies that transcend a particular task and apply to the learning situation and how students act and interact with teachers and peers. Other kinds of strategies have also been identified that can help students overcome difficulties or blocks related specifically to literacy development. These include ways to approach reading, responding to text, writing, and spelling (Kucer, 1995).

Two aspects of learning strategy instruction are important. The first is that teachers must consciously choose particular strategies to incorporate into their instruction, for example, providing advance organizers or consciously summarizing each day's lesson, or modeling note-taking skills on the board. The second is that students must also become aware of and familiar with the strategies, and consciously begin to make use of them as they approach academic and curricular tasks. This can happen only if teachers draw attention to the strategies presented and help students name and use them in everyday work.

Strategy instruction is particularly effective when used by all teachers in a program or building. Coordinating the use of strategies across classrooms increases the chances that students can make connections across content areas, helping to build student confidence that they have tools they can rely on to approach any learning task.

Other Second Languages

In most schools, the second language program is aimed at teaching English as the second language. However, a growing number of bilingual programs are seeking to develop Spanish (or French or Japanese, etc.)

proficiency for native English speakers. Parents' decisions to enroll their children in these programs are strongly influenced by the sociopolitical context, by expectations about who bilingualism is for, and by the value placed on different languages in the broader community. Depending on the context, parents may rush to place their children in Chinese or Hebrew classes, but hesitate to enroll them in a Spanish-English bilingual program. The ambivalence that many people have about the value of particular languages and the benefits of bilingualism, as well as the kinds of cross-cultural interactions in which they want their children to participate, play out in the nature and level of quality of second language programs. Maintaining the majority community's interest in having children participate in bilingual programs requires that the context in which first and second language students work be noncompensatory, and that these programs show results in terms of second language acquisition, as well as academic achievement.

In most bilingual programs there is usually a great disparity in the second language expectations of students from the two language groups. For example, while native Spanish speakers must always become proficient in English (ESL) in order to achieve academic success, native English speakers are seldom expected to learn enough Spanish (SSL) to do any academic work. This difference in expectations has important ramifications in terms of overall program effectiveness, and the climate for learning in general. Occasional, catch-as-catch-can lessons, and the lack of academic content instruction and accountability for content mastery in Spanish for English speakers, for example, sends the message to all students that Spanish is not really a serious language for learning. In addition, in programs where the burden of learning a second language falls only on non-native English speakers, these students always tend to be in the position of knowing less than their English-speaking counterparts, who are then always seen as the experts. This affects students' attitudes, not only about learning a second language, but about the language itself and the status of those who speak that language.

In contrast, when all students in a bilingual program are expected to learn academic content in both languages in order to achieve academic success, the nature of the program changes. For example, in a Category I program where biliteracy is the goal for students from each language group, the criteria and the organizational plan for, say, Spanish instruction parallels that of the English program, with Spanish as second language students being expected to develop language, literacy, and content expertise in Spanish. When everyone is expected to gain knowledge and accomplish school tasks in both languages, the status of the languages becomes more balanced and Spanish is validated as a language for learning important information. In such programs, everyone gets to experience the frustration and difficulty of learning to function in a second language, and everyone also experiences the positive feeling of being experts, able to help their peers struggling to acquire a second language.

As will be discussed in the next chapter, it is far easier to plan instruction when the program also includes goals for the development of bilingualism for native English speakers. When the expectations for both groups are similar, there is increased flexibility in grouping students for different aspects of instruction, since each group will need a parallel set of experiences.

ISSUES UNIQUE TO EACH PROGRAM CATEGORY

Thus far, the discussion of second language learning has not dealt directly with what is occurring in the primary language. But across the four program categories decisions about how programs will be configured must encompass the relationship of the two languages to one another. As developed more fully in Chapter 7, growth in each language can be represented along a continuum beginning with basic oral communication skills, moving toward the use of oral language for the expression of more abstract ideas, and later to reading and writing at increasing levels of sophistication. While the developmental paths for each language are similar, the level at which students are functioning in one language or the other is rarely equivalent. This difference between proficiency in the first and second languages occurs because students rarely enter school fully bilingual. Older second language learners, for example, may have advanced skills in literacy in their primary language but be limited in their ability to read and discuss English text. These students still need to acquire the vocabulary, syntactic structures, and sound system required to make sense of their English reading. While such students may be able to talk in abstract terms about a topic in their primary language, their emerging second language abilities will usually confine them to expressing only very concrete and basic levels of meaning in English.

The relationship between languages within the curriculum affects the role each will play in instruction as well as expectations for its use. The balance of the two languages shifts depending on program category and on students' changing levels of development. The more limited the opportunities for primary language instruction, the greater the need to teach the concepts and content of the academic curriculum through the second language. In programs with little primary language support, second language development is a slower and more deliberate process in which students will need more help in order to express these concepts and ideas clearly (Collier, 1995).

Students' access to the primary language for content instruction affects the focus of second language oral, content, and literacy instruction. Finally, the relationship of the two languages in instruction has implications for transition criteria as well as for the nature of the transition period. In the following discussion the balance of languages, the language learning contexts, and the transition elements unique to each program category will be discussed.

Category I: Full Primary Language Foundation

Balance of Language Use and Contexts. When primary language instruction is available for non–English speakers, these students can depend on their background of experiences and strengths in the primary language to move new ideas forward and to fully develop their linguistic and cognitive repertoire. Daily planned opportunities to develop second language proficiency are also an integral part of the curriculum. In Category I, the initial goal of the second language program is to develop a strong oral base in English, while the foundation for literacy and concept development is advanced in the primary language. Second language instruction time should focus not on presenting the basic content, but rather on helping students develop the ability to think through the second language, develop the vocabulary and structures they need to talk about the ideas being elaborated in their primary language, and participate in spontaneous discussions of a topic. A strong oral language component provides students these opportunities to learn how to interact with ideas and concepts introduced across content areas.

As students progress through the grades, they will also begin to interact informally with English literacy by listening to stories, interacting with ambient print, and perhaps picking up an English book during free-reading time. Over time, the emphasis will shift from informal literacy experiences to a transition into formal English reading, as described below.

Transition to English Literacy. In a Category I program, where students receive primary language content and literacy instruction, the transition period involves the shift from primary language–only literacy instruction to the addition of informal then formal second language reading and biliteracy. If students are in a short-term program, a second phase of transition will occur from primary language instruction to all-English instruction.

The distinction between informal and formal reading is particularly significant in programs where primary language support is provided, because, as discussed in Chapter 4, concurrent formal literacy instruction at the beginning levels is detrimental to the development of a strong primary foundation (Escamilla & Medina, 1993). During second language instruction and in other parts of the day, students will have many informal opportunities to encounter print and text in English, and they will undoubtedly show an interest in trying to read it. This interest is important to the overall success of a second language program, but it does not indicate a readiness for *formal* English reading. The issue is not that children shouldn't have these informal experiences with English print, but rather that when they do, such experiences do not take over or displace their primary language literacy development before that literacy is fully in place. Unfortunately, the quality of the foundation established in the primary language is often ignored. As we have discussed, there is a tremendous pressure to move into English whether it is the most sound academic decision or not. By recognizing the distinction between informal and formal reading in a second language, teachers can plan more appropriate choices for students, choices that will allow them to enjoy their exploration of English books without undermining their literacy development in the primary language.

For children who are beginning readers, it will typically take several years to reach the beginning of the transition period. During this time, students' oral second language development and informal reading experiences are the focus of English language development. Certainly children progress at different rates, but in general it might be reasonable to expect that students will be ready to begin formal English reading after approximately 3½ to 4 years of literacy instruction in a strong sustained primary language program. For older students, this transition may occur more quickly, depending on primary language literacy level and English language proficiency.

Category II: Primary Language Support—Literacy Only

Balance of Languages and Contexts. In a Category II program, students develop initial literacy in their first language with a focus on content in their primary language. Content reading can provide the opportunity to meet and develop understanding of new concepts that will then be dealt with primarily in English. Because much of the content instruction is conducted in English, the second language program carries a greater responsibility for developing content-area vocabulary and concepts than in a Category I program. In a Category II program, formal literacy instruction will not be the initial focus of second language lessons. Instead, second language time should focus on oral language development, balanced between spontaneous (language-sensitive content lesson) and scaffolded (content-enriched language lesson) opportunities to use content vocabulary and ideas based on instructional themes. In this way students are provided maximum access to the main ideas and vocabulary of the curriculum in English. Informal reading activities also become a more important element in students' English instruction with opportunities for group "writing" being a strong supporting feature.

Transition to English Literacy. Although students in programs where only primary language literacy is offered will have had greater informal exposure to English text and vocabulary, the transition to English literacy should follow the same basic guidelines as in Category I. Gaps in students' understanding of content material will be likely, both because students must learn content mainly through their second language and because their base in their primary language is not as fully elaborated as that of students with a full primary language program. Because the primary language is available only on a limited basis for the discussion and learning of abstract concepts, the transition period to all-English instruction should be longer than in Category I in order to guarantee that students will have sufficient opportunity to consolidate conceptual knowledge in their second language. Attention to the possible gaps in understanding, to the depth of understanding regardless of oral fluency, and to not rushing too quickly into formal English literacy is particularly important in this program category.

Category III: Primary Language Content Reinforcement

Balance of Languages and Contexts. A Category III program provides students with some, albeit limited, access to conceptual knowledge in their primary language. Initial literacy instruction will begin immediately in English. This means that just as students are beginning to gain meaning through their second language, they will also be expected to begin to put those ideas into print. Coordinating the curriculum across languages continues to be critical in order to ensure that during second language instruction students can work on the same concepts and content themes that they will be discussing during primary language time, thus using the primary language to full advantage. Students will need substantial experience with oral language and vocabulary development in English, as well as exposure to new concepts and many opportunities to act on information related to the main content themes. Concept comprehension as well as scaffolded oral expression lessons should be balanced in the second language program.

The modified Language Experience Approach described above should play a central role in organizing the literacy component of second language instruction in Category III. The experiences that form the core of the LEA should be based on content themes. The success of these lessons will depend on the comprehensibility of instruction and on providing students with multiple opportunities to access meaning and interact with new learning. Reading aloud to students from a variety of texts and materials in order to expose them to the range of genres that they will eventually have to be able to read and write about on their own will be very important. In addition, a specific component that focuses on the sound-symbol correspondence and literacy conventions of English will have to be included.

As discussed in Chapter 4, the need for support from family and community members is even more critical where there is little primary language support in school. An important role that second language teachers can play is to actively enlist and encourage this participation of parents and others in helping students explore and extend their knowledge of content themes in the primary language. Personnel responsible for primary language concept reinforcement instruction can assist teachers in providing parents with ideas and suggestions for the kinds of questions to ask and the types of discussions to encourage in the home language around particular topics. These questions and discussions will help to develop the underlying schema necessary to support knowledge about the content in the second language.

Transition to No Second Language Support. For students in a Category III program there is no transition to English reading since students begin literacy immediately in their second language. There is a transition period, however, that begins when students are ready to receive all of their content instruction in English without additional support. Because the demands of English also increase as oral proficiency and grade-level requirements increase (becoming continually more abstract and decontextualized), monitoring and mediating understanding of unfamiliar content and language will still be a support needed by students.

Category IV: All-English

Balance of Languages and Contexts. Students in Category IV programs have virtually no formal access in school to the funds of knowledge they have developed in their primary language. In order to enhance their access to the content of the academic curriculum, they need to spend a greater amount of time in lessons designed to support second language learning. Lessons that focus on language, others that support concept comprehension, and others that focus on initial literacy instruction all should be part of their total program. The strategies discussed throughout this chapter present the framework for instruction in a Category IV program. All settings in which second language learners are instructed should provide for comprehensible input, active participation, and the monitoring of understanding. This does not mean that students need to be moved to another room or to other teachers, but rather that appropriate instructional and grouping strategies are employed.

When students encounter themes, topics, and vocabulary across the day, they have a greater chance to make meaning out of their instruction. As in Category III, thematic units and the modified Language Experience Approach to reading are important organizing structures for the integration of oral interactions, literacy instruction, and content. Where there are sufficient numbers of second language learners in a school or at a particular level, it may be feasible to organize sheltered content instruction for a specific subject or a portion of a unit. Care must be taken, however, to assure that students also have opportunities to interact with native English-speaking peers in meaningful activities on a regular basis (see Chapter 6).

Again, as in Category III, the role of parents and community in Category IV programs takes on ever-increasing importance. In order to help prepare families and others to assist in reinforcing the main concepts of the curriculum, it is useful to be able to anticipate upcoming content themes and to communicate this information to parents. Joining with parents as partners in the learning process requires advance planning. It is enhanced by including other community and district resources to translate information and open lines of communication in parents' home languages. It is also important to remember that even in a school with no formal primary language instruction, schoolwide efforts can be made to acknowledge and respect the existence of the multiple languages and cultures in the building, for example, through signs, announcements, and visual images.

Transition to No Second Language Support. The transition period in Category IV is similar to that in Category III. Students will begin initial literacy instruction in English right away and the transition period will support them in becoming ready to receive all their content instruction in English without second language support. Students in Category IV programs have very little access in school to the funds of knowledge they have developed in their primary language. They must rely on their second language to carry all their academic development, which, if we think back to our Chinese example in Chapter 4, is a tremendous task. For these reasons, it may take several years for students to be ready to make the shift to formal instruction in all content areas in English without support. Steps can be taken on a schoolwide basis to ensure that in the halls and in every classroom, teachers attend to students' need for comprehensibility, and provide multiple ways to access the meaning of instruction.

Decision Making on Your Own

1. Questions that highlight major issues regarding second language development include: How does your program meet the varying needs of students from different backgrounds? What strategies do you employ to assure that instruction is understandable to second language learners? How have you organized instruction so that students gain both linguistic and academic competence in their second language? How do you help students begin reading in their second language?

In order to answer these questions about your setting you will need to add the following information to your school profile: students' circumstances of being in the United States, language proficiency assessment data, number of students at each language-proficiency level, initial placement information, level of literacy development in the primary language, support services offered by the district, which teachers have training in working with second language learners, and available materials and resources.

2. Think about the Basic Premises and major elements presented in this chapter on second language. Generate a list of additional questions that will help you to decide how best to serve your students.

3. Compare your list of questions with those of a colleague and refine your list. Are there any major issues you haven't addressed?

4. Form a small group and brainstorm the optimal second language practices possible in your setting. Use the Basic Premises highlighted in this chapter to weigh your decisions.

5. List two or three changes that might have to be made.

6. What are the implications of your decisions for other areas, for example, assessment, the utilization of staff, and scheduling?

7. Add these data to your school profile.

CHAPTER 6

Curriculum and Content Development

Key Premises to Consider

• *Premise 1—Active Learning.* Knowledge is best acquired when learners actively participate in meaningful activities that are constructive in nature and appropriate to their level of development.

• *Premise 2—The primary language foundation.* The more comprehensive the use of the primary language, the greater the potential for linguistically diverse students to be academically successful. There are always ways to nurture the primary language regardless of school resources.

• *Premise 4—Strategies for second language development.* Second language development creates an added dimension to instructional decision making. Instruction must reflect specific strategies designed to meet the needs of second language learners.

• *Premise 5—Contexts for second language development.* Second language instruction must be organized to provide students the time, experiences, and opportunities they need to fully develop language proficiency. This requires a range of social and academic contexts in which both language and content are emphasized.

• *Premise 6—First and second language environments.* Bilingual academic proficiency requires that clear, distinct, and meaning-enriched contexts for each language be created during instructional time.

• *Premise 10—Planning for cross-cultural interactions.* Instruction must be organized to help students understand and respect themselves and their own culture as well as the cultures of the broader society. Planned cross-cultural interactions are an essential component of programs for all students.

Perspectives on curriculum in programs for linguistically diverse students are intertwined with prevailing attitudes and tensions in the broader educational community about what content should be taught, where the emphasis of learning should be placed, and what methods should be used for the delivery. (Sinclair & Ghory, 1987; Sleeter, 1991) The issue of what to teach and how to teach it extends beyond a single teacher or grade level. It involves how the curriculum will be articulated across grade levels within a program, and how it will be coordinated among different teachers and other service providers. The goal of the decision-making process is to create a rigorous curriculum that prepares students to be academically successful, while at the same time respecting and affirming the multiple perspectives present in their communities.

Content-area learning requires sophisticated levels of language use and comprehension (Chamot & O'Malley, 1994). In content-area classes (social studies, science, math, etc.) students are asked to read and understand ideas often far removed from their experience. They are asked to solve problems, to analyze, evaluate, and synthesize a wide range of information, and to apply their knowledge to new situations. In the give-and-take of discussion they are required to ask and answer questions about the information they are reading and learning, and to present and defend their ideas orally and in writing. As they progress through the grades they are required to engage in these more difficult tasks with fewer visual supports and examples. In order to gain experience and flexibility in these areas, students must engage in specific kinds of activities that will help them develop these academic competencies.

Content-area instruction is important not only for linguistic and cognitive development, but also for the rich opportunities it offers students from different language and cultural backgrounds to interact with one another, sharing knowledge, perspectives, and language. Organizing instruction to take advantage of all these possibilities and to account for language use is the focus of this chapter.

Planning for the interaction of bilingualism and academic content competence is challenging. It requires accounting for first and second language development, balanced within a cross-cultural context. The Concept Development Strategy (CDS) presented in this chapter provides a framework for curriculum planning that accomplishes these several purposes.

Decision Making: Ask Yourself

What types of content tasks will students be expected to accomplish in each language?

How can depth of content knowledge, and the ability to express it, best be developed?

What opportunities do students need in order to be successful in these tasks?

How can instruction across languages be balanced to provide these opportunities?

What particular attention should be paid to language use?
Where possible, how can content delivery be organized to foster bilingualism for all students?

PERSPECTIVES ON CURRICULUM AND CONCEPT DEVELOPMENT

In every setting, the choices and decisions that must be made about the content, perspectives, and purposes of instruction are as important as the methods that will be used to deliver it. Curriculum is, in essence, how we put into practice our beliefs about how students learn and how teachers should teach, and there are many ways in which it can be approached. In the perspective we embrace, instruction should be sensitive to student needs, and students should be actively engaged in activities that utilize their creativity, intellect, and skills to learn new material. Teachers actively guide learning, always urging students forward by providing opportunities and contexts that build on prior knowledge, consolidate new meanings and understandings, and apply new knowledge (Connelly & Clandinin, 1988).

A major issue in current discussions about education is what constitutes an appropriate educational program for the increasingly diverse population of today's public schools (Liston & Zeichner, 1991; Nieto, 1992). Much of the debate centers on the definition and scope of multicultural education. It is clear that some methods of instruction are better suited than others to a curriculum that seeks to support equity and empowerment. As Banks (1994) indicates, a multicultural curriculum must support the development of critical thinking, and consists "of the methods, activities, and questions teachers use to help students to understand, investigate and determine how implicit cultural assumptions, frames of reference, perspectives and biases within a discipline influence the ways in which knowledge is constructed" (p. 9). That is, a multicultural curriculum helps students "to understand how knowledge is created and how it is influenced by the racial, ethnic, and social-class positions of individuals and groups" (ibid.). Instruction should give students the opportunity to think critically, to test and question ideas, to interact fully with the content, to learn to understand the perspective of others, to discriminate among ideas, and to form and defend their own points of view.

For bilingual students, academic development is enhanced when specific opportunities are organized so that students can interact in all the aspects of instruction described above, in both their first and second languages. As discussed in Chapter 5, for second language learners, the development of academic proficiency in the content areas also requires a range of lessons that shift the focus of instruction between understand-ing ideas and concepts and the ability to communicate those ideas and learnings. These different aspects of linguistic and academic development require different types of lessons, necessitating a range of different be-haviors and responses from students and teachers alike.

When lessons focus on concepts, the emphasis is on the understand-ing students are gaining from the information they may be hearing, or reading, and the activities they are experiencing. These lessons are planned to provide ways for students to use this knowledge, and to dem-onstrate their understanding of key concepts. Students might be talking and sharing, but they are just as likely to be observing, listening, reading, or silently concentrating on performing a task. The role of the teacher in content-focused lessons is to organize and present content-area knowl-edge in a way that makes concepts understandable to students. There-fore, they might be demonstrating, telling, or questioning. Communicat-ing information to students and checking their understanding are the focus of teachers' attention.

In lessons that focus on language and expression, on the other hand, students extend their facility in expressing their knowledge and ideas, and must acquire a variety of ways to talk *about* the information they are learn-ing. Emphasis is placed on students' ability to communicate their ideas by organizing, editing, and refining them, first orally and then in writing. In lessons that develop communicative proficiency, students are continu-ally talking and sharing, listening to each other in order to respond to each other. Students learn ways to ask better questions, to give more complete and well-reasoned answers, to present the information they think is im-portant, and to expand their knowledge of vocabulary and structure. In lessons with a language focus teachers are more likely to be listening, modeling, and prompting. They minimize their own talk, encouraging and supporting as much student talk as possible.

As an example, let's examine aspects of a science experiment on the difference between solutions and mixtures. In a content-focused lesson a teacher could, by talking aloud through the process, use a science ex-periment to identify the properties of solutions and mixtures and model for students how they might think about what they were doing. She might also have students experiment with each, and observe the properties for themselves, describing what happened and how the solutions and mix-tures looked similar or different from one another.

In a language-focused lesson, on the other hand, she would use the science experiment with the purpose of having students learn to explain what they observed in detail to each other, retell the steps they went through and the observations they made, or practice asking each other questions and refining their ability to give good answers and reasons for responses.

ISSUES ACROSS PROGRAM CATEGORIES

The way in which curriculum issues are handled varies across school settings. In some districts the question of what will be taught is pre-scribed in great detail, and teachers are held closely accountable for following established guidelines. In others, curriculum objectives are broadly stated and teachers are given a tremendous amount of flexibil-ity in designing their lessons. No matter what the setting, the decision-making process for content-area instruction for linguistically diverse students should encompass three major dimensions: determining the content to be taught, providing the types of lessons that will lead to full academic content competency, and organizing for the optimal use of each of the students' languages.

What to Teach

The question of what to teach is influenced by many factors, including national, state, and local standards, published guidelines for particular content areas, a multicultural perspective, the availability of resources, and textbook policies. In programs for students from diverse linguistic and cultural backgrounds, there are also additional concerns that impact the curriculum decision-making process. These include how to plan for ap-propriate language use, how to adjust curriculum to meet the needs of a wide range of language proficiency while still providing a rigorous cur-riculum for all students, and how to provide a curriculum that is inclu-sive of multicultural and community perspectives.

These concerns pose very real challenges. For example, in order to facilitate student understanding, teachers will often have to adjust the instructional program to make it clearer and more accessible. Or, in order to be sensitive to the diversity of their students, they may find it necessary to adjust traditional curricula that reflect a monocultural per-spective insensitive to their students' history, language, and culture. As a result of such adjustments, the curricula in bilingual and second lan-guage programs often look different from those of the monolingual English program.

Although the reasons for making these adjustments or modifications are important and valid, they have wide-ranging ramifications, and can raise a number of concerns. Teachers must be able to understand and justify their actions. For example, parents of linguistically diverse students who, like all parents, are interested in what their children are learning in school don't want them to receive a watered-down, simplified curriculum just because they may not yet be fluent in English. They want their children to receive a curriculum that is similar and parallel in content, experiences, and expectations to that of all other students within a school or district. In addition, for many the content of the mainstream curriculum reflects the culture of power and possibility (Delpit, 1988), and they do not want them to lose out on something they feel everyone else gets. While in many cases their children are receiving a better instructional program than they would in more traditional classrooms, parents' feelings about their children having access to knowledge and ideas should be recognized and respected.

Teachers, particularly those in the upper grades, may also express concerns about modifications to the curriculum when it affects their own instructional program. For example, as students progress through the grades moving out of second language programs (and perhaps out of bilingual ones), teachers may find that even students who have been in school for a number of years have gaps in prerequisite knowledge, even though they may have acquired basic literacy and academic skills. Instead of recognizing that they may not have been taught the concepts and vocabulary, teachers tend to see the students themselves as somehow lacking. These tensions in curriculum development highlight the need to specifically balance the various goals in students' programs. All curricular modifications must be carefully considered to assure that students will be provided with the basic information and knowledge base needed to be academically competitive, within a culturally and instructionally sensitive curriculum. How, when, and where to make curricular modifications are necessarily important aspects of the decision-making process for programs and schools.

Because of the need to create a more appropriate and inclusive curriculum, teachers who make the commitment to effectively serve linguistically and culturally diverse students often must also take on tasks that create an added dimension to their work. For example, where school district goals do not account for the needs and perspectives of all students, efforts will have to be made to influence the direction of districtwide curriculum toward a more multicultural perspective. This can happen most effectively when teachers and community members join together in efforts to expand and modify the curriculum for all students in a district. As will be discussed in Chapter 8, when schools are directly in touch with the needs and desires of their families and communities, they can play a proactive role in advocating for a more inclusive curriculum that can benefit all segments of the total community.

Language Use

The second area of concern in developing curriculum is that of which language should be used, and when, for instruction. The issue of clearly defined and enriched language contexts is perhaps most apparent in the area of content development. The argument has been made that the language students use while learning new content is less important than the quality of the content with which they are engaged (De Avila, 1983; De Avila & Duncan, 1980). There is no doubt that both the nature of the tasks in which students participate and the mode of instructional delivery are crucial. Poor programs and poor educational experiences will bear poor results whether they are conducted in first, second, or mixed language situations. Curriculum planners, however, cannot ignore the relationship between what is thought about and language as a tool for that thinking and cognitive development.

It is important to remember that bilingual proficiency does not mean that an individual uses both languages interchangeably at all times. Full bilingualism reflects a command of two separate language systems with a fluency and flexibility that allows the speaker to communicate effectively with monolingual speakers of either language, as well as with other bilinguals. Academic bilingualism implies the ability to engage effectively in the study and discussion of content in both languages, an ability that requires a sophisticated level of language use in each one.

The development of defined language contexts for acquiring content knowledge is important for all bilingual students, but it is particularly important for linguistically diverse students who, because of inconsistent instruction, have not had opportunities to develop substantive academic proficiency in either their primary or second language. These are the students who are often referred to as mixed-dominant. Although they may have background knowledge of the content topics studied, they may not have sufficient experience or academic vocabulary in either language to be able to express themselves fully during content instruction. Very often they have difficulty staying in one language to communicate what they know, a detriment if they are not among other bilinguals who share their linguistic base. For mixed-dominant students, rather than reflecting a sophisticated linguistic ability, code switching or borrowing may be the only way to completely express their ideas. For these students, gaining full proficiency does not mean drilling them on the vocabulary they are perceived to be lacking, but rather providing contexts that engage them in the active exploration, analysis, and expression of their ideas in each language.

Reexamining Translation Practices

Particularly in the content areas, a lack of language-use planning and policies has led to the use of the primary language mainly for translation, perpetuating the "do what's momentarily convenient" mentality in many programs. The argument most often heard in defense of translation is that it provides second language learners with quick access to the main concepts of the curriculum. However, teachers who try to translate as they teach find that because of time constraints they can rarely fully translate what is to be learned. What passes for translation can be more accurately described as partial explanation, the paraphrasing of large chunks of information, and shorthand explanations of complex ideas. Isolated facts rather than whole ideas and concepts tend to be communicated. In addition, these translations almost always go from English to the primary language, further limiting access to the rich description and linguistic detail in lessons that English speakers have access to daily (Escamilla, 1994). As a result, students accumulate slightly wrong facts, half-analyzed information, and bits and pieces of whole concepts. The long-term consequences are obvious—students don't have equal access to the concepts of the curriculum.

Even if translation could be done fully, students would then in effect receive *all* of their instruction in the primary language, leaving the question of when they would be able (or need) to learn their second language. This lack of instruction in English would undermine their ability to function proficiently in monolingual English-content settings. Constant translation of content materials also undermines the power of the primary language and sends another strong message to students—that their primary language is not really a language to learn through, but rather a prop that is necessary because they are not proficient enough to learn like everyone else. Although a quick fix in some instances, translation can create a dependency in students that does not let them fully develop their abilities to communicate clearly in either language.

Goals for Content Instruction

Across all program categories, content-area instruction for linguistically diverse students must accomplish four major goals. These goals relate directly to the Basic Premises and serve as the basis for the Concept Development Strategy that guides decision making for content-area instruction and language use. The first three goals have major implications for the nature of instruction, and the balance between linguistic and conceptual aspects of academic development. The fourth goal addresses the importance of cross-cultural interactions.

Goal 1: Fully Understanding and Interacting with Content (Premises 1, 2, 3, 4, and 5). This first goal is one all teachers have for their students. Linguistically diverse students, like all students, need to fully understand and interact with content. This is facilitated in bilingual programs where students have access to conceptual development in their primary language. Where students cannot use the primary language for content learning, a time set aside on a regularly scheduled basis for this is important in helping them to acquire the important key academic concepts with a depth of understanding. Planning for such instruction requires organizing and presenting content in a way that assures understanding.

Goal 2. Learning New Content Through the Second Language (Premises 3 and 4). Whether primary language support is available or not, all students need to be able to effectively interact with content in English. Goals 2 and 3 reflect two major aspects of this process, which include receiving opportunities to learn new content through their second language and developing academic proficiency in that language. Goal 2 focuses on the students' need to engage in activities that help them gain the ability to think through their second language, rather than always having to depend on their first language as the mediator of meaning. In addition, as discussed previously, simply being in an English setting is not adequate for developing deep understanding. The flow of a second language may seem overwhelming in quantity and complexity, and lessons designed to provide multiple means of communicating understanding are most important for helping students gain a high level of understanding of new content.

Goal 3: Developing Second Language Academic Proficiency (Premises 2, 3, 4, and 5). Another critical dimension of second language proficiency is acquiring the ability to articulate ideas clearly and logically, and to effectively express knowledge, ideas, and understandings orally and in writing. Students without such proficiency are often considered lacking in academic potential. For many students, however, the opportunities to engage in English *academic* discourse both in and out of school are limited. For example, research indicates that at school, teacher talk often dominates classroom discourse, thereby limiting students' opportunities

to gain experience and practice in voicing their ideas, opinions, and jus-
tifications. In addition, the diminishing emphasis on oral language development as students progress through the grades (in both regular and
second language classrooms) further constrains these experiences. At
home, opportunities to hear and use academic language may also be limited, depending on parents' academic background and experience.

When students have limited opportunities for developing the skills
of verbal expression in their second language, they may find it difficult
to comfortably ask for information, or to express the knowledge and ideas
they have, in either language (Herzog, 1995). Limited opportunities to
develop oral expression around content ideas can affect students' abilities to express themselves in writing, since they are less likely to have a
firm grasp on the vocabulary and organizational frameworks needed for
written work (see Chapter 5). The first three goals not only dictate that
students must have opportunities to use language in a variety of ways;
they also interact significantly to assure that students develop a broad
knowledge base and repertoire of language competence.

Goal 4: Cross-Cultural Interactions (Premise 10). Purposeful planning of
instruction includes how students will be grouped across learning contexts. The presence of students from two (or more) linguistic and cultural
groups opens up many opportunities for cross-cultural interactions. When
planned and organized effectively, instruction in the content areas can
offer an important vehicle for sharing ideas and perceptions, interaction
and cooperation around class projects, and the development of language
with native-speaking peers. Although in many programs students spend
much of their time in cross-lingual/cross-cultural groups, these interactions
are not always conducive to learning and sharing. Differential abilities in
students' language proficiency or background experience can create
distance, rather than closeness, between students.

As the literature in cooperative learning demonstrates, simply being
together in a classroom or a group is insufficient to foster cross-lingual or
cross-cultural understanding (Cohen, 1986; Kagan, 1986). Cooperative
learning is, in fact, a powerful tool in providing opportunities for cross-
cultural interaction, but it takes explicit planning to be successful. One
issue that arises is how groups should be formed. While it is sometimes
beneficial for students to be able to choose their partners for small-group
work, there is a natural tendency for individuals to choose those students
they know and understand best. The goals for cross-cultural interaction
and having native models will be undermined if students choose to work
only with other students from their own language or cultural group. This
also precludes the necessity for second language learners to ever use

the target language for interactions. The following vignette highlights this dilemma.

Bringing Students Together

Ms. Shell teaches a bilingual class that is fairly ethnically and linguistically balanced. In order to support her students' concept and second language development, she uses cooperative group learning activities extensively, especially during social studies and science times. Ms. Shell thinks that cooperative groups give students the opportunity to interact, share their knowledge, work on problem-solving tasks together, and make for a better sense of community in the classroom. Because she wants students to have opportunities to make choices and to be comfortable in their learning settings, she allows students to pick their own groups. This seemed to be working quite well at the beginning of the year as students got into the habit of working in groups, sharing information, and assuming the various roles required in the group process. Recently, however, Ms. Shell has noticed that the students have actually segregated themselves. Native English speakers always group with English speakers and Latino students, most of whom are Spanish-dominant, always group together. In addition, there is a predominance of all-boy and all-girl groups. This, she realizes, does not allow for either social or language interaction among the different groups of students. During Spanish lessons, for example, the dominant English-speaking students are constantly asking her for clarification and try to pull her away from working with all of the students in the class. Because they have no native Spanish speakers in their groups, she is the only resource they have.

Although she hates to assign students to groups herself, she realizes that her broader goals for cooperative learning are not being met. She decides to institute the rule that students may still form their own small groups but the groups must be balanced by gender and language, and she explains her reasons. At first students resist and complain about not being able to work with their friends, but they comply. When they begin to slip back into old patterns, Ms. Shell says "Remember how to mix yourselves" and they quickly integrate themselves. After several weeks, she observes that once again problems in understanding are being worked out between students; they are sharing ideas and negotiating meaning among themselves. In addition, on the playground and in the lunchroom students seem to segregate themselves less often.

This case highlights the need for balance across a broad variety of sometimes competing educational goals. Although it is important for students to make their own choices, it is also important that they do not limit their options for new learning and expanded understanding. Making a shift and leading students to make better choices in selecting their groups can contribute to a more positive and interactive cross-cultural environment.

Planning to meet all four of the goals is the real challenge faced by teachers of linguistically diverse students. A framework is needed to provide a guide in balancing the multiple objectives we have for students, and for assuring that the various instructional settings created for learning build on and benefit from each other.

Organizing to Meet the Goals: The Concept Development Strategy

The Concept Development Strategy (CDS) presented here is an effective means to organize instruction specifically to help students develop academic proficiency in the content areas. The strategy provides a vehicle for utilizing students' language proficiencies for optimal academic concept learning. As indicated in Figure 6.1, the CDS focuses on the four basic learning goals described above. Meeting these goals is accomplished through three different types of lessons: Concept Comprehension Lessons, Integrated Group Lessons, and Scaffolded Oral Expression Lessons.

The lessons that comprise the CDS are not added on to the regular curriculum, but rather form the core of classroom instruction in the content areas and second language development. The CDS is an important element in all program categories, but the nature of each of the three lessons will change in bilingual and all-English settings. For example, for

FIGURE 6.1. Concept development strategy: Types of lessons and corresponding learning goals.

LESSON	GOAL
Concept Comprehension	Goal 1. Understanding and using new concepts
Integrated Group	Goal 2. Learning content through the second language
	Goal 4. Cross-cultural interaction
Scaffolded Oral Expression	Goal 3. Developing proficiency in the language of academic content

students working in their primary language, the Concept Comprehension Lessons are the focus of content instruction, and may include literacy. Integrated Group Lessons also can be done during the regularly scheduled social studies/health/science or math period, and Scaffolded Oral Expression Lessons can form the core of the second language curriculum. In all-English settings, Concept Comprehension Lessons are part of a total overall ESL curriculum and represent language sensitive content lessons (see Chapter 5) that are balanced with Scaffolded Oral Expression Lessons (content-enriched language lessons). Each of these lessons will be described in greater detail below.

The CDS lessons are not taught in a linear fashion. They are most effective when they are cycled throughout a unit of study, giving students a chance to participate in a balance of each type of lesson. The strategy can be utilized to its best advantage when curriculum is organized thematically, with each lesson containing some unique aspect of the broader topic or theme. Using a thematic approach for concept and language development also has the advantage of creating an authentic need for using vocabulary and ideas in different situations throughout the day. This increases students' opportunities to gain flexibility with those ideas and language. It is also most effectively implemented using a team teaching approach with different teachers responsible for different types of lessons and/or languages of instruction.

CDS Lessons in Bilingual Settings

In bilingual settings, Categories I, II, and III, the Concept Development Strategy allows students to

- discuss and develop the more abstract ideas about the concepts in their primary language using the language tool they can use most effectively;
- experience learning new aspects of a concept by having to use the second language spontaneously for thinking and processing new information through comprehensible input in an integrated group;
- use the language of the Integrated Group Lesson in second language lessons, at their own level of ability in a nonthreatening context, comprised of only second language learners.

Concept Comprehension Lessons. These lessons deal directly with the main concepts of the content-area curriculum, and focus on higher-level thinking skills supporting goal 1. Techniques for these lessons focus on discussions based on content materials that add depth to the understanding of the concept being studied. In addition, they provide an opportunity for the extension and development of more sophisticated vocabulary in the primary language. Although the possibility of expanding students' vocabulary is an important aspect of these lessons, Concept Comprehension Lessons are not vocabulary lessons. They are lessons that focus on the "big ideas" or key concepts of a theme. They draw the students into thinking, talking about, and acting on the most important information that is being taught. These lessons are conducted in *homogeneous* language groups to provide a time in which students can fully develop their primary language.

Integrated Group Lessons. Integrated Group Lessons are conducted in groups where both native and second language speakers are working and learning together (goal 4). These lessons are taught at the fluency level of the native speaker and constitute a "mini-immersion" experience for second language learners (goal 2).

Since this is a native language lesson for some students and a mini-immersion situation for others, the nature of the activities selected are very important and should be chosen carefully. In order to be understood by students from a wide variety of language proficiency levels, lessons present concepts utilizing concrete, hands-on activities. Visuals and demonstrations are used to aid understanding for all students and to ensure comprehensible input and opportunities for interaction for the non-native speakers. Questions are directed not only at the level of native speakers but at the appropriate language level of second language students, so that all can participate spontaneously in the activity. This is a language-active rather than a language-passive lesson. Hands-on participation through interaction in the lesson is encouraged. Understanding of the concept is accomplished by watching and doing, rather than simply by listening.

In a full, two-way bilingual situation (Category I), students would engage in Integrated Group Lessons in each language. These are not the same lessons twice, but are a different extension of the theme. For example, if the theme is the Civil War, a lesson in English might involve a re-creation/role play of the underground railroad. The lesson in Spanish might focus on identifying the northern and southern states and the features of their economies that made slavery desirable or not.

Team teaching works particularly well in bilingual settings, because two distinct language settings are provided for primary and second language lessons. A teacher who speaks the student's first language can team with a monolingual teacher in charge of second language instruction, thereby extending school resources. Teaming, of course, requires time for planning and coordination among teachers. Team teaching also helps to solve another problem that often arises in bilingual programs. This problem has to do with the fact that many bilingual teachers are English-dominant, and teaching content in the students' first language may require extra effort and preparation on their part. When teachers receive all or most of their own concept instruction in English, they will most likely have to work harder in order to present content with the fluency of a native speaker in the other language. The advantage of team teaching in this situation is that rather than having to deal with content in two languages, with two sets of vocabulary and materials, these teachers can concentrate on the topic in one language and have the opportunity to become better at the vocabulary and expression of ideas, thereby helping to extend students' knowledge, experience, and language in the content area.

Scaffolded Oral Expression Lessons. How do second language learners receive support in acquiring the flexibility and fluency to participate effectively in the Integrated Group Lessons? A major part of the answer lies in Scaffolded Oral Expression Lessons, which address goal 3. In these lessons students learn to use the vocabulary and practice the language structures related to the theme of the Integrated Group Lessons. These lessons are content-enriched language lessons and can form the core of students' English (or other language) as a second language program (e.g., ssl). Students work in homogeneous second language groups and concept vocabulary is used at the level of the students' second language proficiency. This gives students the opportunity to hear these words more distinctly and to actually use them at their own particular level of proficiency and out of competition with native speakers.

These lessons provide opportunities to use forms of language and vocabulary that students are not generally comfortable or fluent in using and that are different from what they would usually use in social conversations. They help students become familiar with and, fluent and proficient in academic language. A rule of thumb is that if students can already say it, the lesson should be adjusted since it is not helping them to add to their repertoire of language. Although teachers monitor students' understanding of the concepts in these lessons, they do not spend scaffolded language expression time in reexplaining those concepts. Rather, they take note that students need additional concept-focused lessons and plan additional Concept Comprehension Lessons. Planning for first and second language settings and interactions is a new, different way of thinking about curriculum for most teachers.

The following two vignettes give examples of how content instruction might be organized through the Concept Development Strategy.

Gearing Up

The third-grade unit on technology was coming up. Delia and Fran, a bilingual team, were getting ready to plan their 4-week unit.

FRAN: I would really like to give students some hands-on activities that get them in touch with the physics required to make machines work.

DELIA: Let's have some activities on pulleys and fulcrums. That would give the kids a chance to try some simple machines for themselves.

FRAN: That sounds like a great idea, but first we need to figure out what the total unit will look like. I've asked the kids informally what their favorite machines are and why, but I think we should start by asking them to list the machines they know, how they think they work, and how they think they might go about making a new machine.

DELIA: That sounds like a good idea. The kids come from so many different backgrounds that I think we will see a pretty big range in the experiences they have had with a broad range of different types of machines. It would really be important to have them talk about this background knowledge and experience in their primary language.

FRAN: You know, we don't have all of the same materials in both languages. I have a lot more in English. Is that going to cause a problem?

DELIA: I don't think so, in fact I think it may be a benefit. If we plan carefully we can use the Spanish materials for the Spanish speakers in Concept Comprehension Lessons, for the Integrated Group Lessons in Spanish, and some might even fit well into ssl lessons. We can do the same with the English materials. Hands-on activities and machines that the kids can build themselves will also be more fun and engaging. If we balance our materials carefully we will actually have more to offer the kids.

As the teachers continue their planning they brainstorm additional activities and experiences they want students to have. They decide to do the background experience in the homogeneous first language group in Concept Comprehension Lessons. They will also explore some of the ideas of weight and matter in these lessons. During the primary language literacy block, they will have students read about different types of machines and make a book about the machines they are learning about.

They choose two pulley and two fulcrum activities for the Integrated Group Lessons. One of each will be done in Spanish, and the others in English. For example, they have bought several different sizes of pulleys and are looking forward to students' using them to lift objects of different weights, and then to specifically explore the ratio of one pulley to another. By having two activities for each topic, students learn the language for each topic in each language.

In the Scaffolded Oral Expression time, besides working on pulleys and fulcrums and what they do (e.g., "I can lift twice as many pounds with the larger pulley"), they also decide to focus on vocabulary for different types of machines and on phrases such as, "A [bulldozer] is used to [move dirt]." "If you need to [get messages] you can use an [answering machine]." "What machine do you need to [bake bread]?" They decide to group the machines students talk about and select different groups for their lessons. They plan similar lessons in SSL. In following lessons they will also have students compose a couple of language experience information charts.

As reflected in the example above, at the beginning levels of literacy, the CDS is focused on learning concepts and language, not on literacy activities for second language learners. It is aimed at developing strong primary language literacy and strong second language oral, speaking, and thinking skills. Teachers must plan together in order to balance activities and ensure that they support and reinforce each other across languages. They also need to coordinate the use of the materials available to them. Having all material in both languages is not necessary, and may inhibit good lesson planning because covering all content in both languages in the same way is unproductive.

As students' proficiency increases, however, the Concept Development Strategy becomes an important tool in students' continued development of bilingualism and biliteracy. The following vignette shows the process of thinking through a Concept Development Strategy lesson in a middle school that offers first and second language instruction for students who have been involved in a two-way program for some time.

Advancing Bilingualism

On a middle-school bilingual team, teachers were looking for a way to help students refine their writing process, a major focus of their school's improvement goals. They also wanted to work on selected learning strategies. They began their plan with how to organize instruction to focus on metacognitive strategies. They used their team planning time to brainstorm a set of lessons that focused on helping students with organization (sequence and coherence) and comparing and contrasting information. They chose the topic of comic books with the goal of having students analyze and discuss comics as a genre—who reads them and why, as well as how information is presented. They decided they would model how to organize a storyboard with a plot and how to create dialogue. Then they would have students create comics both together and individually. Eventually, they would have students publish and share their comics, analyzing their own and those of their peers for the elements indicated above.

Since the goals of the program were to help both Spanish- and English-dominant students develop first and second language skills around this curriculum focus, they had to decide which lessons would be taught in the students' first language, and which could be used for integrated groups. For the integrated lessons in each language it was important to choose activities that were interactive with meaning supported by visuals and hands-on activities. Teachers were also concerned with developing second language lessons that would help students use the concepts and language they had learned. In the end, they decided that the discussion of the genre, organization, and purposes was best accomplished in the primary language (*Concept Comprehension*). They would break down the parts of a comic and model the aspects of putting a comic book together in integrated groups with overheads and visuals in whole groups and in small cooperative groups (*Integrated Group*). In their second language, students would create their own simple comic strip with dialogue, while talking about the process and the parts (*Scaffolded Oral Expression*). They would specifically target students' use of verbs and adjectives, since they have noticed that students' language tends to be brief and narrow.

CDS in All-English Settings

In an all-English setting (Category IV), the Concept Development Strategy allows students to meet all of the goals for concept development, although as indicated below, there is a significant difference in the Concept Comprehension Lesson from programs where the primary language is utilized. In all-English settings, Category IV, the Concept Development Strategy allows students to:

• engage in significant concept learning through *sheltered* content lessons;
• experience learning new aspects of a concept by having to use the second language for thinking and processing new information through comprehensible input in an integrated group;

- use the language of the Integrated Group Lesson in second language lessons, at their own level of ability in a nonthreatening context comprised of only second language learners.

In all-English programs, Concept Comprehension Lessons, rather than using the primary language for concept development, engage students in significant concept learning through sheltered content lessons. These Concept Comprehension Lessons are more than just language lessons, however. Their focus is on the depth of understanding students have about the concepts and ideas they are learning (Gordon & Tobias, 1993).

As in Categories I–III, Integrated Group settings for Category IV also provide opportunities for students to experience learning new aspects of a concept by having to use the second language for thinking and processing new information, through comprehensible input in groups with native English speakers. In a Category IV program, second language learners spend most of their time in these groupings (unless they are in a fully sheltered situation).

In order to support all-English instruction in integrated group settings, a comprehensive second language program must also include sheltered and language learning opportunities. Such a program balances both Concept Comprehension and Scaffolded Oral Expression lessons, which are critical to students gaining full access to understanding, participating and communicating effectively in classroom activities.

In all-English programs, a basic level of coordination must exist within the ESL curriculum to balance content and language expression lessons. When ESL is part of a pull-out program, this coordination becomes even more critical. Forty-five minutes of services will not be enough to provide sufficient instruction in the content areas. The general education classroom teacher will need to share responsibility for providing students with Concent Comprehension lessons to support in class learning and to supplement external ESL lessons. The following vignette shows how one teacher organized his classroom to meet the concept and language learning needs of his second language learners.

The Classroom Teacher

Mr. Taft has in his class 13 students who have limited English proficiency. Although with help they seem to be able to do the activities, they rarely talk or ask questions and he worries that they do not really understand the underlying concepts. Because they are often overpowered by native English speakers and always seem to fade into the background, he decides to address their instruction in two ways. First, he decides to institute a time every day when he can meet with these students in a small group. He has chosen a time when other students are working independently, and he has been able to carve out 20–30 minutes daily. He alternates the focus of these small-group sessions to meet goals 1, 2, and 3. On one day he introduces new concepts and prepares students by giving background understandings of the topics they will be learning about in the main lesson with the whole group. He does this by focusing on the most important ideas he wants the students to learn, and presenting them with an activity that introduces them to the concepts. The activity is related to but different from the main lesson. Since he uses thematic units to organize his content, he is able to establish a baseline of understanding that also allows him to check for students' grasp of the ideas they are working with, before they go on to new concepts in the unit. On alternate days, he helps students develop the vocabulary they need to participate. He does this by thinking about words and phrases that he knows will be important for them to know and be able to use. He then models questions, answers and dialogue from the lesson and gives the students opportunities to practice in the small group. During the Scaffolded Oral Expression Lessons, Mr. Taft incorporates structures and vocabulary that he knows will help students participate in discussions, and ask and answer questions about the content. These lessons give students a chance to practice in a safe environment where they can make mistakes and build confidence.

The area of concept development opens up unlimited opportunities to develop critical and creative thinkers. The quality of lessons and the depth of knowledge students acquire will be key to their academic success. In programs for linguistically diverse learners, organizing for quality includes not only excellent teaching, but also direct attention to the use of languages in instruction. As discussed, this area of program planning is unfamiliar to most teachers, and will take concerted time and effort for full utilization. The outcomes for students, however, can be dramatic. Working together, teachers can help each other to accomplish this important goal for empowering students. Figure 6.2 summarizes the use of languages for each type of lesson as adapted for each category.

ISSUES UNIQUE TO EACH PROGRAM CATEGORY

As discussed above, understanding and expressing that understanding are the cornerstones for the development of content-area instruction. In bilingual programs (Categories I, II, and III), as students become increas-

FIGURE 6.2. Concept development strategy difference by program category.

Category I

Two-Way bilingual programs
Concept Comprehension: Primary language
Integrated Group: Lessons balance between Primary language and
                            English
Scaffolded Oral Expression: ESL and other SL

Bilingual for linguistically diverse students only
Concept Comprehension: Primary language
Integrated Group: In English only
Scaffolded Oral Expression: ESL

Category II
Concept Comprehension: Primary language
                            Primary literacy directly connected to content themes
Integrated Group: In English only
Scaffolded Oral Expression: ESL

Category III
Concept Comprehension: Primary language, abbreviated
                            Sheltered second language, as necessary
Integrated Group: In English only
Scaffolded Oral Expression: ESL

Category IV
Concept Comprehension: Sheltered lessons regularly
                            No regularly scheduled primary language instruction
Integrated Group: In English only
Scaffolded Oral Expression: ESL

---

ingly proficient in their second language, the instructional balance between languages shifts. Where the primary language was once almost exclusively utilized to help students understand underlying concepts, over time the second language becomes more and more able to handle the cognitive load. When program goals include the development of bilingualism, the two languages move into a 50–50 balance across content areas. Where bilingualism is not the goal, English gradually becomes the only language of instruction. In all-English programs (Category IV), the shift occurs not in the language of instruction but rather in the types of settings in which students learn content. The balance shifts between receiving substantive support in small second language groups with sheltered methods, to the ability to fully understand and participate in content learning in lessons at the native, monolingual English level, with no sheltered support. This process takes a good deal of time and careful monitoring.

In order to demonstrate the adaptations of the Concept Development Strategy across categories, in the following section the same theme and set of lessons is developed for each program category. As described below, in every case there is a six-step process for developing instruction. The first step is the selection of a *theme*. In these examples, the theme selected is ecology and the food chain, and the specific topics are predators and prey and the food chain pyramid. In the second step it is important to *brainstorm* a range of activities that might be used to teach this theme and its underlying concepts. Brainstorming works best in teams or groups where people can share ideas. Generating a broad list of activities and lessons to teach the topic can help connect these topics more effectively to district and mandated curriculum. Once the outline of specific concepts and lessons is developed, decisions can be made about the most *appropriate language* to use for each lesson (more abstract in the primary language, more interactive in integrated groups). Decisions regarding the targeted language for *second language* lessons can also be made. *Developing lessons* is the next step, with the final step being to *organize* them for instruction. Figure 6.3 presents an overview of the steps taken for the ecology theme, with potential lessons and the language and setting that seem most appropriate for each. Using the lesson elements in Figure 6.3, adaptations for each program category are discussed below.

Category I: Full Primary Language Foundation

In bilingual programs, all students may be provided the opportunity to develop bilingual skills. In a full two-way program both linguistically diverse and native English-speaking students are offered the opportunity to develop bilingualism. In order to demonstrate the Concept Development Strategy in such programs, the following Spanish–English sample lesson set is presented. Primary language is indicated by L1, second language is indicated by L2.

Concept Comprehension—L1:	Introduce and discuss predators and prey
Integrated Group—Spanish:	Create a predator
Scaffolded Oral Expression—L2:	Learn to express descriptions and contrasts between characteristics of predators and their prey

FIGURE 6.3. Example of steps in developing a concept development strategy theme.

1. Choose Themes: Ecology and the Food Chain—Predators and Prey

2. Brainstorm potential lessons

3. Decide on appropriateness of topic and language for each type of lesson (depends on Program Category)
   Discuss meaning of predator, prey (CC)
   Look at predators and prey and their ecological adaptations: camouflage, body shapes, other defense mechanisms (IG)
   Discuss difference between herbivores and carnivores, insectivores and ominvores (CC)
   Identify physiological characteristics of herbivores and carnivores, insectivores and omnivores (IG)
   Make the model of a predator (IG)
   Match habitats to animals (IG)
   Match predators to prey (IG or CC)
   Discuss the importance of a natural balance and primary producers (CC)
   Introduce and discuss pyramid as a conceptual model for the food chain (CC)
   Read books on predator/prey, to and with students (IG and CC depending on proficiency)

4. Select Scaffolded Oral Expression Lesson vocabulary, structures and discourse patterns
   Learning names of a variety of animals
       lion, gazelle, hyena, antelope, fox, chickens, eagles, small rodents, etc.
   Identifying them as predators or prey in relation to each other
       The lion preys on the _____.
       The gazelle is the lion's prey.
   Use comparatives to describe differences between predators and prey in matching sets
       The lion is bigger, stronger and has sharp teeth and claws.
   Use connectors to describing a food chain
   Use adjectives in describing habitats and give reasons for why they might protect prey or give predator an advantage
       The forest floor protects the . . .

5. Develop the lessons (steps 5 and 6 need to be done together)

6. Organize lessons for instruction

Concept Comprehension—L1:	Introduce and discuss pyramid as a conceptual model for the food chain
Integrated Group—English:	Create a food chain pyramid mural—English
Scaffolded Oral Expression—L2:	Learn to describe elements of the food chain

Two Integrated Group Lessons are necessary in a two-way program, because Integrated Group learning opportunities are necessary for both groups of second language learners. Where no opportunity for second language is afforded to monolingual English speakers, Integrated Group Lessons would be conducted in English only.

Category II: Primary Language Support—Literacy Only

Category II programs provide students the opportunity to use their primary language for literacy. Since content-area instruction for these students is primarily in English, it is essential that literacy instruction be linked to content themes, in order to assure that these areas of content learning are supported and in order to take full advantage of the primary language for concept development. Because a greater amount of content-area instruction may be done in English, concept development in the second language may have to be supported by occasional sheltered (language-sensitive) content lessons.

Concept Comprehension—L1:	Introduce and discuss predators and prey
Integrated Group—English:	Create a predator
Scaffolded Oral Expression—L2:	Learn to express descriptions and contrasts between characteristics of predators and their prey
Concept Comprehension—L1:	Introduce and discuss pyramid as a conceptual model for the food chain
Integrated Group—English:	Create a food chain pyramid mural
Scaffolded Oral Expression—L2:	Learn to describe elements of the food chain

Category III: Primary Language Content Reinforcement—No Literacy

In Category III programs, students spend the majority of their time in all-English settings, mainly in integrated groups. They do, however, have a regular opportunity to use their first language to focus on the "big ideas" or central concepts.

Concept Comprehension—L1:	Introduce and discuss predators and prey
Integrated Group—English:	Create a predator
Concept Comprehension—L2:	Present sheltered lesson in which students compare a variety of predators to their prey

Scaffolded Oral Expression—L2:	Learn to express descriptions and contrasts between characteristics of predators and their prey
Concept Comprehension—L1:	Introduce and discuss pyramid as a conceptual model for the food chain
Concept Comprehension—L2:	Present sheltered lesson in which students create a food chain with predators and prey selected from previous sheltered concept comprehension lesson
Integrated Group—English:	Create a food chain pyramid mural
Scaffolded Oral Expression—L2:	Learn to describe elements of the food chain

In Category III programs, the second language curriculum is important not only in providing comprehensible lessons in the integrated language group, but in balancing *content-focused language lessons* (Scaffolded Oral Expression) and *language-sensitive content lessons* (Concept Comprehension). The overall second language (ESL) program should provide time in which these two goals are balanced.

Category IV: All-English

In programs where primary language resources are not available, the full load of concept development is carried through English. Deliberate planning for second language content support is a critical aspect of instruction, and must become a regular part of the students' program.

Concept Comprehension—Sheltered:	Introduce and discuss predators and prey
Integrated Group—English:	Create a predator
Scaffolded Oral Expression—L2:	Learn to express descriptions and contrasts between characteristics of predators and their prey
Concept Comprehension—Sheltered:	Introduce and discuss pyramid as a conceptual model for the food chain
Integrated Group—English:	Create a food chain pyramid mural
Scaffolded Oral Expression—L2:	Learn to describe elements of the food chain

Decision Making on Your Own

1. Questions that highlight major issues regarding the curriculum and concept development include: What kinds of tasks will students be ex-

pected to accomplish? What opportunities do students need to be successful in these tasks? How can instruction across languages be balanced to provide these opportunities? What particular attention should be paid to language use? Where possible, can content delivery be organized to foster bilingualism for all students? Is language accounted for across the content areas? If so, how? How can the curriculum and linguistic resources be organized more effectively? How is program quality assured?

In order to answer these questions about your setting you need to add the following information to your school profile: what content students are being taught; who makes curricular decisions; how the curriculum is articulated across content areas, instructors, and grades; how language is accounted for across the content areas; what students are expected to know; whether the curriculum is culturally relevant to students; the numbers of students in each primary language group; how the primary language is currently used in the school; whether languages have clear and distinct contexts for instruction; teacher proficiency in students' primary language; textbooks and materials available in the primary language; additional community resources, political climate, and so forth.

2. Think about the Basic Premises and major elements presented in this chapter on curriculum and concept development. Generate a list of additional questions that will help you to decide how best to serve students in your setting or school.

3. Compare your list of questions with those of a colleague and refine your list. Have you considered all the major issues?

4. Form a small group and brainstorm the optimal curriculum delivery practices possible in your setting. Use the Basic Premises highlighted in this chapter (1, 2, 4, 5, 6, 10) to weigh your decisions.

5. List two or three changes that might have to be made.

6. What are the implications of your decisions for other areas, for example, oral language development, community involvement, or assessment practices?

7. Add these data to your school profile.

CHAPTER 7

Assessment

Key Premises to Consider

• *Premise 1—Active Learning.* Knowledge is best acquired when learners actively participate in meaningful activities that are constructive in nature and appropriate to their level of development.

• *Premise 7—Transitions and redesignations.* Decisions regarding transition to formal second language reading and redesignations that exit students from programs cannot be made arbitrarily.

• *Premise 8—Instructional assessment.* Instructional assessment must be based on students' first and second language development, rather than on grade level or predetermined criteria. An appropriate assessment plan should address language and literacy development as well as content knowledge.

• *Premise 9—Parents and community.* Parents and community must play a major role in the learning and schooling of their children.

• *Premise 12—Teachers as decision makers.* Teacher are decision makers. As part of a learning community they are all equally responsible for decisions regarding the instructional program for linguistically diverse students.

Another key element in program planning for linguistically diverse students is assessment and accountability. In order to make decisions regarding student performance and instruction, a firm grounding in the multiple aspects of program quality is necessary.

Educational assessment serves a wide variety of purposes. Although measuring individual student performance in the classroom is a major goal, evaluation of a school's performance is also important. Assessment also encompasses a myriad of other purposes: reporting student achievement to parents, informing curricular decisions, statewide testing of individual and group performance, and often various criterion-referenced district requirements.

How the measures used affect students' motivation for learning, how they result in the grouping and tracking of students, and whether the results of such measures tell a true story are questions that are continually being raised about assessment across the country. Central to the scope of this chapter is how appropriate decisions about assessment practices are to be made with regard to linguistically diverse students.

Decision Making: Ask Yourself:

What do we want students to know and value?

What types of assessments truly inform instruction and also provide accountablity data?

What assessment practices accurately measure the entry level of linguistically diverse students, the progress of students in both their primary and second languages, and the readiness for formal reading in the second language?

How can quality assessment practices avoid the tracking of linguistically diverse students within low levels of instruction and /or at beginning levels of a dual language program?

PERSPECTIVES ON ASSESSMENT

Traditional forms of assessment used throughout this country are derived from the same behaviorist framework of instruction that has driven the American educational system for most of this century. Both instruction and assessment focus on the parts rather than on the whole. The prevailing graded and compartmentalized assessments are based on the belief that students learn prescribed sequences regardless of age, socioeconomic background, learning styles, linguistic differences, or disabilities. Expectations are built into the system that students will reach these prescribed levels at predetermined times. These assessments are usually imposed, are external to the learning environment, occur at preset times, and have very little relationship to the curriculum of the school. Students remain at the periphery of such assessments, displaced by the grade-level expectations, test scores, and ranks themselves.

Standardized, norm-referenced tests that result in a population distribution along a normal curve are often used to sort and track students, with long-term consequences for student achievement. For the most part, the content of these assessments focuses on right and wrong answers, and tests very limited levels of thinking and language. When instruction is organized to accommodate these tests, what often results is a superficial curriculum and a tendency to "teach to the test" (Shepard, 1991). Grade levels, norm-referenced tests, letter grades, and rankings are all forms of classification that assume that every student can be placed into a slot.

When expectations are determined on the basis of arbitrary grade levels or rankings rather than on clear standards of achievement that are set for all students, then students who do not fit the "average" profile are often categorized as poor learners and remain at the lower levels of expectation. These practices are barriers to continuous progress and set students up for failure. This is particularly true for students who may be at risk, come to school speaking a language other than English, or have had very little formal education.

Tracking of linguistically diverse students into reductionist curricula both in and out of bilingual programs has been a consequence of a focus on sorting students into high, medium, and low groups. Tracking has also resulted from setting arbitrary criteria for the redesignation of students out of second language or bilingual programs based on time periods rather than on students' development. Such criteria are often established in response to policies driven by political concerns that often override what educators know to be good pedagogy with regard to linguistically diverse students (see Chapter 1; Miramontes, 1993a,b). For example, decisions may be made about the movement of students through bilingual programs based on funding sources or controversies such as those regarding immigrant children, rather than on the results of specified outcomes for first and second language development. The inappropriate instruction that ensues often relegates students to low-level or remedial classes where they remain indefinitely.

Another common policy that often results in student tracking is based on the notion that somehow older students do not require primary language instruction, or even a specialized program of English language development simply because they have less time remaining in school. This is a function of the fact that secondary education becomes increasingly geared to course completion and graduation requirements. This leaves little room to address the specific needs of students. As a consequence, many students at the secondary level simply drop out of school (Fine, 1986; Ochoa, Hurtado, Espinosa, & Zachman, 1987).

Instructional decision making should be based on understanding what students comprehend and can do with what they have learned. This requires forms of assessment very different from the traditional norm-referenced and mastery tests often used today. Assumption 1, that learning is a process of development that is constructive in nature, implies a different paradigm for assessment, one in which student performance is embedded in the curriculum and where students are active participants in the learning process. As suggested in *Case for Constructivist Classrooms* (Brooks & Brooks, 1993) "[assessment] is part of a curriculum which is adapted to students' needs, seeks and values their point of view, and structures learning around problems of emerging relevance" (p. 35). In this alternative assessment paradigm, the learner is at the center of the process and is held accountable, but this accountability is born out of an environment that asks students to continually assess their own progress, and supports them in the process of learning. Standards for achievement are apparent to students at all times. Such a student-centered instructional program leads ultimately to a process of assessment that is dramatically different from the traditional.

The assessment and accountability process that a school undertakes is one of the most significant of all the reform practices. A key factor in this process is the alignment of curriculum, instruction, assessment, and, ultimately, performance evaluations. Internal to the school is how to design an assessment system whose purpose is not only to evaluate student progress, but also to continually reevaluate the school's capacity to help all students achieve academically. Unless a school has its own internal mechanism for assessment and accountability based on external criteria, the goal of high achievement for all students may fail. This internal mechanism for continuous improvement must be one in which all staff have the opportunity to examine student work across all levels of development with the purpose of continually reevaluating not only student progress, but the assessment practices as well. A state and national vision that strives to help the educational community set high standards for all students regardless of race, language, disability, or socioeconomic level is, without question, a goal that educators and families must embrace. But what a school *does* with those standards is what is crucial.

The form and perspective of assessment are particularly critical to the instruction of linguistically diverse students. When schools plan assessment practices for these students, they must include plans for placement and diagnosis, as well as for curriculum modification and achievement. These issues cross all the program categories as well as having specific impact in each particular category. Important insights about students' knowledge and more substantive information for placement are available when authentic assessments are used—that is, when assessments that focus on what students know and can do in real and meaningful situations are the focus of decision making. A continuous progress mode requires assessments that measure the authentic work of students and that involve them and their parents in the process.

ISSUES ACROSS PROGRAM CATEGORIES

Several important assessment issues cut across all program categories: (1) placement of students, (2) accountability for student performance, (3) developing an authentic process, and (4) measuring school effectiveness.

Placement of Students

Educators and policymakers often assume that all students who enter school speaking a language other than English arrive with no English at all, and only at the beginning levels of schooling. The reality is that they enter at all ages, from all socioeconomic levels, with varying educational backgrounds and with linguistic capacities ranging from monolingual to being able to use either language effectively across domains. That there are so many factors to consider creates dilemmas regarding how to place students, and how to monitor and assess their academic progress, dilemmas educators often find overwhelming. To meet this challenge, a multi-faceted approach that distinguishes second language proficiency from educational ability is essential. Simply put, low-level English language proficiency is not an indicator of ability, or even of achievement.

When all of the factors for the placement of linguistically diverse students are taken into account, a matrix begins to evolve that facilitates the placement of these students into appropriate instructional programs. (See Figures 7.1 and 7.2 for examples of how the matrix is used in different Categories.) This matrix incorporates such factors as age, prior schooling, primary language literacy level, and current levels of second language development. Figure 7.1 gives an example of the matrix in relation to intermediate students, in grades 4, 5, and 6, in a Category I program. Figure 7.2 gives an example for intermediate students in a Category IV program. Note that very different program decisions are indicated for students with different backgrounds and in different program categories.

With such a matrix, the needs of younger versus older students and of those who enter not only with limited English proficiency but with limited educational background can all be accounted for. For example, a student with advanced primary language proficiency and literacy will need a more accelerated program of English than a student entering with more limited proficiency in the primary language. Bilingual students who not only have varying patterns of proficiency in each language but are experiencing difficulties in both, will need different opportunities to develop their languages than those who are clearly proficient in one language or both.

Students placed on a matrix don't become simply a point on a linear continuum, but are considered for placement as individuals who come with cognitive strengths, values, and rich cultural experiences. They are regarded as having the capacity to achieve high standards in both languages given the appropriate access and opportunity to learn. Important insights about what students know and more substantive information for placement are available when authentic assessments are used—that is,

FIGURE 7.1. Sample student placement matrix—Program Category I, grades 4, 5, and 6.

Literacy Proficiency [1]	Non English Speaking	Limited English Speaking	Fluent English Speaking	Placement for Mixed Dominant [2] Students with Difficulties	Placement for Native English Speakers
Proficient	L-1 literacy	L-1 literacy	L-1 enrichment literacy	Experiencing difficulty in both languages	L-1 English literacy
	CD Strategy or L-1content	CD strategy for content	CD strategy for content		CD strategy for content
	L-2 oral and informal literacy	L-2 oral and formal literacy	L-2 formal literacy		L-2 oral and informal literacy
Developing	L-1 literacy	L-1 intensive literacy	L-1 intensive literacy	Experiencing difficulty in both languages	L-1 intensive English literacy
	L-1 content	CD strategy for content	CD Strategy for content		L-1 English content, primarily
	L-2 oral	L-2 oral and informal literacy	L-2 formal literacy		L-2 oral and informal literacy
Limited or None	L-1 literacy intervention strategies	L-1 literacy intervention strategies	L-1 design an individual program	L-1 design an individual intervention program with strong oral language and concept development focus	L-1 intervention English literacy
	L-1 content	L-1 content	CD strategy for content		L-1 content
	L-2 oral	L-2 oral	L-2 informal		L-2 oral

[1] Levels of proficiency are indicated for primary language literacy (L-1) and for second language oral development.

[2] Decisions regarding this student's placement will depend on careful assessment of home language use, and prior instruction in first and second language.

FIGURE 7.2. Student placement matrix—Program Category IV, grades 4,5, and 6.

Literacy Proficiency[1]	ORAL PROFICIENCY: Non English Speaking	ORAL PROFICIENCY: Limited English Speaking	ORAL PROFICIENCY: Fluent English Speaking	MIXED DOMINANT:[2] Students with Difficulties
Proficient	accelerated oral informal literacy CD strategy for content[3]	accelerated oral accelerated informal to formal literacy CD strategy for content	Oral academic language development, as necessary Accelerated literacy CD strategy or content with no L-2 support services	Experiencing difficulty in both languages
Developing	Oral—beginning Initial informal literacy CD strategy for content	Oral—extended Informal literacy CD strategy for content	Oral academic language development Formal literacy CD strategy or content with no L-2 support services	Experiencing difficulty in both languages
Limited	Oral—extended CD strategy for content	Oral Informal literacy CD strategy for content	Academic oral language development Intervention literacy & CD strategies	Intensive oral Intervention strategy Sheltered content

[1] Levels of proficiency are indicated for primary language literacy (L–1) and for second language oral development.
[2] Decisions regarding this student's placement will depend on careful assessment of home language use, and prior instruction in first and second language.
[3] CD strategy includes sheltered content and academic oral language development lessons.

assessments that focus on what students know and can do in real and meaningful situations. These will be discussed in greater detail later in this chapter.

Besides helping to determine instructional needs for individual students, when schools are trying to select an appropriate category of program, the placement matrix is useful in helping to better identify the specific needs of the range of students to be served. Placement matrices for all age groups and proficiency levels of students can be very useful in determining the direction and priorities a staff will take. In this way decisions can be made based on student needs, not simply on factors such as available resources, teacher preference, and readiness for change.

Later in the chapter there will be a discussion of standards and learner outcomes in the first and second language. Learner Outcome Profiles are presented that provide criteria for student movement through a program based on their performance of a wide variety of tasks. As a school community decides to develop learner outcomes for the program they are planning, a placement matrix can be a useful tool in mapping out the development of the learner outcomes in the appropriate languages.

Accountability for Student Performance

Inherent in the concept of site-based decision making presented in Chapter 3 is the understanding that along with the empowerment engendered by such a process goes the responsibility for successful student outcomes. School accountability includes the framework for expectations, student achievement criteria, and overall indicators of a school's effectiveness.

The process for change undertaken by an individual school is set within state and national reform efforts. Much of the movement toward educational reform calls for setting standards of excellence for student performance (U.S. Department of Education, 1994). Because students will ultimately be held responsible within these broader frameworks, it is the responsibility of the school to use these frameworks, content standards, and holistic outcomes to design specific outcomes for students, based on the school's individual needs. But caution should be exercised. Although state and national reform efforts are laudable, the move toward standards-based education has largely ignored the elements that are fundamental to providing effective instruction for linguistically diverse students (August, Hakuta, & Pompa, 1994; Gandara; 1994). It is therefore incumbent on school personnel to become informed and knowledgeable regarding the first and second language issues reflected in the Basic Premises.

For students who receive primary language instruction, a system of assessment that has set high standards of performance in both the first and second language and has systematically assessed that performance along the way should be able to accurately demonstrate the strengths and weaknesses of students as they progress through the grades. This progress must be monitored in the primary language relative to the second language. For example, in a high-standard, continuous-progress system, linguistically diverse students who entered the elementary level at age 9 speaking only Spanish would receive instruction appropriate to their stage of language and literacy development and prior schooling within an age-appropriate setting.

For students who do not receive primary language support, the development of a second language for academic purposes is the focus of outcomes. This process is recognized as different from the process of being able to use the first language for new learning. It implies a critical need for monitoring progress with regard to oral language, literacy, and concept understanding, over time.

Even though some of the reform literature would place the locus of control, and ultimately of accountability, at the school site (Sizer, 1984), schools exist within systems. In the long run, schools cannot succeed unless the broader community is involved and shares accountability for students' success. The process of accountability for student performance should be conducted by an entire school community. Broad representation of staff, parents, and other community members is essential. The decision-making process encompasses several steps: establishing standards and learner outcomes, developing an assessment process and selecting assessment measures, and developing criteria for evaluation.

Early in the process of deciding to move to nontraditional forms of assessment, the impact of the two-pronged purpose of student performance assessment—the monitoring of individual student progress and the assessment of overall program effectiveness—must be considered by the whole school. Thus, early planning must include the means for constant reevaluation and adjustment of instruction based on the assessment results, as well as a means for extrapolating composite data for program monitoring and public reporting.

Establishing Standards. From the development of a comprehensive vision presented in Chapter 3 flow the accountability questions: What do we want students to know? How do we want them to perform? What do we want them to value when they leave school? The answers to these questions take the form of standards. These standards are often developed at the local level, but are also derived from standards at the state and national levels. For example, a standard in language arts for primary grades might be "give oral book reports following a prepared format" or "use four-step writing process either individually or in cooperative groups." At the upper-elementary level, possible standards could be "read at least one book per month, independently" or "write in daily journal." Standards are discussed, changed, and finally developed with input from a broad representation of the community. In addition, it is important in all schools, and especially so in those with substantial populations of second language learners, that the valuing of cultural and linguistic diversity and bilingualism be pervasive throughout the standards.

Learner Outcomes. The next step in the accountability process is the development of learner outcomes based on the external standards in each content area. It may not be feasible to develop standards and outcomes for all content areas simultaneously. By using the resources available through national standards, state frameworks, and district standards, the school can begin the process of selecting particular content areas from which to embark. In a school with large numbers of linguistically diverse students, especially at the elementary level, language arts is the logical choice. Learner outcomes for oral language, reading, and writing are necessary. It should be noted that standards in all content areas are the same for all students, but the outcomes may vary for different types of students. In programs providing primary language development, outcomes that clearly demonstrate the expectations for the process of acquiring both the first and second languages are critical. In programs with no primary language resources, the learner outcomes for second language proficiency are a major focus.

The development of outcomes for second language learners is a challenge, especially because it is easy to confuse outcomes with standards. While it is important to establish a single set of standards for all students, the specific outcomes will depend on whether they are being accomplished in the student's first or second language.

Why is it insufficient to have the same outcomes for second language learners as for native English speakers? If identical outcomes are required for all students, those students without the fund of native language experiences (see Chapters 4 and 5) are asked to perform the same tasks and are assessed by the same criteria as native speakers. Because their English development is following a different, second language path, assessment will be unreliable and will not give accurate information without measureable outcomes, evidence, and benchmarks specific to that second language process. Using native English-speaker criteria will yield little information on second language learners' actual academic progress. A way to legitimately monitor their progress, therefore, would not be available until their language proficiency and work began to approximate that of native speakers. The following example illustrates this point.

Accounting for Second Language

Several teachers were discussing the prospect of their district going into a standards-based system. One teacher mentioned that the district had directed the schools to develop learner outcomes for their respective sites based on the content standards provided by the central office. They were wondering whether they were expected to write separate outcomes for the second language learners.

Several individuals in the group felt that distinct outcomes should be developed for the linguistically different students; others disagreed. One teacher admitted that she had little experience in teaching English as a second language, but she thought that if she were asking the students to write a friendly letter, the expected outcome would be the same for all students writing the letter. The second language learners would be given as much support as possible to accomplish the task, and their work would be accepted in their portfolios at the level of their capability.

Her colleague said, "I don't think writing a friendly letter is really an appropriate outcome for someone who is just barely able to communicate in English."

Outcomes and assessments should be designed to advance the specific needs in learning and development for second language students. Some tasks are more appropriate and important at these students' beginning level of second language development than others. They are tasks specifically designed for the second language learner. While it is important that the instruction and assessment of these students be tied to the content of the overall curriculum, in the scenario above, it is likely that instead of writing a friendly letter, a more appropriate and profitable task would have been to role play inviting a friend to a party.

As discussed, where students receive primary language instruction, their linguistic and cognitive background experiences support literacy development. Although language development is an important part of all readiness and literacy programs, familiarity with the meaning, sound, and structures of their native language gives students a head start they don't have in their second language. Students in all-English literacy programs (Category III or IV) will not have the equivalent or necessary background language skills, concepts, and strategies to move rapidly into all-English instruction without support. The path of the criteria to the standard, then, is different for the student in a program offering only second language instruction. In order to be successful in English literacy where there is no access to primary language literacy, students will need substantial instruction focused on their needs as second language learners. Therefore, the development of the prerequisite oral language and informal reading outcomes becomes an extended process. The natural transfer of concepts and skills from the first language to the second will have to be replaced with a protracted and intense development of English language acquisition.

For example, such students will need an extended English oral language phase with many opportunities for practice in a variety of contexts. They will also need a rich, curriculum with a focus on communication and vocabulary development since the transfer of extended vocabulary from the first to the second language will be minimal. In Category III and IV programs, an extended phase of informal reading will also be necessary in which students receive consistent scaffolding of the oral, reading, and writing process in English. Strategies such as shared reading, language experience, and cooperative learning take on a much more critical role in the instructional process. The oral discussions in which the students' background and experiences are explored before the reading of any text are also a necessary element of this phase. It is important to remember that for older students who come to school with well-developed primary language literacy abilities, however, the process of English language acquisition can be similar to that of a Category I or II program.

Once outcomes and assessments are developed for first and second language, they become the basis for determining appropriate criteria for movement through instructional phases. They also become the basis for determining exit from primary or second language services to all-English instruction. The criteria for these two important decisions should be based on outcomes and student performances that reflect sound pedagogical principles. They should reflect student development in both the first and second languages, and not simply be criteria that are politically motivated. The program categories defined in this book present a range of possible instructional plans in which the first and second languages are used at varying levels, given the populations of students, the available resources, and the decision-making process used. The designation of appropriate student outcomes for each program category allows decision makers to identify criteria and make sound decisions about ongoing instruction and movement through a program. Changes in category of program generate the following questions: How will the criteria for progression into English reading be different for a Category I versus a Category IV program? Should the criteria for students receiving primary language instruction be different from that for those who don't? Or is it the path to the criteria that is different?

The Learner Outcome Profiles presented in Figures 7.3 and 7.4 provide an example of student outcomes across the phases of a program. Since a major determiner of the path for outcomes is the level of primary language development, different profiles are presented for Categories I and II and for Categories III and IV. The profiles also indicate the path toward the decision points, that is, from oral language to informal reading, from informal reading to formal reading, and to all-English instruction. In Category I and II programs the relationship between the first and the second language forms the basis for the criteria of movement. It is important to note the striking differences in development between the two profiles.

Developing an Authentic Process

Given the issues presented, how do school staffs identify and assess linguistically diverse students' progress over time, while maintaining a systematic and consistent perspective of first and second language development? Also, what kind of student work reflects thinking, oral language development, and comparative levels of progress in both languages? A constructivist framework requires forms of assessment that have the capacity to produce a portrait of learning outcomes and learning processes. These are often referred to as "authentic" assessments because they enable the viewers of the work to see what students are capable of doing and how they think, work, and develop. Wiggins (1989) suggests that student work might take several varied forms to which a common set of standards must be applied, and Palmer-Wolfe (1989) sees more authentic forms of assessment as "pictures of children's work" (p. 37) over time. These types of assessment are especially important for students who are learning in more than one language, since they allow for a display and comparison of performance across languages.

Applying a set of standards is the reverse of more traditional models of assessment where the curriculum is designed to meet the criteria of the test and ultimately student work becomes geared to those criteria. Forms of assessment that meet the criteria of being authentic, performance-based, and student-centered provide a broad view of student performance and include many pieces of evidence that reflect the student's process of thinking over time. Because these types of assessments demonstrate what students can do and how they are progressing, rather than focusing on all of the things they may not yet be able to do, they set parameters that are inclusive of all students. Such assessments can play a significant role in the assessment and inclusion of exceptional students in bilingual and second language programs. One particularly valuable form of assessment is the use of portfolios.

Portfolio Assessment. Portfolios are defined by Paulson, Paulson, and Meyer (1991) as "a purposeful collection of student work that exhibits the student's efforts, progress and achievement in one or more areas. [The process of collection] must include student participation in selecting contents, the criteria for selection, the criteria for judging merit and evidence of student self-reflection" (p. 16). A collection of student work that demonstrates progress over time and reflects thinking, learning style, and problem-solving ability provides significant information about the language learner's development. Literacy development, for example, can be monitored in terms of strategies for reading that cannot be measured through more traditional assessments. Including observational records in a portfolio provides a means of assessing fluency and metacognitive strategies. Self-reflection that demonstrates writing confidence, independence, and abilities to self-correct, for example, can only be assessed progressively over time.

The following dialogue represents a typical conversation with a student about her portfolio, and demonstrates both the role of the student and how a rubric is applied.

Involving the Student

TEACHER (T): Esmeralda, I'd like you to select one of your essays that you would like for your portfolio.
ESMERALDA (E): I would like the one about the whales.
T: OK, tell me why you selected that one and remember to tell me which one of our rubrics you will select for your work.
E: Well, I chose it because it's about my favorite animal, whales—and I really worked hard on it. I think I will give it "experienced writer" because I didn't just describe the whale, I talked about how people feel about the whale when they see one and I talked about how we have to protect all whales.
T: Those are good reasons. Now let's look at some other things. What else do you see?
E: I didn't make any spelling mistakes, but I am missing some capitals and commas.

FIGURE 7.3. Learner Outcome Profile—Program Categories I and II. Notice that the criteria for formal English reading and for redesignation are different in Category I and II programs than in Category III and IV programs (Figure 7.4) due to the development of skills in the primary language.

Primary Language	BEGINNING		INTERMEDIATE	ADVANCED
Understands information presented orally	Expresses ideas with a command of language	Uses conventions of language	Shows confidence in speaking, active participation	Confident, effective speaker
Expresses ideas orally	Uses some conventions of language confidently	Comprehends language subtleties: humor, idioms	Increasingly uses academic vocabulary	Expresses ideas with a high level command of language
Understands that oral language can be written	Dictates a variety of personal stories	Understands and uses academic vocabulary	Reads a variety of genre w/ comprehension	Is able to use & synthesize information from texts
Makes initial connections between meaning & print	Can read simple books independently	Asks and answers questions about content confidently	Gathers information from text	Reads in all content areas, locating and drawing on a variety of sources
Shows interest in reading	Self-corrects semantic miscues	Reads books with confidence	Reads independently from a variety of sources	Consistently self-corrects miscues by applying multiple strategies independently
Can read own dictated stories	Uses some comprehension strategies with confidence	Begins to self-correct miscues by applying multiple strategies.	Consistently self-corrects miscues by applying multiple strategies	Exhibits critical awareness as a reader
Uses invented spelling in journal entries	Beginning to use word identification	Can write own stories	Written work exhibits organization, variety, and control of vocabulary	Uses a wide range of techniques in writing to engage the reader
Writes simple thoughts & phrases		Can write summaries & book reports	Predominantly uses conventional spelling and punctuation	Exhibits a thorough command of the conventions of language and purses own interests
		Uses basic standard sentence mechanics in writing	Revises/edits writing based on feedback	Understands reading as a generative, problem-solving activity
		Begins to revise and edit writing based on feedback	Writes for a broad range of purposes	Predominantly uses conventional spelling & punctuation
				Written work exhibits organization & control of vocabulary

To Begin Formal English Reading

Redesignation for Early Exit Programs

Advanced skills are continually being developed and refined

Developmental stages (read across): **Second Language** → **To Begin Formal English Reading** → **Redesignation to Fluent English Speaker**

Second Language

- Responds appropriately to oral directions
- Uses appropriate words to identify objects
- Begins to take risks with language
- Describes pictures using phrases and simple sentences
- Understands that oral language can be written
- Gives a simple description of own drawing

- Follows multiple directions
- Uses increasing vocabulary related to personal interests/needs
- Retells a story with confidence
- Takes risks with language
- Makes predictions about simple read-aloud stories
- Asks and answers questions

- Asks & answers questions confidently
- Dictates a variety of personal stories
- Contributes facts to small group academic discussions
- Joins in the oral reading of predictable books
- Responds to questions before/during/after a book is read to him/her
- Maintains dialogues of increasing length/complexity
- Can talk about content area materials with confidence

To Begin Formal English Reading

- Uses most syntax & vocabulary correctly
- Summarizes oral material
- Reads English books with confidence
- Begins to self-correct semantic miscues
- Increasingly uses strategies for solving unknown words
- Can write own simple stories
- Can write summaries & book reports
- Use basic standard sentence mechanics in writing

Redesignation to Fluent English Speaker

- Shows confidence in speaking active participation
- Increasingly uses academic vocabulary
- Reads a variety of genre w/comprehension
- Gathers information from text
- Reads independently from a variety of sources
- Usually self-corrects miscues by applying multiple strategies
- Written work exhibits organization, variety, & control of vocabulary
- Uses some conventional spelling and punctuation
- Revises/edits writing based on feedback

- Confident, effective speaker
- Expresses ideas with a high level command of language
- Is able to use and synthesize information from texts
- Reads in all content locating and drawing on a variety of sources
- Consistently self-corrects miscues by applying multiple strategies, independently
- Exhibits critical awareness as reader
- Uses a wide range of techniques in writing to engage the reader
- Exhibits a thorough command of the conventions of language & purses own interests
- Predominantly uses conventional spelling and punctuation
- Written work exhibits organization & control of vocabulary

Advanced skills are continually being developed and refined

FIGURE 7.4. Learner Outcome Profile—Program Categories III and IV.

Second Language

BEGINNING				INTERMEDIATE		ADVANCED
Responds appropriately	Follows multiple directions	Asks questions confidently	Asks and answers questions confidently	Integrates new vocabulary into speech	Understands and uses increasing academic vocabulary	Confident, effective speaker
Uses appropriate words to identify objects	Uses increasing vocabulary related to personal interests/needs	Dictates a variety of personal stories	Maintains dialogues of increasing length/complexity	Uses most syntax & vocabulary correctly	Comprehends language subtleties, humor, idioms, irony	Expresses ideas with a high level command of language
Contributes words to small group hands-on activities	Retells a story with confidence	Contributes facts to small group academic discussion	Can discuss content area materials	Summarizes oral material	Shows confidence in speaking, active participation	Is able to use & synthesize information from texts
Begins to take risks with language	Takes risks with books	Joins in the oral reading and pre-dictable text	Reads pre-dictable text	Reads books w/ confidence	Consistently self-corrects miscues by applying multiple strategies	Reads in all content areas locating & drawing on a variety of sources
Describes pictures using phrases and simple sentences	Contributes simple phrases to language experience story about content related subjects	Responds to questions before/during/after a book is read to him/her	Beginning to use word identification strategies w/prompting	Begins to self-correct semantic miscues	Reads independently from a variety of sources	Consistently self-corrects miscues by applying multiple strategies, independently
Understands that oral language can be written	Takes risks with language	Labels own drawings with assistance	Begins to build meaning w/teacher support	Increasingly uses strategies for solving unknown words	Read a variety of genre w/comprehension	Exhibits critical awareness as a reader
Contributes simple phrases to language experience story	Dictates story with at least 3 sentences/themes/subjects	Dictates story with at least 3 sentences	Begins to select books independently	Can write own simple stories	Gathers information from texts	Uses wide range of techniques in writing to engage the reader
Shows interests in books	Makes predictions about simple read-aloud stories	Uses invented spelling in journal entries	Writes simple phrases about group activity or shared story w/assistance	Can write summaries & book reports	Understands reading is a generative, problem-solving activity	Exhibits a thorough command of the conventions of language and pursues own interests
Dictates simple description of own drawing	Copies letter/numbers/words from class activity		Writes thoughts in journal	Uses basic standard punctuation in writing	Predominantly uses conventional spelling & punctuation	Writes for broad purposes/audiences
					Written work exhibits organization & control of vocabulary	Advanced skills are continually being developed and refined
					Revises/edits writing based on feedback	

To begin formal English Reading (between BEGINNING and INTERMEDIATE)

To Exit Second Language Support Services (between INTERMEDIATE and ADVANCED)

---

[1] Note the additional criteria for beginning formal English reading and for exiting the program between the Category III and IV programs and the Category I and II programs (Figure 7.3) due to the absence of primary language literacy development.

190

T: Let's look again at the rubric—it says under experienced writer that "some errors in mechanics are made," so I still think you are accurate in choosing that rubric.

This brief dialogue between teacher and student exemplifies a much more responsible role taken by the student about her work. It communicates that Esmeralda understands the standards of expectation and is making connections about how her writing approximates the rubric or exemplar of the standard. By being engaged in a discussion about her work, the choices she made, and the content of her piece, Esmeralda and her teacher have a much deeper understanding of her performance than the teacher alone would have gained from a test.

Portfolios for students developing proficiency in first and second language begin with learner outcomes developed collaboratively by staff members for both languages. These reflect targets of high expectations matched to those for all students in their primary language. They also take into account the unique developmental path for students in their second language. Pieces of work that reflect the standards are prescribed to be included in the portfolio throughout the school year, for example, by genre: a personal narrative, expository paper, or a poem. Students, however, are involved in the selection of the particular pieces for their personal portfolio. Their reflections on the process of their work in first and second language are highly encouraged and become integral to the assessment process as these new practices become internalized. These reflections may have to be modeled by the teacher or initially include prompts to the student, particularly in the second language. But over time, they become more specific and insightful, and are a consistent means for students to think about, talk about, and eventually put into writing feelings about, attitudes toward, and reactions to their work.

Portfolios can also contribute greatly to understanding and monitoring students' second language oral proficiency. Oral language development in the second language is a process that has traditionally been measured as discrete points along a scale of vocabulary, grammar, and syntax. As discussed in Chapter 5, however, proficiency in oral language represents a complex constellation of skills. Audio, video, and observational techniques are methods that can result in substantive evidence of progress in second language acquisition. These assessments are embedded in the day-to-day curriculum of the classroom and can measure natural language ability, confidence, and nuances of language use.

Portfolio assessment has been presented as an example of a process that follows learning over time and that allows for student choice and reflection. For this kind of assessment to be successful, however, the contents of the portfolio must be developed and articulated through a schoolwide process, with indicators selected collaboratively and directly tied to the learner outcomes.

Observations. The portfolio includes evidence of student work that reflects progress over time, based on preset standards. As portfolios are being developed, a number of other techniques can be used concurrently to assess performance-based tasks. For example, observational techniques are uniquely conducive to recording student responses, dialogues, and performance through hands-on tasks. To be able to use observations effectively requires that teachers create student-centered classrooms in which the setting and structure offer multiple opportunities to observe and record student progress consistently.

Checklists can be a helpful tool in observation. Rather than being skills-oriented, however, checklists should reflect strategies for performance on a particular task. Caution must be taken to avoid the use of checklists in a perfunctory manner to mark off behaviors in a one-time setting. Instead, they are a tool teachers can utilize to observe student use of strategies over time. The following example illustrates possible strategies on an observation checklist for students learning a second language:

Informal reading—student can: predict outcomes with teacher input; choose pictures of pertinent words; retell story in sequence with teacher input; produce books and storyboards and create art pertaining to the story; think and/or write questions in cooperative groups; read short passages from story independently after being exposed several times (teacher reading, listening post, small-group reading).
Formal reading—student can: make predictions and inferences and summarize familiar stories; identify beginning, middle, and end of stories; identify setting, characters, story problems, and solutions; use picture clues, phonics, and context clues to gain meaning.

Exhibitions. Exhibitions are another powerful means of assessment. Geared more appropriately to older students, the exhibitions of work display or communicate a comprehensive project or production over time. In programs for linguistically diverse students, these culminating exhibitions of work in first and second language over a sequence of schooling (i.e., elementary, middle, or senior high) can be a critical means of assessing overall performance at all levels of language proficiency as well as content knowledge.

Culminating, thoughtful exhibitions and portfolios are significant means of offering teachers an in-depth look at how students are performing relative to each language along several dimensions that need to be considered in both languages. A schoolwide accountability system that is articulated upward to the next educational level has the capacity for telling a very complete and thoughtful story about student progress. Its use can provide specific information for developing and adjusting curriculum and instructional strategies appropriately. Understanding the Basic Premises and implementing a communitywide plan for assessment and accountability establish the framework for instructional improvement.

Articulation. Articulation, the sharing of student progress between levels of schooling, has remained a serious problem in education. Teachers participating in the following dialogue are beginning the discussion about how to connect their individual assessment practices to a school accountability process.

Making Connections

TEACHER (T) 1: The portfolios of my students are really showing some very good progress in English writing. I believe they are ready for transition.

T2: (transition teacher) But I don't use portfolios. How will I be able to judge if they are ready?

T3: (mentor teacher) I have been giving this issue a lot of thought. I think we need a process that we all use to assess student performance and that will help us determine when students are ready for transition or any other types of redesignations.

T1: But where do we start?

T4: Well, we can't really create assessment measures without first knowing what expectations we have for students.

T3: How does everyone feel about using our next nonstudent day to begin to develop student outcomes for language arts?

T5: Isn't there anything already published we can use?

T3: Certainly, there are the state frameworks that we would need to guide us and the national standards work, but we have to think about our own population of students and what criteria we will use for continuous progress of the English language learners that we have been talking about.

Articulating the achievement of linguistically diverse students requires a more complex set of considerations. Although teachers and other staff may wholeheartedly adopt the notion of authentic assessment and maintain portfolios and other types of effective assessment practices in their individual classrooms, if these are not shared and purposefully used they have little value in helping to provide appropriate instruction to students over time. And, unless these assessments are developed, implemented, and maintained schoolwide, true school accountability and instructional improvement are improbable.

Developing Criteria. The fourth step is the development of criteria for assessing performance, such as rubrics—descriptors of student work over time. A rubric provides a detailed description of what work that meets the standard should look like over time. For example, "developing writer" would be a descriptor that could encompass several criteria including, among other things "labels own drawings with assistance" and "work demonstrates simple sentence structure, fragments, simple limited vocabulary." Even though the outcomes and rubrics are developed by staff, they include student input and at all levels students are made fully aware of the expectations, and are included in the assigning of the rubrics. As opposed to a grade, percent, or rank, portfolios give a portrait of performance that communicates development and growth.

Specific measures to assess the chosen outcomes must then be selected. These should include the forms of authentic assessment embedded in the curriculum that measure what a student knows. These measures must be able to reflect language development at both the receptive and productive levels. Thus, language measures are necessary that demonstrate the students' oral language development in natural contexts, as well as reading, writing, and concept development over time. If students are at the center of the process, the assessment measures will also consistently provide opportunities for them to reflect on their work.

In order to ensure reliability and validity in the portfolio assessment, exemplars of students work, called anchors, must be generated. Anchors are samples of student work that demonstrate the criteria established for the rubrics. The creation of rubrics and the selection of anchor papers that reflect student development over time must be done collaboratively by the entire school staff. It is most beneficial to involve parents and community members early in this collaboration, as well. In order to assure that these rubrics and anchors continue to represent the expected outcomes, they must be reviewed and renegotiated regularly.

Such a process can be effective only if school staff and other participants view it as an advantageous means to consistently monitor student progress and ultimately to plan for program improvement. Careful planning is a critical factor in its success. Although it requires considerable careful deliberation, and is time-consuming and difficult, the payoff comes in substantially increased student achievement.

Using the Data. An essential part of the assessment process in primary and second language programs is the adjustment of instruction to the needs of changing student proficiency and shifting curricular demands. Using schoolwide assessment practices to make continuous adjustments calls for a purposeful system designed specifically to monitor the progress of students. This requires that a school establish procedures to regularly review second language learners' progress. An effective way to approach this process is through a *second language team*, particularly in the initial stages of developing a comprehensive instructional process for these students. Such a team can help staff work through issues reflected in the Basic Premises and become more proficient in correctly determining student needs.

The second language team, with broad staff representation, meets regularly and has the responsibility for making recommendations regarding initial placement or ongoing program reassignment of second language students. In this schoolwide team process, assessments such as portfolios are an effective source of data on which the staff can make decisions. Judgments regarding student instruction should be based on the learning outcomes developed by the staff as a whole, guidelines for program development indicated in the Basic Premises, and the actual progress indicated through the portfolio and other performance-based measures. These determiners are not based on individual judgment or predetermined program criteria.

The development of assessment practices within the reform process requires that a school adopt an inquiry approach to its day-to-day activities. This approach should represent an interactive process where individuals feel safe and comfortable critically analyzing their situation as they work toward restructuring. This type of inquiry can be used regularly within the school community to keep change efforts focused on real and specific learning needs of all students. During the process, the staff's inquiry is centered on student work over time. This type of discussion can generate information on how the school uses assessment to inform teaching, as well as provide a means of monitoring the school's performance in relation to the district and state standards.

As an example, in one school that had already implemented schoolwide portfolio assessment and student outcomes in language arts and math, but had not yet included the entire staff in an opportunity to review samples of student work across levels, the inquiry process focused on how to involve the entire staff. They dedicated one of their staff development days to have teams from across the school work together to examine student portfolios and discuss student progress, anchor papers, and the validity of the rubrics. Noncertificated staff and parents acted as reflectors, giving ongoing feedback to the teachers about the process itself, as well as the discussion about the work of students. These reflections allowed the staff to closely examine the continuity of the outcomes they had developed and their assessment practices as a whole. It also provided an opportunity for noncertificated staff and parents to be intimately involved in the process.

After a school has devised a schoolwide assessment system, a giant step is to begin to design ways of extrapolating data from the performance-based assessment results. For example, it is appropriate to be able to report on the percent of students who have advanced on the schoolwide rubrics and have reached various language bench marks. Data from rubrics, exhibitions, and observation records, rather than from grades, can form the basis for evaluating student progress on a schoolwide basis. These data, unlike traditional grades, can be accompanied by substantiating evidence. Given the kind of systematic approach to assessment discussed, the reliability and validity of the data can be established and this information focus can be used to validate the success of the schoolwide program.

Informing Parents. Informing parents about student progress is integral to the internal process of accountability. If a staff begins examining the potential for moving into performance-based assessments, it will ultimately have to consider a change from the traditional "report card." The continued use of letter or number grades that represent a tracking, sorting system will send a mixed message to the community.

In order to move to a nongraded reporting system, the staff will have to plan for how to provide opportunities for parents to review the portfolio exhibitions and performances. Intensive effort must be made to ensure that parents are involved in the assessment process, that they attend conferences, and that communication about student progress is available in their language. Often, when limited staff or volunteers are available who speak the language or languages of the community, cooperative efforts have to be made to ensure that these bilingual individuals are available on a rotating, shared basis among teachers to discuss the portfolio and other performance-based results. It is only through the experience of following the process with their own child that parents will be able to embrace this new practice.

Measuring School Effectiveness

Ultimately the effectiveness of school reform rests on the results of students' academic achievement and the school's ability to respond to the needs of its total community. Several means for reporting data on school effectiveness are available. A multifaceted approach should be utilized that includes indicators of attendance levels, surveys of parent and staff satisfaction and involvement in decision making, dropout rates, nontracking indicators, distribution of students across courses, involvement of businesses and agencies in the school, and so forth. With regard to programs for linguistically diverse students, indicators of how effective the school has been in involving the culture or cultures of the community in the curriculum also are needed. For example, have Latino or Asian business leaders been drawn into the school community? Have health and human services been coordinated to provide optimum service to students?

With respect to the reporting of student achievement data, a major challenge to schools is to accommodate the data from traditional, norm-referenced tests within a performance-based system. Advocacy for one position or the other will result in wasted energy since, as a society, we do not yet seem prepared to move away from normative measures. It is, therefore, important for educators to include such data in reporting total school effectiveness. Most normative measures emphasize skills and do not reflect the second language acquisition process. When progress on these skills is reported, it must be balanced with student performance on more substantive and authentic thinking tasks in their primary language. Staffs should spend time analyzing the results from the standardized tests and linking those data to the performance-based data for an overall view of student achievement. Reporting must also demonstrate the precise progress of linguistically diverse students in relation to the process of second language development, as well as indicating how and when second language learners will be expected to reach the benchmarks that indicate they have developed native-like English language proficiency and academic achievement.

ISSUES SPECIFIC TO PROGRAM CATEGORIES

The following discussion will draw from the previous analysis of assessment practices as they relate to the linguistically diverse student in general, but will give specific criteria and benchmarks for each program category (as reflected in Figures 7.3 and 7.4) and indicate the path of continuous progress for students within each program category.

Category I: Full Primary Language Foundation

In this category, the full range of assessment specific to bilingual instruction is required. Content standards in each of the content areas including literacy must be developed. Learner outcomes are derived from these standards. Learner outcomes in the primary language should reflect what is expected for all students in math, science, social studies, and language arts. Those for second language development reflect a substantially different progression of outcomes through the transition levels. Performance-based assessments must be established for all the benchmarks in both the first and the second language. These benchmarks indicate the path to bilingualism or the point at which a student has achieved a solid foundation in the primary language and is able to function academically in English.

Category II: Primary Language Support—Literacy Only

Since only literacy instruction in the primary language is offered in this category, it becomes a major vehicle for language and concept development. Because of the limited scope of primary language instruction, a special effort must be made to ensure that the standards and learner outcomes reflect a range and depth of genres, vocabulary development, and experiences with writing. All of the expectations should drive a curriculum that provides students extensive flexibility in literacy. An integrated approach in which content is embedded in the language arts curriculum is necessary so that students' developing knowledge of content and concepts in their second language can be assessed. Special attention should be paid to primary and second language interaction by closely monitoring the benchmark step of movement into formal English reading and where necessary to all-English, as indicated in Figure 7.3. Throughout the process it is important to ask yourself: Has the appropriate foundation of literacy and concepts been established in the first language to support the transfer into the second language, and has there been the necessary oral language development in the second language?

Category III: Primary Language Content Reinforcement

In programs where little or no primary language instruction is offered, the development of English language and academic proficiency will be a slower and more deliberate process, which will be reflected in the assessment outcomes (see Figure 7.4). In this category, assessment will focus much more on second language development and the primary language serves a more supportive role. In Category III, where there may be primary language content reinforcement, information derived from this limited but critical experience is useful to staff when making decisions about program modifications. For example:

> A second language team is reviewing the portfolios of students in a Category III program with the purpose of deciding whether the students qualify to move into the transition phase of the program. They have noticed that one student's work appears to place her on the border of the benchmark to move into the transition phase. A representative on the committee has brought to the discussion information about how the student functions in her primary language reinforcement activities. It is reported that the student is highly verbal in her primary language, brings many in-depth concepts to school, and is very proud to speak her mother tongue.

The important information that she has many strengths in the primary language may be the deciding factor in moving the student into the transition period.

In Categories III and IV the emphasis of the assessment process will be on English language proficiency and academic development through English. Because the aural–oral language phase must initially be relied on to carry all content and understanding of instruction, it must go far beyond a basic communication curriculum and must be based on the content of academic curriculum. Opportunities for oral language development must not be allowed to be replaced by formal reading. Rather, an informal reading phase that builds on meaning established through the oral language curriculum is critical. Precise learner outcomes must be developed to reflect what is expected and measurable at this phase.

Category IV: All-English

As indicated above, in an all-English situation assessment focused on academic English is paramount. In this category, the assessment process is entirely in English. Since the second language is the vehicle for all content and understanding of instruction, content must be the focus of spontaneous and scaffolded language development. Opportunities for oral language development must also continue for several years as a support for literacy development, and should not be displaced by formal reading. Precise learner outcomes must reflect the second language process, and must be continuously measured.

In programs where there is no formal instruction in the primary language, it is also still important to have information about the use of the primary language at home and in other contexts outside of school. Running records included in the student's portfolio can provide invaluable insights, and can be used to involve parents in the assessment process. Investigating how a student uses the primary language in these various contexts, for example, can add an important dimension to the assessment process. This is especially important for students who have limited proficiencies in both languages. As discussed in Chapters 4 and 5, these bilingual students are often assumed not to need any second language support, and gaps in language and vocabulary are often ignored. Oral language development, discussion of topics before engaging in text, and constant monitoring of comprehension are all critical to the development of these second language learners.

Decision Making on Your Own

1. Questions that highlight major issues regarding assessment include: Does your staff have common expectations or standards for student achievement? Are they delineated for bilingual instruction? If so, are the standards and outcomes different for the linguistically diverse students? Do the assessment practices in your school accurately measure the entry level of the linguistically different students, the progress of students in both L1 and L2, and the readiness for formal reading in L2? Are there practices in your school that result in tracking students? If so, how do these practices affect the second language learners? Do your assessment methods lead to the sorting and tracking of these students or do they help avoid it?

In order to answer these questions about your setting, you will need to add the following information to your school profile: areas of the curriculum taught in the primary language and in English; general assessment practices in place in your school; instruments currently used to assess primary language and second language development; ways that teachers and parents are involved in the assessment of students.

2. Think about the Basic Premises and major elements presented in this chapter on assessment. Generate a list of additional questions that will help you to decide how best to serve students in your setting or school.

3. Compare your list of questions and those of a colleague and refine your list. Have you considered all the major issues?

4. Form a small group and brainstorm the optimal assessment practices possible in your setting. Use the Basic Premises highlighted in this chapter to weigh your decisions.

5. List two or three changes that might have to be made.

6. What are the implications of your decisions for other areas, for example, progress reporting, curriculum, program and performance evaluation, community engagement, and articulation with the next level of education?

7. Add these data to your school profile.

CHAPTER 8

Community Outreach

Key Premises to Consider

• *Premise 2—The primary language foundation.* The more comprehensive the use of the primary language, the greater that potential for linguistically diverse students to be academically successful. There are always ways to nurture the primary language regardless of school resources.

• *Premise 9—Parents and community.* Parents and community must play a major role in the learning and schooling of their children.

• *Premise 11—Sociocultural and political implications.* Sociocultural factors and political context must be considered in making decisions regarding every aspect of program planning.

Instructional programs do not exist in a vacuum. Rather, they exist within schools that are situated in communities that can be defined along several dimensions. There is the geographic community that physically surrounds a school; there are the ethnolinguistic communities that comprise the student population; and there are the institutions, services, leisure activities, and commercial enterprises that constitute the life of the broader civic community. In this chapter, we link the instructional program to outreach strategies and explore some of the reasons why a strong emphasis on community is so important to the education of second language learners.

Traditional parent involvement programs are often based on a mainstream, middle-class model that assumes that parents have particular outlooks, resources, and time frames available for schoolwork. There are also preconceived notions about what roles parents will play in the decision-making process of the school, their values about education in general, and their status in relation to teachers. Typically, parent involvement policies and opportunities are dictated by a small group of people in the schools, acting alone without the consultation of the communities they serve (McLaughlin & Shields, 1987).

The perspective presented in this chapter is distinct from these traditional views on parental involvement. We use the term "outreach" to describe a program of engagement that requires school personnel to go out and draw parents, other family members, and the community at large into the school arena as partners in the decision-making process. In this view, the community outreach program is tied directly to the school's vision for the academic achievement of its students, not as a singular goal, but as a perspective that permeates the entire vision. A guiding assumption in this chapter is that school policies must go beyond giving lip service to the importance of collaboration and reflect active steps to reach out to and bring in families and community members to foster academic success.

Decision Making: Ask Yourself

What are the implications of a community outreach rather than a traditional parent involvement perspective for the broader inclusion of community partners?

Who should be involved in schools, and at what levels of involvement?

What is the impact of bringing new people into the decision-making process?

What are nontraditional ways in which parents help children and support schools?

How will the languages of the community be used?

PERSPECTIVES ON COMMUNITY OUTREACH

Parental participation in schooling is positively associated with academic achievement for all students, regardless of home language. The most successful schools embrace the joint collaboration of teachers, students, families, and community (McCaleb, 1994) and view families as assets in the schooling process. They seek ways to foster community partnerships so that parents, families, and others can act in a variety of capacities and settings to enhance children's education.

Parents' and teachers' views of each other are shaped, in part, by their actions in relation to school/community interaction. Not surprisingly, teachers view parents' involvement as a sign that they value educational success (Lareau, 1989). Conversely, teachers who communicate more with parents or are leaders in parent involvement are considered to be better teachers by parents (Epstein, 1984). Some teachers link students' success with the level at which their parents care about them and their schooling (Delgado-Gaitan, 1990).

The ways schools interact with their constituent communities reflect the overall values and beliefs of a school and its staff. These beliefs and values are expressed in both the explicit and the implicit ways educators communicate what the community's role should be in the educational process. In most traditional parent/school groups, teachers and administrators have primary responsibility for seeing that things get done and a few token parents are involved to give tacit approval for decisions that are made.

The ultimate goal of an outreach program is that families and community members work with teachers and staff and play an active role as educational advocates and decision makers, with places on school committees and decision-making bodies. However, a major shift in thinking must occur for parents and community members to begin to take ownership of portions of the work, and for school staffs to accept that they do not have to have control of all the ideas. When outreach efforts are tied to a school's vision for the academic achievement of its students, all groups are held accountable for adherence to the vision.

Obviously, creating a community focus implies a commitment to the ideal of collaborative participation. It will take time, patience, and planning to assure that people along the continuum from totally nonparticipatory to those who seem to want total control can move together toward common goals. An outreach program is aimed at establishing collaborative decision making within an organization. Through the process of developing this kind of collaborative model, school involvement can represent authentic participation in the democratic process.

Understanding Differences

In schools with large numbers of second language learners, differences in ethnicity, schooling, and class between teachers and the communities in which they work can create barriers and misunderstandings. Many immigrants and refugees come here from rural settings and nonliterate backgrounds and do not share common experiences with their children's teachers. In addition, most teachers don't live in and are unfamiliar with the communities of their students. This is very different from previous generations, where teachers and families were likely to encounter each other at the grocery, in churches, or at the park. The physical distance between educators and students' communities means that teachers are probably unaware of the events and activities in the community that do, in fact, support school goals. Breakdowns in communication can allow negative stereotypes to influence practice and seriously hinder potentially successful interactions. Consider the following comments by teachers of immigrant students in the United States.

There just doesn't seem to be an educational environment at home. There's not much input when she leaves class.

He never does homework; he never does anything beyond the classroom. His home environment is not very educational.

Listening to the kids, the parents are probably very good parents, but if they never had any schooling, how can they help them at home? (Commins, 1992, p. 40)

These statements express attitudes that we have encountered repeatedly over the years. Students' home environments are seen as insufficient to prepare them for academic success, and families who don't speak English are thought to be unable to help their children with academic work.

Indeed, very often non–English speaking parents are not actively involved in school-based activities. Unfortunately, educators often mistakenly interpret low levels of participation as indicating a lack of caring or willingness to be involved on the part of parents. Those teachers who are accustomed to working with families from mainstream, middle-class backgrounds come to expect that parents will take the initiative to communicate with them, help with schoolwork, volunteer in the classroom, and attend school events and meetings (Lareau, 1989). Or, instead of seeking a reciprocal relationship, teachers want parents simply to cooperate with them on the school's terms. However, many low-income and working-class families do not have the resources and confidence about the educational process that many middle-class parents take for granted.

A lack of familiarity and comfort with the school setting is one reason that many parents are reluctant to get involved in school activities. Some parents consider teachers to be disinterested and unresponsive to their children. They may feel that their own beliefs about education are ignored or undervalued. For parents, especially younger ones, who did not have particularly pleasant schooling experiences, just walking in the doorway of a school may evoke painful memories of disenfranchisement and neglect, as illustrated by the vignette below.

Unhappy Memories of School

It's the first day of school and Diana, a 21-year-old mother of a kindergartner, is taking her daughter, Amanda, to school for the first time. Diana, who dropped out of school in 11th grade because she was pregnant, is more apprehensive about entering the building than Amanda is. She can recall going to school the first day, not speaking a word of English, confused and frightened in the huge building filled with people she couldn't understand.

Diana has no fond memories of school and feels disconnected. Her parents never went to school, uncomfortable speaking only Spanish in its all-English environment. Even when she was placed in a bilingual program in fifth grade, her parents remained uninvolved, not able to overcome their uneasiness at entering the school. Diana's teachers assumed her parents just didn't care. No one expected her to succeed or noticed if she was absent. When she got pregnant, no one encouraged her to stay in school.

Now that Amanda is ready for kindergarten, Diana has gotten her GED and has plans to attend classes at the local community college. She is determined that school be a better experience for her children than it was for her, but she can't overcome her unhappy memories on that first day. When Amanda's teacher greets her at the door with a "Bienvenida" and tells Diana how much she looks forward to working with her that year, Diana smiles, but is skeptical.

For parents like Diana to feel welcome and become active members of the school community, schools must attempt to build common understandings and establish trust. Indeed, reform efforts aimed at increasing community collaboration take for granted that most parents are interested in supporting their children, but that many don't know how best to do so (Commins, 1992; Davies, 1988; Delgado-Gaitan, 1992). This is reflected in the comments (translated) of the parents of the same children described by teachers above.

I'd be willing to help them do well in school, but I don't understand their English assignments, and I'm not sure of what I could do.

They say we don't care about our children's education, but they never tell us what we can do to help, and everything they send home is in English.

As these statements indicate, many parents are simply unsure of their roles in relation to schools. They may have limited exposure to the norms of public education in this country or be unable to communicate effectively in English. Parents may also be reluctant to become actively involved in their children's education because of their views on the proper roles of parents and teachers. In many countries, there is a clear delineation between the responsibilities of the school and the responsibilities of parents. Teachers are the educators and parents who try to become involved at school are seen as interfering in the school's business. Family members may, therefore, find it difficult to respond positively to a request to come to school when, in their home countries, such requests are made only when students are in serious trouble. In this country, too, families are typically called on only to solve problems or in times of crisis (Davies, 1988).

When outreach is organized specifically to engage parents from low-income and traditionally marginalized communities, their levels of involvement and participation increase (Brandt, 1989; McCaleb, 1994). Knowing that our actions can make a difference, it seems clear that it is the responsibility of school personnel to find ways to reach out to people and help them to participate in ways that are meaningful. Effective partnerships result when reciprocal relationships are established between families and schools that allow for the development, sustenance, and enhancement of mutual trust (Bronfenbrenner, 1979). In these situations, mutual respect for the contributions members make to the total community can grow and develop. Majority as well as minority group members learn about new ways of thinking and doing. The flow of knowledge and respect becomes a two-way exchange.

Community Outreach in Linguistically Diverse Communities

Organizing for community outreach takes on an added dimension in schools comprised of students from diverse linguistic and cultural backgrounds. In these schools, educators should consider such questions as: What happens to second language learners when they enter schools and embark on the road to English proficiency? What does it mean to become an English speaker, both to these students and to their families? What can we do as a staff to maximize the schooling experience?

Increasing student achievement is a core goal of community outreach, but it can have the added benefit of strengthening family ties, as well. When children who speak a language other than English at home enter school, they move into a new world that may bear little resemblance to what is familiar to them and to their parents. Children of immigrant families in the United States are more likely to learn English and move more quickly than their parents into the new culture. When school activities are conducted mainly or solely in English, it is understandable that parents may feel they no longer have a role in their children's education. This shift can cause severe stress in families and can lead to irreparable rifts between children and their parents (Wong-Fillmore, 1991). Given the multiple issues faced by youth today, the importance of family ties cannot be overstated. Therefore, enhancing—not undermining—families is in the best interests of those who work in schools.

Children's developing proficiency in English can be of great help to families, while at the same time being a source of stress. For example, children are often able to translate at doctors' offices or negotiate with store clerks. While their English skills facilitate communication, they can also place children in unnatural roles in relation to adults. Through outreach programs, schools can help parents understand the implications of their children's being bilingual and bicultural and suggest strategies for how to cope with the inevitable cultural changes their children will experience.

One way to help children and parents deal with cultural clashes is to begin by recognizing and acknowledging them. Conflicts can arise over such things as whether older siblings should be expected to miss school to care for younger brothers and sisters, or whether it is more important for teenagers to work in the family business after school than to do homework. Other issues concern the limits of corporal punishment and what constitutes child abuse. Families who utilize non-Western medical practices, for example, have been accused of physical abuse because of marks made on a children's neck and face that result from coin rubbing, a traditional healing practice.

Once these issues are recognized, the next step is to try to accommodate the varying views of different communities in school programs, as described in the example below.

A Home–School Cultural Clash

The rise in the number of teen pregnancies at a local high school was the impetus for the implementation of a new program for girls called "On Your Way." The thrust of the program was to help girls become independent decision makers and to learn about the many options available to them in the future if they could put off becoming pregnant. The program had the support of several social service agencies, which provided volunteers to work with the girls as both teachers and mentors. Many girls participated enthusiastically in this after-school program. However, following the first four-week session, complaints began to be heard from members of the Hmong community indicating that the program was undermining the community's traditions and values. For most of the families, marriage in the early teens was the norm and the idea that girls would make choices for themselves without consulting elders in the community was an affront. Once these complaints were voiced, school personnel indicated a willingness to respond, but a climate of mutual understanding and trust did not really exist. It took many one-on-one meetings between individual teachers, parents, and clan leaders to establish a solid foundation for communication. Growing out of these meetings, school personnel and Hmong community leaders were eventually able to develop a parent education program around the issue of teen pregnancy and marriage. The program focused on analyzing and discussing the various attitudes different cultural groups have toward these issues and in the end they were able to make some adjustments to "On Your Way" that addressed the concerns of everyone involved.

One goal of outreach, then, can be to break down fears associated with cultural change. Instead of school representing the "other world," it can act as a bridge between mainstream society and students' own linguistic and cultural backgrounds. The sense of community that can develop through school outreach efforts can help reassure families that the school is a safe environment for their children, is understanding and supportive of their values, and is concerned about creating a bridge between them. Part of community outreach is internal to the school. One goal is to ensure that children encounter people in all facets of the school with whom they are comfortable and feel supported.

A vision that affirms the importance of families is based, in part, on the belief that students from all backgrounds arrive at school with a wealth of experiences, conceptual knowledge, and strategies for learning. A strong community outreach program can help teachers to see children as functioning members of their linguistic and cultural communities. When schools believe that all families can help children achieve academic success, they seek ways to build on families' strengths. In a school committed to community outreach, educators ask how students' cultures and languages can be affirmed and reflected in the overall school environment and how these can be actively incorporated into the curriculum.

Understanding the Sociopolitical Context. To create a successful outreach program, educators need to understand their community within the larger sociopolitical context. Issues of status, power, and economic circumstances all play a role in shaping the community. For example, second language learners often live in communities with high concentrations of immigrants. By their very nature these are communities in transition. These transitions occur as new waves of immigrants come in to replace those who have established roots, garnered success, and moved on. Each group of immigrants brings with them the particular issues and circumstances that prompted their coming to this country—whether to escape a war, to find a job, or to complete graduate school. These life circumstances create tensions that range from cross-ethnic conflicts exacerbated by linguistic barriers to matters of the ownership of the businesses that people use every day.

Those second language learners who live in well-established and stable communities may also face tensions in their communities, particularly between long-term residents and recent arrivals. Even among individuals of the same ethnic group, differing levels of acculturation may cause clashes, in part because of the failure of the general public to distinguish between second- or third-generation residents and recent arrivals. The automatic assumption, for example, that someone of Latino origin does not speak English or is not a citizen reflects the prejudices that inflame these tensions. Resentments can also arise if newcomers are seen as undermining the stability of the community or as somehow threatening the gains made by long-time residents.

The high mobility of many immigrant and working-class families is often an issue of concern to educators. Students may be taken in and out of school a dozen times over the course of several years, thereby seriously disrupting their educational progress. An outreach program can help families understand how constantly moving can negatively impact students' academic progress. It may be possible through outreach to encourage families to move less frequently or, if they must move, to stay in the same neighborhood, so that their children can continue to attend the same schools. But, in order to provide families with a real incentive to stay, it is essential that there be a strong instructional program in place that truly meets the needs of their children.

Broadening the Definition of Community Participation. As discussed in the introduction to this chapter, community can be more broadly defined than the immediate ethnolinguistic community of students. A more inclusive definition encompasses the full range of businesses, services, and events that constitute the context of schools. Over the last decade many efforts have been launched based on the ideas that especially in urban centers, the resources available in the broader community can be used to support schools and that schools provide a natural locus for gathering together services, such as health clinics, schooling for parents, and social services. Such efforts have been launched across the country in cities like New Haven, Milwaukee, San Diego, and Boston. An essential feature of all these programs is the active involvement of parents and the broader community in nontraditional ways. James Comer (1984), for example, proposes a comprehensive model for reorganizing schools for community involvement. Its four main components include a representative governance and management body, a multidimensional parent program, involvement of support staff through a mental health team program, and a staff and curriculum development program designed to increase the responsiveness of curriculum by addressing areas in which teachers need or want support. The connection between curriculum development and community outreach is critical. The best community program will not help improve student achievement if sufficient attention is not paid to the quality of the instructional program.

One way to link the instructional program to community outreach is by incorporating what Moll (1990a,b) calls "community funds of knowledge" into the academic curriculum. From this perspective, communities are viewed as rich sources of knowledge, expertise, and information that may be overlooked in traditional approaches to education. By learning about the strengths of the community and attempting to incorporate these funds of knowledge into curriculum planning, educators can reaffirm the importance of families and provide ways for them to authentically participate in their children's education. One example described by Moll involves building on parents' knowledge of many construction trades to create interdisciplinary instructional units centered on building. Similarly, knowledge about agriculture, clothing, or other topics related to the jobs and professions of community members can provide the foundation for their incorporation into the instructional program as active participants in sharing knowledge. This increases the likelihood that parents can support students at home and provides strong links between the schools and the wider community.

Active efforts on the part of schools to bring in more families, businesses, and community service agencies to enlist their support can help to ease tensions and build strong community-school bridges. This happens when all parties become involved in ways that they consider to be useful and meaningful and when involvement lasts over time. A community-centered school can serve as a focus for community renewal.

ISSUES COMMON TO ALL PROGRAM CATEGORIES

Program categories affect the ultimate organization of a parent outreach program, although there is less variability than in the instructional program. Specifically, they impact the ability to communicate in the primary language, the possibilities for involving family members directly in the instructional program at school, and the likelihood that bicultural personnel will be available to act as links with the community. Most elements of community outreach efforts however are reflected across all program categories.

The development of goals for community outreach is an integral part of establishing a vision for the school. This involves identifying the different stakeholders who need to participate in the decision-making process and specifying the kinds of roles teachers, families, and community members can play. It can begin by going to all of the constituents to determine their needs, their dreams, and their vision of how the community can work to reach common goals. For parents it may mean letting them know where the answers to their questions can be found or that opportunities exist for their own education. For teachers it may mean finding resources to support curriculum delivery or garnering additional support at home to assure that assignments are completed. For social service providers it may mean finding ways to assure that families have access to health care or are aware of their rights and responsibilities. And, for businesspeople in the community there may be issues related to student behavior after school hours, or ways that they can offer resources to the school.

Schools as Centers for Community Learning

One of the most effective ways to encourage students to strive for academic success is for them to see their parents actively engaged in the learning process themselves. Public schools provide a natural setting in which to meet the educational needs of adults. A parent education program should be a central feature of any community outreach program.

The program begins with an assessment of parents' educational and schooling needs to determine the kinds of classes and opportunities that can be offered to families. This may include one-time and long-term offerings facilitated both by school staff and through collaboration with community agencies. Classes may include anything ranging from 2-hour hands-on workshops, to family literacy and family math programs, to citizenship classes or more extensive vocational training. These educational opportunities, in turn, can provide a springboard for community renewal and advancement.

Related to this is the recent thrust of reform efforts that focuses on school-to-work transition and making connections between the curriculum of the school and preparation for work and real life. From this perspective school learning must be relevant to the real world. In turn, the demands of the work world should be taken into account when setting standards for what should be expected of students as they move through the grades. This implies that different constituencies should get together to set goals, and opportunities should be provided for learning outside the school.

Involvement in the decision-making process occurs in stages. Premise 1, regarding how students learn, is also applicable to adults in the decision-making process. Since people are at different levels in their experience with collaborative decision making, it will take time to develop a functional and functioning decision-making body within a school. This is a process that requires patience and planning. The more schools offer, the more people are likely to become involved, or to find the one thing that allows them to overcome any inhibitions or blocks that keep them from participating. Once more people are involved, there will be an increasing sense of ownership that expands the possibilities for programs, activities, and interactions. Because participation and involvement occur in stages, it will be necessary to set long-term goals and devise short-term strategies to reach them.

Think about your own school. Are mechanisms in place to identify the needs of parents, community members, businesses, and service agencies? What are the most important issues to the community itself? Are there support systems to meet those needs? How are families and community members viewed—as assets to students' academic success or as nonsupportive of that success? Is there a climate of respect for different languages and cultures in your building? Is trying to address the needs of non–English speaking students seen as a burden? Are written documents translated into all the home languages represented in your community? Are interpreters provided for meetings? Are meetings conducted in the languages of the community? Are activities organized to reflect families' level of comfort in interacting in the school setting?

Creating a Community Outreach Program

Planning for community outreach requires that we take a long-term view. This is a process that takes time, and changes are not likely to occur overnight. It is also important not to become complacent with small victories. While it may be satisfying to see large numbers of parents turning out for a student performance, it should not overshadow the fact that the real challenge is sharing power (Zelazo, 1995).

Some business as usual must go on as people work to assess and improve programs for students. You can only begin where you are. Short-term goals may be for the semester or school year, while multiyear goals will set the stage for where the school should be down the road. What is important is to take steps and keep moving. Often this will seem like fighting an uphill battle, for example, when working with very traditional families that don't see themselves as having a role in school decision making. The fact that many parents, teachers, and community members are not yet comfortable being active decision makers is not, however, an excuse to stop the process. A collaborative decision-making process can also provide the basis for resolving conflicts and finding reasonable solutions to difficult problems.

Changing Assessment Strategies

For several years, teachers at Riverbend Middle School have been working on improving their assessment strategies to provide more accurate and in-depth information about students' academic progress. It has often come up that the current grade reporting system is inadequate to reflect the assessments being done of students' work. In the past, when this idea has been presented to the school's improvement team, many parents have objected to the changes. They argue that they are used to the standard letter grade system and that they don't have a basis for judging students' progress without them. This argument has come very forcefully from the large group of parents of second language learners in the school, since the letter grade system at least bears some resemblance to systems they are used to. Other parents worry that when students go on to high school, they won't be compared favorably with students who come from middle schools that do use letter grades. Because of the tremendous resistance from parents, the issue had been dropped. Most teachers, however, want to move forward and a subcommittee has come to a faculty meeting with a draft of a new report card. The teachers realize that no matter how anxious they are to make some changes, simply changing the policy outright will alienate many parents. They decide to schedule a meeting with the school's governance team. Through their joint discussions they are able to arrive at a compromise. They will conduct a year-long pilot project, to use both the old and the new report cards. They will monitor both teachers' and parents' responses throughout the year. As a first step, a series of workshops on understanding alternative assessments will be offered to both parents and teachers.

When authentic community concerns are a focus of the process, people can be convinced to participate. Therefore, procedures must be put in place to identify the needs of the community, as well as its resources. This can be accomplished through community surveys and questionnaires, as well as one-on-one conversations and interviews with family and community members, business leaders, and service providers. It means working with the established representatives of the geographic and ethnic community groups already in existence in the community. For each stakeholder group, the particular issues and obstacles to participation in the decision-making process and effective outreach must be understood and recognized. In the following section, issues related to each of the three main groups—families, teachers, and the broader community are discussed.

Families

Community outreach is a new way of looking at what has typically been called parent involvement. From an outreach perspective, however, the definition of who should be involved is broadened beyond parents to include members of students' extended families. It is important to recognize that uncles, grandmothers, older cousins, and even close family friends may be the ones participating in school/community activities.

The literature describes many different roles that families can take in relation to children's schooling (Swap, 1987). These roles can be thought of as spanning a continuum that ranges from passive spectators to active decision makers. Some roles involve little more than attendance at school activities and events; others require that family members actively participate in shaping and directing children's education. These more active roles are characteristic of a truly collaborative relationship between schools and families.

Working toward full family participation implies a conscious accommodation of families' current levels of comfort and skills. In designing an outreach program, it is important to accept that for some families, just to walk in the door of the school is a giant step. It will take time and patience for everyone to feel comfortable participating in school-sponsored activities, and even longer before many are ready to give opinions and ultimately become actively involved in a decision-making process or the instructional program. If families do not see themselves in these more active roles, then strategies for helping them to see ways in which to participate must be part of the family program. These include such things as making home visits, conducting parent interviews, and providing a sufficiently broad range of opportunities for parents to become involved at school. This increases the chances that everyone will find something that feels comfortable for them.

Many opportunities exist for families to participate and they can help children with their learning both in and out of school. As discussed in Chapter 5, perhaps their most valuable role is in actively supporting children's learning in their primary language. By discussing the main concepts and ideas of the instructional curriculum with children, family members can help stimulate conceptual development and further develop students' thinking and learning.

Family members can also play an important role as collaborators in assessing their children's progress. This includes providing critical information regarding students' growth and development to help school personnel understand the needs and capabilities of children. They can help in other areas of assessment, as well, such as reviewing and responding to student portfolios. It will often be necessary, of course, to work with families to help them to value this role, especially if they come from backgrounds that view assessment as solely the responsibility of teachers.

In organizing outreach efforts, an important issue is the varying levels of literacy among parents in both English and their primary language. The inability to read and write need not prevent parents from becoming informed and involved in the school setting. Phone calls, word of mouth, and informal small-group meetings are strategies that reach out to both literate and nonliterate families. Once you get people to meetings, many strategies can be employed to help increase parent comfort level with activities that may be unfamiliar or roles they do not see as their own. For example, it is important to ensure that parent voices are heard. This can be accomplished by making a point of going around to everyone for their thoughts and opinions and keeping a written record of comments that can be referred to in later discussions.

To many families, schools are intimidating places. To overcome people's resistance to entering into what might be a stressful situation, it may be important to create an informal atmosphere where people don't feel put on the spot. Holding meetings at community centers or other locations where families feel comfortable and providing food at meetings are strategies that can break down barriers and increase active participation. Inviting families to view student performances also helps bring people in. These performances can include not only schoolwide productions, but also brief student presentations before meetings.

Establishing Clear Patterns of Communication. A critical component of outreach to linguistically diverse communities is how language is used for communication at meetings and events and in written communication. The intent of an outreach program is to get the families of second language learners involved in the schooling process. Raising authentic issues and exchanging important information require that parents' home languages be utilized in order to give them direct access to the process. The issues of what languages will be used at meetings and how English and home languages will be balanced is one that bears close attention. This is seldom an easy process, but this commitment requires planning for the utilization of school resources in order to support and enhance community building. The following discussion illuminates some of the issues that arise and strategies that can be employed when trying to incorporate and accommodate families' home language.

Community Liaisons. One way to facilitate communication with families is to make use of the linguistic resources that do exist in the school and community to act as liaisons to their ethnolinguistic community. These individuals may be native language tutors or paraprofessionals already part of the staff or other members of the community who are designated specifically to act as liaisons. The job of these individuals is to help coordinate activities between the school and the home through a two-way communication process. They communicate to families basic information about schools and curriculum and help school staff understand the customs, traditions, and values of the communities they represent. They can help identify for the schools the issues of greatest concern to the community and they can help families to feel comfortable participating in the schooling process. It is important that the work of the liaisons is tied to the school's vision for academic achievement and not limited to addressing individual concerns.

It is critical that people chosen to act as liaisons have the respect and trust of members of their communities. This can be facilitated when community leaders become involved in the outreach to make presentations about topics of interest to parents or about school policies or instructional practices. This necessitates informing these community leaders about topics with which they may not be familiar and providing them with the means and materials to share with members of their group. Outside experts can help to organize presentations, but to be most effective they should be delivered by community aides or native speakers.

In schools with a number of language groups, bilingual people from a variety of language backgrounds can work jointly to create plans for presentations to the community, or for lessons for students. They all learn together and then provide the material to members of their community in their primary language. The collaboration among aides from different language groups allow for issues to be aired and clarified.

Language Use at Meetings. Whenever meetings involve school personnel and families from different language backgrounds, it will be necessary to decide how to communicate. Unless every single individual is completely bilingual, it will be necessary to use more than one language if all parties are to be fully informed. There are different strategies that can be employed, each with advantages and disadvantages, as described below.

Translation at Parent Meetings

The staff of Riverbend Elementary, a K–8 school with a two-way Portuguese/English bilingual program, placed a big emphasis on community involvement. In creating the school, the staff included a parent leadership group as part of their governance structure. They wanted to assure that all parents from both language groups could fully participate in the discussions that would shape the school's policies and direction. They considered their options to be simultaneous translating both ways, or to separate the two language groups and follow parallel agendas. Some were opposed to translating, feeling it would be very difficult to have a natural flow and interchange of ideas if every minute they had to stop to interpret for the other group. On the other hand, suggestions to separate the groups were rejected by others as promoting segregation between the two language groups. In addition, it would mean that some mechanism be in place for communicating decisions and ideas about issues. At the beginning of the year they agreed to try working in a single group using simultaneous translation, assigning one person to translate from Portuguese to English and another from English to Portuguese, However, after several months staff noticed that nearly all the talk happened in English and the translations were so short that they couldn't possibly be conveying all the nuances of the larger discussion. They also noticed that even if there were more Portuguese speakers than English speakers, English invariably dominated the conversation, partly because most bilingual staff members were more comfortable speaking in English.

They then decided to try to meet separately by language groups. After two meetings, attendance of Portuguese speakers increased dramatically and formerly silent parents began to contribute actively to policy discussions. They were able to work on several issues of great concern to the community that had been overlooked in the previous months.

They learned that they needed to take steps to counteract the segregation that resulted from meeting by language. This included a 20-minute joint meeting following the separate meetings to share what had happened. While it took concerted efforts to coordinate the ideas and decisions, it was preferable to having so many parents left out of an active decision-making role. They also set up special social events to get all the parents together and created a partner family network of individuals who could help each other when one or the other was unable to provide adequate help in their child's second language.

As this vignette illustrates, there are many challenges in working with parents from different language groups. In most groups and schools we have observed, non–English speakers wait patiently and quietly for information to be translated to their language, knowing full well they are getting only part of the story. And even when the interpretations are abbreviated summaries of what has been said in English, many English speakers fidget and show impatience until things return to the language they understand. A part of outreach, then, is to find ways to work with monolingual English-speaking parents to help them gain patience, understand the importance of total participation, and become sensitized to what it is like to want to be involved and be blocked by language.

Teachers

A schoolwide vision that seeks to draw in families and community members requires that teachers embrace the need for community outreach and affirm their roles as outreach ambassadors. The strength of tying community outreach to the school's vision is that it distributes the responsibility for maintaining communication with the community among all the staff. By enacting schoolwide practices based on the common vision and by tying this vision to the overall curriculum and instruction, individual efforts can be supported and individual teachers can rely on strategies that go beyond their own—often limited—time and resources. To be successful, structures must be put into place so that individual teachers' efforts are part of an overall strategy and are supported by resources beyond those available to particular individuals.

As previously discussed, the majority of teachers do not live in the communities in which they teach. They often also do not share the cultural, linguistic, and economic backgrounds of their students. Teaching students from a number of different linguistic and cultural backgrounds may initially feel overwhelming and the prospect of trying to reach out to all of them in ways that reflect a sensitivity to their cultural values may seem daunting. Approaching this task has been given little attention in teacher preparation and it is, therefore, not surprising that teachers often lack confidence in their abilities to interact in multicultural settings. In order to appreciate the role and importance of language and culture, it is necessary to begin to understand how our own language and culture affect our attitudes, values, and beliefs about learning. Educators need to see themselves as having culture and ethnicity and understand how aspects of their own culture impact their basic beliefs. They also need to know how these biases and perspectives influence how they interact with their students. From an anthropological perspective, the success of an outreach plan will depend on how the teachers and community work together to enhance the interaction of their cultures.

While it may not be possible to be completely knowledgeable about every culture in a school, we can all become more conscious of the possibility of cross-cultural differences and seek to understand and accommodate them. We can also maintain the perspective that all families and communities have something to offer in support of children's academic success.

It can be very helpful to develop certain skills to facilitate working with families. For example, for teachers, who must talk as part of their work, learning to listen is extremely valuable in helping family and community members to feel comfortable enough to be willing to participate. Another advantageous skill is being able to admit to what you don't know, and to learn how to ask the right questions to become more knowledgeable. It is also important to learn how to let down one's defenses and step outside of oneself in order to be able to look at and try to take on the perspective of others. Acquiring these skills is far easier to do in a collaborative work environment where there is the assurance that one is not alone in trying to improve and the acknowledgment that far more can be accomplished by working together than when people work in isolation. In this process, everyone can become aware of the resources that exist among the staff—discover who are the natural leaders and to whom to go to ask questions. Teachers' humanity can open many doors.

Taking an active stance in favor of a multicultural approach to education has strong implications for the way in which teachers view their roles and interactions with the communities in which they work. This, in turn, has implications for the ways in which teachers are prepared and what they consider to be part of their job. Where teacher preparation programs have failed to help teachers become effective in multicultural settings and curriculums, schools themselves must create a professional culture that helps teachers assume this role. When staff have not had an opportunity to explore multicultural issues, it is incumbent on schools to take the time to address them as part of staff development and reform efforts.

Broader Community

Community outreach can be organized to garner support from businesses, foundations, and corporations, as well as social service agencies, health care providers, and local celebrities. In fact, businesses and community agencies have a long history of supporting and working with schools. But very often these links have been haphazard or limited to the initiative of good-hearted or civic-minded individuals. To establish truly effective ties with the community means opening a dialogue and developing a plan for activities that can support students and contribute to the well-being of the larger community as a whole. All of these activities must be tied to the school's vision for the academic achievement of students.

An outreach perspective sees schools as being at the center of their communities. School-community partnerships can have many goals, the emphasis of which will vary according to the level of the school (elementary or secondary), the characteristics of the community, and the particular issues that arise. Schools in urban settings are likely to have different issues than rural schools, relatively stable communities different issues than communities in rapid transition. Schools with a predominance of a single ethnic group will have to rely on strategies and resources different from those used in schools in which many different ethnic and linguistic groups are served. The goal is not to seek a single solution to problems and challenges, but rather to develop a process for determining the issues of concern and resources available to address them.

Collaboration is predicated on sharing the common goal of a well-educated citizenry ready and able to take responsibility for their community. This is a two-way process. It does not simply mean what businesses and the broader community can do for the schools. It also includes how schools promote an attitude of participation in the life of the community. This can be accomplished through such activities as including service learning as part of the instructional curriculum. This is one way that students can give something to, as well as learn from, the broader community.

Community links can be created to accomplish multiple goals. These might include having a regular source of volunteer tutors and mentors, providing mental health and counseling services for children and their families, participating in neighborhood cleanup campaigns, conducting oral history and writing projects with senior citizens, housing adult education classes for neighborhood residents, establishing additional funding sources for school projects, or providing T-shirts for a sports team.

Another type of partnership that can be established is with local institutions of higher education. Such collaborations might include providing a site for teachers in training to do field work, garnering resources to conduct research into the topics that are of concern to the school community, and generating a source of role models and mentors of former second language learners who have managed to succeed academically and progress through the system.

Bringing It All Together

As is apparent from the above discussion, there are many facets to community collaboration and a fully articulated outreach program will have a number of components. There should be a process for inviting community input into school governance structures. This, in turn, will imply the need for leadership training and a family education program. Other areas of involvement will be in relation to curriculum enhancement. Addressing the needs of all the constituent stakeholders (teachers, families, and the broader community) will require that schools employ multiple strategies to reach out. These will include such things as workshops, classes, and training sessions; written communication in the parents' native language; and individual mentors. When community outreach and collaboration become articulated goals in a school's vision, then it is possible to establish policies that encourage and facilitate outreach. For example, the Amigos project in Massachusetts includes a bilingual monthly newsletter, a weekly observation day, ESL classes, and Spanish classes. To accomplish all these goals, it may be necessary to reorganize budget priorities to provide for parent coordinators or community outreach liaisons.

No matter what you attempt to do, it will require acceptance, patience, persistence, and, above all, an open-door, welcoming attitude. A process will also have to be put into place to develop an understanding in the majority community that efforts to reach out to all the linguistic and cultural groups in the school are not only necessary, but are extremely beneficial to the well-being of the school and the community at large.

Family Resource Schools, predicated on the belief that academic achievement is connected to factors that exist outside of the school, are an example of an effective and comprehensive outreach program. They assume that in communities that are economically stressed, simply allocating resources to fund the instructional program to pay for teachers, paraprofessionals, texts, and materials will be insufficient to guarantee academic success. They usually encompass several components, such as health and wellness—including mental health counseling services and dental screenings; parent education; after-school enrichment; and providing child care for meetings, classes, and events. The staff of the Family Resource Schools act as advocates for children and their families and do everything possible to help create a sound learning environment. The collaborations that are at the heart of a Family Resource School depend on many funding sources, including local government agencies, corporations, and foundations, in addition to school district monies to support their efforts.

An example of a smaller scale project is the Centro de Aprendizaje de la Comunidad (Community Learning Center) in Boulder, Colorado, which was organized with the support of the city, the county, and the school district. It is housed in a middle school with a target Latino population, and has a full-time site coordinator who oversees community outreach efforts. These include an after-school homework program and organizing meetings for Spanish-speaking families whose children attend one or more of the five schools that primarily serve the Latino community.

If you are just beginning to think about how to organize an outreach program for your school, it is important not to be frustrated by the seeming enormity of the task, or a lack of resources. No project happens overnight. For example, it wasn't until its third year that the Boulder project was able to even begin to establish a mentoring program with local high school and university students. A helpful motto to keep in mind is "if it's important to be done, resources will be found."

By working together, schools and their communities can overcome seemingly insurmountable obstacles. The Linda Vista Elementary School case study in Chapter 11 provides many more examples of how all the parts of an outreach program can come together. The staff's vision of providing service to their total community spawned remarkable cross-cultural enrichment to that community.

ISSUES UNIQUE TO EACH PROGRAM CATEGORY

The basic components of an outreach program do not change substantially across program categories although there are some differences in the possibilities for actual implementation. The major distinguishing factor among the programs will be the way in which fewer resources in the primary language affect the school's ability to reach out to and communicate with students' families.

Category I: Full Primary Language Foundation

Community outreach in a Category I program is greatly facilitated by the fact that many members of the school staff will speak students' home languages, making it easier to establish open lines of communication with their families. Because Category I programs provide both literacy and content instruction to students in their primary language, resource materials are more likely to be available that can be used to enhance family members' efforts to support students' linguistic and academic development in the home. In addition, there are many avenues for family and community members to participate directly in the instructional program, for example, by volunteering in the classroom or making presentations related to the academic curriculum.

Most schools with Category I programs will be working with only one or two language groups. When there are large numbers of people from a single language group it is easier to meet their needs. For example, compiling a list of interpreters and translating written documents is a fairly straightforward process. It is also more likely that there will be agencies in the community that provide services in families' home languages. Outreach efforts can then focus on linking these existing resources with the efforts of the school.

In two-way programs, where native English speakers are actively involved, one of the biggest challenges for community outreach is to balance the input from majority and minority communities. It is critical in these programs to acknowledge and address the fact that native English speakers are generally accorded more power in school settings. As discussed earlier in the chapter, strategies must be put in place to ensure that all voices can be heard in meetings, and in the decision-making process. While both communities must learn to work together, there also must be opportunities for speakers of languages other than English to be able to meet and talk about issues of importance to them in nonthreatening settings where they can fully express themselves.

Category II: Primary Language Support—Literacy Only

The outreach strategies in Category II programs will be very similar to those in Category I programs. There will probably be a substantially large population of only one or two language groups in the school. While there may be fewer personnel available, there will be staff members who can communicate with families in their language. It will be important to assure that while these people have responsibility for direct contact with the community, outreach and communication remain a total school commitment.

Sufficient literacy and content-related materials will also be available to engage families in helping their children explore the themes being studied and many opportunities exist to involve community members directly in the instructional program.

Category III: Primary Language Content Reinforcement

While a Category III program does not include literacy development, there is an articulated component of the academic curriculum that is provided in students' primary language. This means that a combination of teachers, native language tutors, or bilingual paraprofessionals will work together to provide that instruction. The outreach program will have to tap these people to facilitate communication with students' families and community. Resources will have to be allocated so that these individuals can be compensated for the extra time they will be asked to devote to outreach. In addition, strategies will have to be developed to facilitate the training of both these staff and other community leaders to be able to coordinate efforts among the different language groups in the school.

Category IV: All-English

The decision to provide only a Category IV program is usually made because there are not sufficient numbers of speakers of a single language group to provide primary language instruction. Often Category IV programs are comprised of several students from many different language groups. The challenge to identify community leaders, resources, or even translators will be greater than in any other program category. Efforts will have to be concentrated on making the school a welcoming place for students and families from all linguistic and cultural backgrounds to ensure they feel that they belong to the school community. By providing space and time for parents of each language group to meet together at the school, staff can help establish the basis for a positive relationship. Providing for English as a second language classes on-site for adults is another means to bring family members into the school in a way that is nonthreatening.

Due to the language barriers that are common in these programs, it will be extremely important to identify individuals who can act either formally or informally as liaisons with each language group represented. These efforts can be facilitated by working with other schools and district personnel to compile a list or directory of resources available in each language that can be shared across schools. No matter what the circumstances of a school, the same principles for organizing community outreach hold true.

Decision Making on Your Own

1. Questions that highlight major issues regarding community outreach include: What is the nature of community outreach in your school? Who is currently involved in what kinds of activities? What community resources could you use to support primary language development?

In order to answer these questions about your setting, you will need to add the following information to your profile: current outreach efforts, existing organizations for parental involvement, community resources in each primary language, key people in each language community, potential support structures in the business community, materials available for parent education.

2. Think about the Basic Premises and major elements presented in this chapter on community outreach. Generate a list of additional questions that will help you to decide how best to serve your students.

3. Compare your list of questions with those of a colleague and refine your list. Are there any major issues you haven't addressed?

4. Form a small group and brainstorm the optimal community outreach practices possible in your setting. Use the Basic Premises highlighted in this chapter (2, 9, 11) to weigh your decisions.

5. List two or three things changes that might have to be made in your setting.

6. What are the implications of your decisions for other areas, for example, involvement in the assessment process, governance structures, creating a climate supportive of diversity?

7. Add these data to your school profile.

PART III

Decision Making in Practice: Three Case Studies

CHAPTER 9

Hillside Elementary—Bilingual Bound

This chapter and the next provide the reader practice in using the basic premises to test ideas and suggestions for the reorganization of school resources to best serve linguistically diverse learners. The decision-making process proposed throughout the book is modeled through the application of the Basic Premises to two hypothetical schools, each with a different population and resources. Through dialogues and narrative descriptions we will furnish examples of the issues that arise, the questions to be asked, and examples of how to weigh the benefits and drawbacks to particular proposals and ideas.

For Hillside Elementary, three potential plans will be proposed. Two will be analyzed and discussed to model the process. The other we leave for you to analyze. Hillside Elementary is a composite of many schools we have visited and observed. As with many schools, it is missing many opportunities for better utilizing its resources and improving its program.

As you read through the chapter, think about the information you have been gathering for your school profile, and the questions you have posed about your own setting. Reflect on how the issues discussed in the examples below might pertain to your school.

BACKGROUND

About 600 students attend Hillside Elementary, a K–5 school located in a working- and middle-class neighborhood of a medium-size city. About a third of the students are monolingual English-speaking Euro-American students and the rest of the students are Latino. Most, but not all, of the Latino students are from homes where Spanish is spoken at least part of the time. In the total school population, about 20% of the students are monolingual in Spanish, 40% bilingual, and 40% monolingual in English. No other languages are represented at the school. About three-fourths of the school's population is quite stable in terms of mobility with the rest having a fairly high turnover each year. There is a "bilingual" program in which students are placed based on level of English proficiency and parent choice. Those monolingual Spanish speakers whose parents have chosen to place them in all-English classrooms receive 45 minutes of ESL instruction daily, on a pull-out basis provided by an ESL teacher assigned to the school half time. They spend the rest of their time in the monolingual English classroom.

Currently at Hillside, there are 24 full-time classroom teachers, a reading specialist, and two special education resource teachers, one of whom speaks Spanish. Of the four classes at each grade level, two are designated bilingual in grades K–2 and one at grades 3, 4, and 5. Of the nine teachers assigned to the bilingual program, three are native Spanish speakers. The rest are native English speakers. Three of these teachers have passed the district's competency test in Spanish. The other three have only a very basic knowledge of Spanish, but have committed to studying on their own during the summers. A Spanish-speaking paraprofessional is assigned full time to each of the designated bilingual classrooms. The monolingual English teachers each have paraprofessional time for three-fourths of the instructional day. Figure 9.1 presents a summary of the demographics of Hillside Elementary.

Throughout the school times are designated for each subject area during the day, though there is considerable flexibility in how teachers organize their own self-contained classrooms. There is little communication between teachers or across grade levels about the curriculum or program design, except for second grade, where the two bilingual teachers have begun to collaborate by switching students for science and social studies instruction.

There is a range of practices in the bilingual classrooms. In grades K–2, initial literacy instruction is in Spanish for monolingual speakers, and depending on the teacher, bilingual students may begin in English or Spanish. By the beginning of third grade, Spanish-speaking children are considered ready to make the transition to English literacy. At grades 3–5, even in the classes where the teachers are fluent in Spanish, the instruction is conducted primarily in English. If students don't understand a particular concept, they can go to either the teacher or the paraprofessional for help.

The move to restructure the school follows the realization that simply having Spanish speakers in the classrooms and calling it a bilingual program is not working for students. It is apparent that many students are not developing strong primary language proficiency, and their English achievement is also limited. Information from standardized tests, the main source of assessment data, indicates that overall student scores are below average, with second language speakers of English having the lowest scores. The staff is concerned and wants to make changes, knowing that

FIGURE 9.1. Summary of Hillside Elementary Demographics.

---

600 students
  Language proficiency
    20% monolingual Spanish speakers
    40% bilingual
    40% monolingual English speakers

  Ethnicity
    33% Euro-American
    67% Latino
  75% of population stable
  25% highly mobile
  Working and middle class neighborhood

24 full time classroom teachers
  9 assigned to bilingual classes
    3 native Spanish speakers (all are bilingual)
    6 native English speakers
      3 have passed Spanish competency exam
      3 have only basic knowledge of Spanish
  14 assigned to monolingual English classrooms
  1 Reading specialist
  2 Special Education teachers (1 is Spanish speaking)

20 Paraprofessionals
  9 assigned full time to designated bilingual classes
  11 assigned 3/4 time to monolingual English classrooms

---

there are better ways to organize in order to improve instruction. They and a number of parents have already participated in a series of discussions regarding the nature and delivery of instruction. They have read the Basic Premises and want to use them as the basis for examining their school. As the group discussion moves to how they will change their program, a number of suggestions are made. The portion of their dialogue presented below includes discussion about how aspects of primary language instruction might be reorganized, and how second language instruction, content delivery, and assessment might be strengthened. As you read, pay attention to the tensions that arise and the weaknesses and strengths of the arguments presented by the participants.

Hillside Plans

LEADER (L): We've done a lot of work reading and thinking about language acquisition. We have some basic assumptions about the constructive nature of learning and we've thought about the Basic Premises. Now we need to discuss how they can help us reorganize. Maybe we could start by putting on the table some of the possible ways we might offer primary language instruction and analyze the pros and cons.

TEACHER 1 (T1): Well one thing we could do is choose a Spanish reading series, and then we can all just follow it through the grades for consistency.

T2: That might be a good idea down the line, but it doesn't get at issues like who we think Spanish instruction is for, and why we think it's important.

T3: I think we need to identify who wants to teach what, at which grade level.

T4: I don't agree. We need to move away from what we want to teach to what ways of organizing ourselves will be best for the kids.

T5: And we can't just think about how we're going to organize primary language. We need to think about second language instruction, too. We don't even have ESL time in the bilingual program.

T6: Maybe we could group all the monolingual Spanish speakers in one classroom and make it the ESL class and do everything "sheltered."

T7: Then the Spanish speakers never get to interact with other kids.

T8: Well they're already pretty segregated, would it really make that much difference?

T4: But, it's not just about segregating them, it ignores the importance of the primary language.

T9: Well they wouldn't have to be grouped all day like that, just for ESL. It might make it easier to meet their needs. I know that if I have just a few second language learners, I end up teaching to the native English speakers.

T10: It's going to take a lot of effort to always try to make everything understandable to the ESL kids. Some things they're just not going to get!

T7: Well, they may not be able to "get" everything, but I know my teaching could stand to improve. I think some new strategies could help.

T11: We need to start thinking about second language time a little differently. How are we going to meet the needs of the second language learners, and not bore the monolingual English students?

T2: And what about the special ed kids, they need to be pulled for ESL and for special ed. That doesn't give them much time in the classrooms.

SPECIAL EDUCATION RESOURCE TEACHER (SERT): We could offer some sheltered classes and some classes where kids are integrated. Then the students with special needs all along the spectrum might be accommodated.

T9: If we're going to be able to give kids different types of second language lessons, we'll have to reorganize our content instruction, too.

T5: It would help if we could change the curriculum so that we didn't have to divide up for every subject area. If we tried some integrated units it might make it easier for kids to understand what's going on from one hour to the next.

T1: I know from watching Roberto and Beth at second grade, they seem to have less planning to do since they teach the same lesson twice to two groups. We should think more about teaming.

T11: What about Spanish as a second language? We have quite a number of English speakers who say they want to learn Spanish.

PARENT: I'd support Spanish instruction for everyone in the school. It would really be great.

T2: I agree, but I doubt all the parents would go for that. Unlike you, most of the Anglo parents don't seem interested, and a lot of the Latino parents are worried their children won't learn English fast enough.

T1: We'd need to do a parent education program that shows how important a strong foundation in the primary language is. And maybe we could convince more of the monolingual English-speaking parents that we could help their kids become bilingual and they'd be ahead in the job market.

T8: If we had a strong Spanish component for English speakers, we could organize a time of day when everyone was in their second language class.

T1: And if we had the same topics for both English and Spanish instruction, kids would be able to transfer their knowledge from one language to the other more easily.

T3: And we could do more shifting around of students according to their needs.

T6: It does seem that if we could figure it out we might be able to teach from our strengths, especially whether we're fluent in Spanish or not. What we do now really isn't fair to the kids in classrooms like mine where, I hate to admit, Spanish is pretty weak.

T12: You know, I've never been part of the bilingual program and I'm not that dissatisfied with my teaching and how things are going. I don't think I really need to be at these meetings.

T7: All the kids in the building need to get instruction in English some of the time, and there's no reason we couldn't reorganize so that everyone had responsibility for the second language learners.

ESL T: Getting back to ESL. It's overwhelming to think I'm going to have to integrate content from six different grade levels into my classes. I have a language-based curriculum I'm supposed to follow, too. I can't do all this alone.

T12: But I've never really worked with second language learners; how am I supposed to know if they're making progress or not?

T3: There's the standardized test data.

T4: Those tests don't tell us anything; my students always read and write better than what the tests say they can do.

T10: I don't like the tests either, but we still have to give them. Just look at them as one piece of information to add to what we know about students.

T2: We should go back to what we talked about last year, about coming to a schoolwide consensus on what we think students should know and be able to do.

T13: That's right, we talked about establishing benchmarks that we could all use to measure progress.

T5: And there's a district task force trying to establish appropriate outcomes for second language learners, based on the content standards.

T8: I can just imagine what all this will do to our report cards.

T4: It just seems so complicated to try to reorganize everything at once, and each area depends on the other. Can we really come up with a plan?

L: It's clear that we must change, and I think if we work together we can. The first step is to decide how to organize ourselves to move forward. We want a broad range of perspectives but we're too big to work as a whole group. Let's decide on a way to group ourselves, and set a deadline to come back with some plans.

T9: If we're trying to come up with a whole-school plan we probably need to have representatives from every grade level in a group. How about three groups?

T2: And the specialists could divide up among them.

PARENT: I think there should be parents in each group, too.

L: We seem to have reached a consensus. We can use our planning days to meet over the next few months and will check with each other on an ongoing basis. We'll come back together in the spring with the final plans.

Following their initial brainstorming, the teachers at Hillside break into the three groups to discuss reorganization. Over the next several months, they weigh the Basic Premises against their resources, keeping in mind the political context of their district and the issues they have dealt with over the years. By spring each group has a plan to propose. Common to all of the plans is the intention to coordinate the program across the grade levels, and to move to a more integrated approach to content instruction. The plans differ considerably in their use of the primary language for Spanish speakers, the configuration of second language instruction, the kinds of assessment strategies employed, and the ways in which the staff proposed to engage the community.

GUIDELINES FOR ANALYZING THE PLANS

The three plans proposed by Hillside Teachers are presented below. Each is preceded by a brief summary of its key elements. In the first two plans some, but not all, of their strengths and weaknesses related to the Basic Premises are presented. As you read each plan, jot down notes and questions regarding the issues that arise in relation to the Basic Premises. Include what you perceive to be the strengths and weaknesses of the proposals, and focus attention on how the issues that arise in these plans may also relate to your own situation. The key questions listed below can help to guide your inquiry.

Finally, discuss with your colleagues additional ways in which each plan reflects, or doesn't, the Basic Premises in relation to first and second language instruction, curriculum coordination, assessment practices, and community outreach. You should also be looking for whether an articulated decision-making process and other structures are in place that foster collaboration among staff members at Hillside.

For the third plan we leave more of the work up to you. In this way you will gain practice with the kinds of discussions and processes we propose can be used to improve practices in schools with linguistically diverse populations.

Key Questions

In order to guide you in your analysis of the plans, we have provided the following key questions to consider. These questions, which are not meant to be exhaustive, are grouped according to the major areas described above that we consider to be essential in the planning of programs for linguistically diverse student populations.

Primary Language. What is the degree and extent of primary language support? Does the program build on student strengths? How is each language used and in which environments? How are existing resources configured to get the most out of the personnel in the building?

Second Language. How and to what extent is second language instruction included in the content areas? Does the second language program include all components of language—oral, reading, writing, and content? Does the plan incorporate appropriate second language strategies that build on these components? What strategies and criteria are there for movement of students through the program? How is second language instruction connected to the main curriculum?

Curriculum Coordination. Is the curriculum constructive in nature? If so, how is this reflected? Does the curriculum allow students to meet new concepts and ideas across several contexts? How are the nonacademic areas treated in terms of first and second language? Are there organizational structures in place to allow for effective implementation of the Concept Development Strategy? If thematic units are planned, how are they organized to help develop both first and second language?

Assessment. What is the focus of the assessment plan in terms of traditional and authentic assessment? How are the planners able to decide on student expectations? If portfolio assessment is incorporated, how is the evidence of student work to be collected and the kinds of evidence of first and second language progress to be designated? What plan is there, if any, to assess schoolwide effectiveness? Are there clear benchmarks for moving students through and then exiting from the program? If so, what are they? What is the plan for grading? How does it tie into the general assessment plan?

Community Outreach. How have community members been included in the decision-making process? How are their contributions valued and utilized? What kinds of activities are proposed to support families? How are families and the broader community involved in instruction?

Decision Making. Is there an articulated plan for decision making? What kinds of opportunities are provided to the different stakeholders to participate in the process? Have mechanisms been put into place that will allow change to be sustained over time?

PROGRAM PROPOSALS

Proposal A: A Category II Program

The first group proposes a plan for a Category II program that would provide primary language literacy in grades K–3. Advocates of this option, a number of whom have many years working at Hillside, don't think the community is ready for drastic change. They recognize the value of the primary language, and propose to reorganize to provide a stronger foundation in the early grades, but still believe that parents want their children to move into English as quickly as possible. Figure 9.2 provides an overview of the Proposal A, Category II plan.

Primary Language. Kindergarten would have two designated English and one designated Spanish class each morning and afternoon. In order to create an optimal environment to extend students' conceptual development, students would be placed according to language dominance. Those in the Spanish kindergartens would spend most of their time in Spanish in order to provide students a strong conceptual foundation. For 30 minutes each day they would receive English as a second language instruction, orally based, involving lots of games and activities. In addition, twice a week, special activities and games would be organized at recess so that students across the three kindergarten classes can get to know each other.

In first through third grades, there would be a 1½ hour language arts block every morning. Primary language literacy instruction would be provided for monolingual Spanish speakers, and for bilingual students whose parents request Spanish literacy. The most fluent Spanish-speaking teachers in the school would be assigned to teach in grades 1–3. Teachers would be paired (two pairs per grade level), and one teacher in each pair would provide the Spanish literacy instruction for the whole group.

For students who begin their literacy development in Spanish, English literacy instruction would begin in second grade, during ESL time (see below). During third grade, the amount of time in Spanish literacy would be reduced to 45 minutes and students would receive formal English reading instruction for the other 45 minutes.

For monolingual Spanish speakers who enter in grades 4 and 5, primary language literacy instruction would be provided by the reading

FIGURE 9.2. Overview of Proposal A: Category II Plan.

Primary Language
  primary language literacy in grades K–3
  K: 2 English & 1 Spanish K in am & pm
      students placed according to language dominance
      all but 45 minutes spent in Spanish
  Grades 1–3
      Teachers paired—1 team per grade level
      1 teacher provides Spanish literacy for whole group
      1 1/2 hour block devoted to primary language literacy
      By grade 3 Spanish literacy is reduced to 45 minutes per day.
  Grades 4, 5
      45 minutes primary language literacy for monolingual Spanish speakers

Second Language
  K: 45 minutes/day of ESL, orally based activities, games
      2 times/week special mixed group activities
  Grades 15
      Content based ESL program
      One of four teachers designated as L2 teacher at each grade level.
      All Spanish dominant students assigned to ESL teacher during content block
      Content ESL block subdivided into oral language, content lessons
      English literacy beginninng in second grade

Assessment
  Placement: language proficiency and oral language assessment in each language
  On going: grades 2–5, writing sample upon placement and every 6 weeks in language
  of literacy instruction
  Use of reading series assessment package in both languages

Community Outreach
  Increased communication through parent newsletters

Curriculum Coordination
  Content themes at each grade level
  Yearly timeline, individual planning
  ESL curriculum based on content themes
  Grade-wide culminating activities
  Utilizes current site council to commmunicate information
  Includes Spanish speakers on the council
  Monthly newsletter in English and Spanish
  Classroom teas

specialist for 45 minutes a day during the language arts block. For the other 45 minutes they would receive ESL instruction from the ESL specialist.

Second Language. In order to increase second language learners' understanding of the content areas, this Category II program proposes moving to a content-based ESL program. At every grade level one of the four teachers would be designated the second language teacher. During the content block (1½ hours each day) all of the monolingual Spanish students as well as those bilingual students who have been in this country less than four years would be assigned to that teacher. The 1½ hours would then be subdivided into English oral language development, content lessons, and, starting in second grade, English literacy instruction. In this class, students would prepare to participate in the culminating activities for the content units with the rest of the students from their grade level.

Curriculum Coordination. In order to provide students with repeated access to ideas and vocabulary, and a more coherent framework from which to construct meaning, the teachers have decided that they could move toward having content themes at each grade level. They would agree on the units, set up a time line for the school year, and share ideas about what would be taught. Each teacher would then be responsible for planning the actual instruction for his or her classroom. The themes would also provide the basis for the content-based ESL program. Every 6-week unit would have some sort of culminating activity that would involve students across the grade level. Students would receive math instruction and art, music, and physical education in integrated English groups in English formed from their paired classes.

Assessment. In order to make sure that students receive appropriate services, all students whose Home Language Surveys indicate that Spanish is spoken in the home would be given the Language Assessment Scales (LAS) test in English. These students would also do an informal oral language sample (telling a wordless picture book story) in each language to help determine placement in English or Spanish reading. Students in grades 2 and up would also be asked to do a writing sample at the beginning of each year and once every 6 weeks in the language in which they receive literacy instruction.

In addition, this group recommends that the school select a reading series with parallel versions in English and Spanish K–5, allowing them to be able to rely on the assessment package included in the series. This would provide continuity and guidance for where students should be each year, as well as help teachers to use common literacy assessment strategies across languages.

Community Outreach. The school's current Site Improvement Council will be the main forum for communicating the information regarding the proposed plan. The plan will be presented in light of what the staff believes to be the current desires of the community. A concerted effort will be made to include more Spanish-speaking parents on the council, thereby developing more leadership among these parents. In addition, in order to keep lines of communication open, a monthly informational flyer in both languages will be sent home.

As a means of starting the year on a high note, the staff is proposing to have classroom teas to present the new program on a more intimate level. These will be conducted in both languages, and parents will be invited to volunteer in the program throughout the year.

Analysis of Proposal A, Category II Program Plan

Analysis: Primary Language. This Category II program would be a marked improvement over the existing program. For example, it shifts to a more focused use of the primary language and it provides clearly defined contexts for each language. By offering literacy instruction through the third grade, this plan provides more support than is currently available. However, it discounts the range in the pace of children's literacy development by arbitrarily cutting off all primary language support at third grade, assuming that every student will be ready to exit into an all-English program. There are no criteria for the decision, and no plan for a transition period. There is also no plan for content instruction in Spanish, which means that while Spanish-speaking students will be able to learn to read and write in their primary language, they will not be given the opportunity to explore in depth the concepts and ideas that are central to the academic curriculum. These limitations are compounded by the fact that this group proposes to use only a leveled reading series for this Category II program, with no indication that additional sources related to the content themes would be incorporated into literacy instruction. The vision for the use of the resources available in the school is limited, as demonstrated by plans presented by the other two groups.

Analysis: Second Language. One of the strengths of the Category II plan is that there is a designated time set aside for second language instruction, and that teachers have indicated their intention to provide differentiated instruction for oral language, literacy, and content instruction. In addition, they propose to coordinate the second language curriculum with the main program. Unfortunately, there is no reference made as to how nonacademic areas are taught, nor is there an articulated plan for the transition to English reading, and the movement into all-English instruction at fourth and fifth grade.

Analysis: Assessment. The assessment strategies proposed in the Category II plan go beyond total reliance on standardized language tests. The recommendation to incorporate both oral and written natural language samples broadens the information about student performance considerably. In addition, the plan calls for ongoing and consistent sampling throughout the school year. However, there is no decision on student outcomes, and as a result there is an overreliance on the publisher's assessment package.

Analysis: Curriculum Coordination. This Category II plan indicates that teachers will make a solid effort to collaborate with one another to coordinate their efforts. A major strength of this plan is its reliance on a thematic approach to organizing the curriculum. However, there is no indication of an intention to coordinate the content themes with primary literacy instruction. This limits the possibility for fully utilizing the Concept Development Strategy in instruction. In addition, there is no clear connection between the culminating activities of the units to the overall assessment plan.

Analysis: Community Outreach. In organizing this plan, proponents have accommodated what they believe to be the desires of the community, and taken a rather cautious position. They have also proposed to increase communication with Spanish-speaking families, and are seeking to increase their involvement in governance. Teachers are assuming what parents want, rather than including them in the larger discussion, or presenting them with a variety of options. In addition, outreach is focused mainly on the plan itself, and not on long-term strategies for involvement. For example, there is no mention of the possibility of a parent education program.

Proposal B: A Category I Program

The second group returned in the spring with a plan for a Category I bilingual enrichment program that would involve a reorganization of the entire school. In this plan, the goal would be bilingualism and biliteracy for all students from both language groups. Through surveys and discussions with members of both language communities, proponents of the Category I plan have discovered that many parents would be willing to enroll their children in such a bilingual program.

This program would provide literacy and content instruction in both languages appropriate to students levels of development K–5. This Category I program would rely on the grouping and regrouping of students, sometimes by primary language, sometimes in integrated groups, to assure that they would receive instruction tailored to their needs in both languages, as well as opportunities to work with native models of their second language. Because of the limited number of fluent Spanish-speaking teachers, the reorganization would begin at K–3 the first year and be phased into the upper grades as students progress through the program. Figure 9.3 presents an overview of the Proposal B, Category I plan.

Primary Language. In this Category I program, students would work in their primary language in a number of settings with a slightly different configuration at each grade level. In order to assure that all students receive a firm foundation in literacy, the program would begin with a stronger emphasis in the primary language, and by fourth grade half the instruction would be provided in each language. On a given day the actual time spent might be more or less depending on the language for integrated group content instruction, but over time it would balance to the agreed on percentage for that level.

Students in K–2 would spend an average of 80% of the school day in their primary language. They would receive initial literacy instruction, math, and a portion of their content instruction in the primary language. The remainder of the day would consist of second language enrichment time and content instruction (including art and music projects) in integrated groups in their second language.

Grade 3 students begin to move closer to the goal of becoming academically fluent in both languages. The amount of instruction in primary language groups would be reduced to 60%. The amount of time spent in integrated groups would then increase so that students would receive more second language time instruction.

In subsequent years, at the fourth and fifth grades, two teams would work together to provide appropriate settings for primary language literacy. To balance the reduction of time in Spanish caused by all students' receiving math in English, an added arts and drama component would be incorporated in Spanish, for all students. Those students in the final year of the program would have one period of English language arts and one in Spanish. Most of this time would be in integrated groups, but occasionally students would be separated by primary language to allow for enrichment of concepts and ideas.

Second Language. As indicated above, in order to provide students with the greatest access to concepts and vocabulary, in this Category I pro-

FIGURE 9.3. Overview of Proposal B: Category I Plan.

Primary Language
    Bilingual enrichment—bilingualism and biliteracy for all students
    Monolingual teachers paired with bilingual teachers—students assigned to teams of teachers
    Strong emphasis on L1 in the initial grades
        Ratio of 1st to 2nd language decreases across grades
        Time in primary language: K–2: 80%; 3rd: 60%; 4th/5th: 50% eventually
    Integrated group content instruction included from the beginning, increasing over time

Second Language
    Emphasis on comprehensible input and interaction
    Second language instruction based on general school curriculum
    Begins with 45 minutes daily at kindergarten and extends to 1 1/2 hours by
    K–3: Two teams (four teachers) work together for second language instruction
        Students placed by proficiency
            1 ESL class
            1 SSL class
        Bilingual students rotate between first & second language for enrichment
    Grades 4/5: 20 minutes per day oral language plus integrated group content time
Students entering at 4/5, second language instruction dependent on proficiency level

Assessment
    Two fold process:
        Letter grades for progress reports
        Norm Reference Test (NRT) data for public reporting, grades 2–5
            Remediation based on this data
        Portfolios with oral and written samples in first and second language
            Primary language—one oral and three written samples
            Second language—three samples (not specified oral or written)
            Primary and second language—content unit samples of student work
            Students choose four pieces for baseline data for following year

Curriculum Coordination
    School wide articulation of content themes
    Team teaching
    Cross age groupings
    Extended K

Community Outreach
    Belief that with adequate information community will support program
    Community survey for funds of knowledge and resources
    Uses NRT data for public accountability
    Spanish as a second language classes for English speaking parents

---

gram, second language instruction would be based on the overall curriculum plan for the program. A portion of the day (45 minutes to 1½ hours depending on grade level) would be set aside for second language development. In addition, integrated group content instruction would be designed to maximize the use of hands-on activities and other strategies designed to promote comprehensible input and interaction.

At kindergarten through third grade, teachers from two teams would work together to group students according to their levels of proficiency. Among the four teachers they would offer ESL and SSL classes, as well as language enrichment classes in Spanish and English for students who are already bilingual. Bilingual students would rotate weekly between the English and Spanish classes. This time would be focused on oral language and vocabulary development. Beginning in the two-three combination classes, second language literacy lessons related to the content themes would be added to the ESL and SSL classes.

It is expected that by fourth grade, students who entered as monolingual speakers in kindergarten will have made substantial progress toward full proficiency in their second language. Most second language instruction would occur during the integrated group content time, as well as in a daily 20-minute language lesson where students would be grouped by native language for an enrichment period that would be balanced between the two languages. For students who arrive at the school at fourth or fifth grade, two possible routes could be taken. Those already literate in their primary language would receive second language instruction that would begin with a strong oral language component, but move quickly into formal literacy development using a modified Language Experience Approach. For those students not yet literate in Spanish, their second language instruction would focus on oral language and content themes, and then move into a Language Experience Approach once a strong foundation in Spanish literacy was established. These students would spend a portion of the Integrated Group Content instruction time in a sheltered content class taught by one or two of the teachers at those levels.

Curriculum Coordination. In an attempt to provide a more appropriate curriculum, teachers would reorganize to work in cross-grade teams (K–1, 2–3, and 4–5), four at each level. Students would be assigned not to an individual teacher, but to a team consisting of two teachers, one monolingual English and one a fluent Spanish speaker. Each teacher would be assigned to work in one language or the other to assure that distinct contexts would be created for each language, and to facilitate the planning process for teachers.

Critical to the success of the Category I program would be a school-wide articulation of the content themes to be taught at each level. This would provide continuity to the program and create a meaning-centered environment essential to language development. The four teams at each level would collaborate on overall themes and intended student outcomes. Then each two-person team would create their curriculum assigning a portion of its delivery to one language or the other. As part of the process of deciding on eventual themes, staff and parents would enlist university support to put together a survey of parents to discover their areas of expertise and funds of knowledge. Because this plan includes cross-age grouping, unit planning would be carefully sequenced over a 2-year time span to avoid repetition of content.

Assessment. Proponents of the Category I program think that because this would be such a dramatic change from the way things have always been, it would be important to prove that students are successful on those measures the district and the public look to judge academic success. Therefore, they propose a twofold assessment process. Students would receive letter grades on their day-to-day work. These would be summarized on quarterly report cards. Teachers would also maintain portfolios throughout the school that would include oral and written samples in each language. Every year students would be given an informal oral assessment in both languages. Three formal writing samples would be collected in the primary language and three samples from work during second language instruction would be collected yearly. A sample of students' work from each content unit in each language would also be included. At the end of the year teachers and students would review the portfolio, and students would choose four pieces to be saved as a baseline for judging the following year's work. The rest of the items in the portfolio would be sent home to parents.

As an additional measure, each spring, all students in grades 2 and above would take a standardized reading achievement test in English and Spanish to document both first and second language growth. Those students not making expected progress at the end of their third year in the program would be referred to the reading specialist, who would work in small groups to give intensive supplemental primary language literacy instruction for bilingual students during the second language block.

Community Outreach. Proponents of the Category I proposal recognize the need to be more inclusive of parents and other community members. By conducting a survey of community expertise, leadership, and resources, the staff believes they will be able to tap into these and draw them into the school. They also believe that by conducting the survey in both languages, Spanish-speaking parents will be identified and included. They also plan to offer Spanish classes in the evening to interested parents.

One goal of this plan is to improve communication. They propose two major ways to disseminate information. They would distribute a bi-weekly newsletter in both languages to all families. In addition, to increase accountability, this group proposes to find ways to more effectively communicate the results of standardized testing to parents and to the school's Site Council.

Analysis of Proposal B, Category I Plan

This plan for a Category I program provides strong support for primary language development. At the same time, it holds the promise of bilingualism for both language groups, with few (if any) additional resources than are currently available. In addition, cross-grade grouping increases the possibility that students can progress according to their needs. It falls short of a nongraded school in this aspect, but nonetheless provides much more flexibility in the placement and grouping of students.

Analysis: Primary Language. This plan provides for a two-way bilingual program that includes all students. It provides clearly defined contexts for each language and includes primary language instruction at all grade levels, in all areas: language, content, nonacademic. While the overall framework appears to be strong, there is no clear description of language use on a day-to-day basis.

Analysis: Second Language. The program is organized to provide second language instruction to all students in the school. Not only is there a strong ESL component; there is an articulated Spanish as a Second language component as well. In addition, the plan is for teachers to work in teams to provide for student needs. Instruction is organized to maximize students' access to and understanding of content. There are a variety of settings planned for instruction including integrated groups and sheltered instruction that incorporates content themes beginning in the 2–3 combination classes. However, it is unclear why the teachers have proposed to wait until 2–3 to incorporate the content concepts into the oral language lessons. In addition, it is unclear how instruction for the bilingual students would be organized.

Analysis: Curriculum Coordination. As with the Category II plan, strengths of the Category I program are its intention to articulate the curriculum across grade levels, to work within level to further clarify and coordinate the themes, and to use teams of teachers. In addition the sequencing of units over a 2-year time span assures that students will not repeat content in their second year at a level. The nature of the methods for delivery of the overall curriculum or reading program is unclear.

Analysis: Assessment. One of the strengths of this proposal is the two-fold plan for accountability. Its greatest strength lies in the inclusion a defined process for maintaining portfolios that would be used school-wide, from grade to grade. The inclusion of oral language samples over time provides an added dimension not usually considered in assessment data. Unfortunately, this plan uses only standardized tests to decide whether students need intensive instruction, instead of also relying on the broader range of information available in the portfolios. Teachers have chosen to maintain letter grades on student work, rather than designing a means to delineate the desired student outcomes or devising ways to help parents understand the information that portfolios provide. In addition, waiting 3 years to determine whether students are experiencing difficulty can leave many students far behind.

Analysis: Community Outreach. The willingness of this group to propose such a dramatic reorganization reflects the belief that with proper information the community will support the program. Their proposal includes an open-door policy and several articulated strategies to communicate with, and draw in, community members, as well as to provide accountability. While it is commendable to try to offer Spanish language classes, it is unclear why they are not offering classes in English, or why there is no plan for a parent education program.

Proposal C: A Category I and II Combination Program

As you read through the following plan, remember that the analysis of the strengths and weaknesses will be up to you. Use the questions in the Key Questions section of this chapter to guide you in your analysis.

The third plan proposes a combination of options. It would provide a Category I program (literacy and content in the primary language) for K–3 and a Category II program (literacy only in the primary language) in grades 4 and 5. Proponents think this would be the best way to prepare students to move into the all-English middle school at sixth grade. The program would be offered to all native Spanish speakers. In addition, it would provide some exposure to Spanish as a second language for English speakers in bilingual classrooms. At each grade level, 1–5, one class would be designated a monolingual English class and the other three would be part of the bilingual program. The three bilingual program teachers would work as a team to provide instruction with the most Spanish-fluent of them teaching Spanish language literacy and/or content. As part of the change process, all the staff would make the commitment to create English-only and Spanish-only environments, and encourage students to stay in the language of instruction. Figure 9.4 gives an overview of Proposal C, the combined Category I and II plan.

Primary Language. In the kindergarten, Spanish-dominant students would spend the majority of their time in Spanish, with 45 minutes of ESL daily. During this time period, for three days a week, native English speakers in a paired classroom would have Read Aloud in English, and the other two days they would receive some introductory Spanish as a second language instruction. These would be oral language lessons, mostly songs and games to familiarize them with some basic vocabulary in Spanish (numbers, colors, body parts, etc.). In this way teachers believe they can begin early on to instill the value of bilingualism for all students. During recess and other free time, the teachers in these two classes would organize some cross-group activities to assure that students from each language group are not completely isolated from each other.

In grades 1–3, in order to provide a strong initial foundation, students in the primary grades would receive one hour a day of formal literacy instruction in their primary language. Advocates of this plan think they could create a more authentic environment for literacy development if teachers move to a literature-based program. They have already identified a number of titles in Spanish related to the agreed-on content themes, and these would be reserved for each grade level. In addition, teachers would rely on stories from a reading series in Spanish to assure that there are sufficient grade-appropriate reading materials. Paraprofessionals would be used at every grade level to help create small groups that would rotate between teacher, aide, and independent centers.

A separate 2½ hour content block would be provided for all of the students. They would spend the first part of this content time (1/½ hours at first grade, 1 hour at second grade, 45 minutes at third grade) with the same teacher they had for language arts. During this time, monolingual and Spanish-dominant students would receive instruction in their primary language, including math and lessons from thematic units.

During the second part of the content block, all of the instruction would be in English. Each of the teachers would select a different topic-related activity to teach and students would rotate among the three teachers in integrated groups for 2-week periods. In order to better address the needs of the second language learners, they would attempt to do as many hands-on activities as possible, and students would be introduced to a number of learning strategies.

FIGURE 9.4. Overview of Proposal C: Combined Category I and II Program Plan.

Primary Language
    Category I program for K–3
    Category II program for 4 and 5
    Offered to all native Spanish speakers
    Some exposure to Spanish for English speakers
    At each grade, one class designated as English only and 3 as bilingual
    Bilingual teachers work as a team to provide Spanish literacy/content
    Separate language environments
    Literature based, with content themes
    Paraprofessionals used for small group rotation
    Grades 4, 5 primary language reduced substantially

Second Language
    Grades 1–3: daily 30 minutes second language enrichment time for ESL & SSL
    paraprofessionals work with bilingual students who rotate between languages
        biweekly Grades 4, 5: similar plan, but attempts to accommodate incoming
        monolingual Spanish speaking students, ESL scheduled during English language
        arts, focus on literacy

Curriculum Coordination
    Grades 1-3 provides a 2 1/2 hour content block divided between English and Spanish

Assessment
    Outcome based for first and second languages
    Focus on language arts
    Use of portfolio assessment
    School-wide rubrics/benchmarks
    Samples collected throughout the year
    Benchmarks established for transition
    Language Development Team:
        Intervention referrals include review of portfolio in first and second languages
        Assist in designing an intervention plan
    Standardized tests given at grades 3–5, Spanish version administered

Community Outreach
    Involves parents in decision making
    Monthly parent education program
    Outreach includes home visits, parent volunteers, regular written communication
    Emphasizes use of both language to improve communication

In grades 4 and 5, Spanish-dominant students would receive 45 minutes of daily formal literacy instruction each language. Content instruction would be conducted exclusively in English. For students having difficulty understanding the content, a special time would be set aside at the end of each day to meet with the teachers and paraprofessionals for explanations of assignments and clarification of concepts.

Second Language. In grades 1–3, they would designate a 30-minute second language development time each day. Two teachers in the bilingual triad would teach ESL, and one SSL, and a paraprofessional would be assigned to work with the students considered to be bilingual, rotating between English and Spanish every two weeks.

As in the earlier grades, in fourth and fifth grade there will be a second language period. Because it's expected that many students will have gained substantial fluency in each language, one teacher would teach ESL, one SSL, and the third would rotate between the two languages every 2 weeks. Since this would be the largest group, two paraprofessionals would be assigned to the third teacher at this time to be able to break the class into smaller groups. In addition to the second language development time for all students, monolingual Spanish-speaking students and students with fewer than three years of instruction in English would receive ESL instruction during the English language arts period. The focus would be on initial English reading using a modified Language Experience Approach and activities related to the content units.

Curriculum Coordination. This third plan is based on the view that students' ability to learn concepts and vocabulary will be increased through the use of thematic units. The plan relies heavily on team teaching, with students moving among teachers during the school day. Teachers at each grade level would decide on thematic units and then work to create a common curriculum, with each teacher taking responsibility for a portion of the instruction. One teacher would be designated the second language specialist whose content class would be delivered using a sheltered approach.

Assessment. Assessment under this plan would be based on outcomes specified for first and second language development across levels K–5. The teachers have decided that the initial focus of the revamped assessment plan would focus on language arts, and that benchmarks and outcomes for other subject areas would be developed in later years. The basic assessment strategy would be the use of portfolios for which student work would be drawn from each language where appropriate. Writing samples would be collected four times a year, and one product from each content unit would be included for every student at every grade level except kindergarten. Writing samples would be judged against a rubric to be developed by a schoolwide team. Beginning in second grade, students in Spanish literacy would be assessed to assure they have reached a threshold of competence to signal a beginning to formal English reading. Students would then begin to make the transition whenever they are ready, from in the middle of the second grade to the end of third grade.

Students not making progress would be referred to the Language Development Team, who would represent a schoolwide mechanism to assess the specific needs of individual students. The team would consist of second language and reading specialists who would review the progress of individual students through an analysis of the portfolios and conferences with teachers and parents. They would initially recommend changing or modifying instructional plans within the regular classroom, and provide planning guidance and coaching for teachers in strategies they might use to meet students' needs.

Recognizing that the district still places a strong emphasis on standardized test scores, classes in grades 3–5 would spend 20 minutes every Friday practicing the skills needed to do well on the tests that are administered each spring. Students receiving Spanish literacy instruction in grades 3–5 would take a Spanish version of the test.

Community Outreach. This combination plan includes a concerted effort to include parents in the decision-making process. This effort will be two-pronged: parent education and parent outreach. The education program will assess parent needs and design a monthly education program conducted in both languages to meet those expressed needs. The second aspect of the proposal is to reach out to all parents through a variety of activities including regular home visits, a family volunteer program, regular written communication, and a thoughtful plan for addressing how parents are greeted and made to feel welcome on campus. The proposal also focuses on the importance of all communications being conducted in the language of the parents. As parents become more knowledgeable and feel more comfortable, the staff has made a commitment to ensure that parents are included in the actual decision-making process. Before you go on to the next section, stop and analyze the strengths and weaknesses of this third plan.

SUMMARY DISCUSSION OF ALL THREE PLANS

All three of the plans proposed for Hillside Elementary seek to incorporate the primary language into the regular instructional program. Each contains a shift in strategies designed to accommodate students' changing needs as they progress through grades. Though the three plans differ considerably in the actual level of support, they all provide clear and distinct contexts for the development of each language, by designating teachers and times that are to be used for English and Spanish.

Time is set aside each day for second language instruction for all native Spanish speakers in the school, and each plan provides opportunities for oral language, literacy development, and content instruction. Another common strength is that all plans stress the coordination of the second language curriculum with the content of the main instructional program, increasing teachers' ability to utilize the Concept Development Strategy outlined in Chapter 6. Each plan represents a move toward a more authentic assessment system, with the third plan offering the strongest framework for improving assessment practices.

The entire process undertaken by the staff at Hillside Elementary is a strong example of the kind of decision-making process that can occur among staff and community members. It represents an authentic attempt at collaboration. Its strengths include the use of a leader, discussion that relies on the basic premises to guide decision making, cross-grade grouping of the planning teams, and involvement by a broad segment of the school community.

In the next chapter you will see how this type of collaboration and decision-making process can be further extended to include teachers and community members from more than one school.

Decision Making on Your Own

Make a chart showing the strengths and weaknesses of each of the three proposals. For each plan use the Premises and the key questions to help you in the analysis. Discuss your analysis with a colleague. What are major points of similarity and difference in your analyses? How do the plans proposed by the Hillside teachers relate to your own situation?

CHAPTER 10

Lakeview Junior High—
A Multilingual Challenge

In the previous chapter, we examined an elementary program whose population and resources made it possible to organize a Category I or II program. In this chapter, we focus on a secondary school program in a much different setting. Given the numbers of language groups represented and the varying sizes of the populations of each group, the best-suited proposals for reorganization will be for Category III or IV programs.

BACKGROUND

Lakeview Junior High (LJH) is located in a growing immigrant community on the outskirts of a large city in the Northeast. Over the last 10 years, this once all English-speaking suburb has become home to hundreds of families from at least 15 different countries. As a result, the schools in Lakeview have undergone a radical transformation. The district has realized that it needs to invest in resources and personnel to create effective programs for its multilingual/multicultural students, who represent over a fifth of the school's population. Initially, district reorganization efforts were focused at the elementary level, but it has become increasingly apparent that failing to address issues at all levels from the beginning has been shortsighted, and attention is now being turned to the junior and senior high levels. Teachers, staff, and parents from Lakeview Junior High have decided to work with representatives from Shoreline Elementary (SE), one of their feeder schools, to try to formulate program improvements for the school. An important aspect of this case is in demonstrating how a program can be articulated from elementary to secondary school. Through a series of discussions, the staff at each school hope to come up with ways to collaborate to better meet students' needs.

In preparation for their meetings, the principal has prepared the following overview of Lakeview: The school serves 750 students in grades

7, 8, and 9. This year they have 60 Russian, 55 Chinese, 25 Vietnamese, and 20 Korean students, as well as an additional 50 English language learners representing nine other languages, ranging in proficiency from beginners to intermediate and advanced. About 75 students in the school have been identified as having special education needs; among them 20 are second language speakers of English. In addition, the age range in the school is wider than is typical for a junior high, since many of the second language learners are older than native English-speaking students at their grade level. Currently the school staff consists of 30 full-time teachers and 10 paraprofessionals. The district has promised to provide additional paraprofessionals who can act as native language tutors for the next school year. There are four teachers in each of the core subject areas—social studies, science, language arts, and math. There are two ESL teachers, three special education teachers, two PE/health teachers, three foreign language teachers, one full-time computer teacher, and six half-time elective teachers, who offer classes in industrial arts, life skills, art, music, and keyboarding. One of the social studies teachers is a native English speaker who is fluent in Russian and one of the two ESL teachers assigned to the school is a native Chinese-speaker who was a biology teacher in Taiwan. The academic core areas work as independent departments, though recently there has been some talk about creating a two-period course that would link the language arts and social studies curriculum at each grade level. In its current configuration, Lakeview offers no primary language instruction to any group. All ESL instruction is delivered through a pull-out program with a curriculum based on a popular commercially published program. There is no organized sheltered content instruction in the school. Figure 10.1 presents an overview of Lakeview Junior High Schools demographics.

Beginning the Articulation

LEADER, LAKEVIEW JUNIOR HIGH PRINCIPAL (LJH-P): I want to
welcome the Shoreline Elementary staff to the first in our series of
joint discussions on the reorganization of services for second
language learners here at Lakeview Junior High. While this type of
collaboration may be unusual, we all feel it can be potentially very
beneficial.

SHORELINE ELEMENTARY PRINCIPAL (SE-P): Thank you. As you
know, we've undergone a lot of changes at Shoreline. What most
of us thought would be impossible just a few years ago is now
becoming a reality. We have been able to provide some level of
primary language instruction for all the students in the elementary
school and our second language program accommodates lan-

FIGURE 10.1. Summary of Lakeview Junior High demographics.

---

750 students
Ethnicities and Languages Dominance
    60 Russian students
    55 Chinese students
    25 Vietnamese students
    20 Korean students
    50 students representing 9 other languages

75 students with special education needs, 20 are second language learners
Range of ages wides than typical junior high

30 full-time classroom teachers
    16 content area teachers
        4 social science
            1 is an English speaker fluent in Russian
        4 each science, math, language arts
    2 ESL teachers
        1 native Chinese speaker, former biology teacher in Taiwan
    3 Special Education teachers
    2 p.e./heath teachers
    3 foreign language teachers
    1 full time computer teacher
    6 half time elective teachers: industrial arts, life skills, art, music, keyboarding

---

guage, literacy, and content development. In addition, we have gone from a school where second language learners were once seen as a threat, to one where cultural and linguistic diversity is seen as an important asset. None of this would have been possible if we hadn't decided as a staff to work together to come up with solutions to the challenges we were facing.

LJH-P: We've talked a lot already this year, and we've agreed we need to make some changes to better serve our students. Maybe we can start by opening the floor to some concerns.

9th SOC ST-T: One thing that bothers me is that we keep hearing about how the students need all this specialized second language instruction, but there are only two ESL teachers in the school and it doesn't seem like they could do it all in their classroom.

5th/6th-T: What we came to realize at Shoreline was that all of us were going to have to understand about second language development and that we'd all have to take responsibility for the second language learner's instruction.

7th MATH-T: But, I'm a math teacher, not a language teacher. How can I be expected to help these students with their English? And besides, I don't want to lower my standards or make my content suffer.

3rd/4th-T: It took us a while to accept that especially in content instruction, we'd all have to use strategies that would help students understand.

8th SCIENCE-T: I don't see how I can help, but I'm willing to learn more about second language instruction. I have had a lot of these students in my classrooms and they seem really nice and willing to work hard.

8th MATH-T: Albert and I have both had some coursework in second language acquisition and I've even taken a methods course. I've already started making some modifications to my instruction to make the curriculum more understandable to students and it seems to be paying off.

ALBERT: I agree. It's been really helpful to have some insights into the needs of these kids. I think as a whole staff we'd need to have some additional in-service training or even be able to take a class together.

1st/2nd-T: And, we had to create a schedule that would allow us to coordinate second language instruction with the other parts of the curriculum.

ESL-T: I know you've told us that you don't do pull-out for ESL. I can't imagine how you accomplish that. With a junior high schedule it seems impossible not to have the kids separated out.

SE-P: First we had to create a more interdisciplinary curriculum. We used our staff development time and money to talk about the basic content and themes that we wanted to cover K–6. Once we decided on the core curriculum for the school, then we were able to figure out how to organize to deliver instruction according to students' needs. And this didn't just include second language learners. We also were able to look at how to better serve the needs of all the students including those in special ed.

3rd/4th T: Then we agreed that we would all have a 2-hour language development block and a 1½-hour content block in the morning. During this time students are grouped and regrouped. So, for example, everybody is in literacy instruction, most in their primary language, and all the teachers are following similar themes tied to the content block.

1st/2nd-T: And since we've gone with cross-grade groupings, we had to design the curriculum in 2-year sequences, so we could cover all the content without repeating ourselves each year.

7th SOC ST-T: I don't see how that kind of schedule would work at junior high, but it would be really nice if we could also articulate the content themes K–8 to avoid repetition. It was pretty frustrating this year to embark on a major unit on Latin America as part of world geography and find that the sixth graders had just done the same topic last April.

8th SCIENCE-T: But don't you lose a lot of your autonomy as a teacher when you have to follow along the same thing everyone else is doing? I teach earth science; how am I going to coordinate with the seventh-grade English teacher?

SE ESL-T: Well, certainly it would be different at the junior high level, but the basic idea we started with was how to make life more predictable for the second language students. And we found that by coordinating our efforts, the monolingual English students benefitted from the fact that we were able to add more depth to the curriculum.

LJH-P: We've mostly talked about your second language program. I'm really interested in how you provide primary language instruction to your students.

7th MATH-T: Me too. It seems like there are just too many languages in this school for us to possibly organize any kind of bilingual education.

8th ENGLISH-T: And we know that in the high school there is no chance for primary language instruction. These students are going to have to function completely in English in just a year or two.

LJH ESL-T: We shouldn't limit ourselves just because of what won't exist in the future. I think we should provide the strongest program possible in the time we have.

7th ENGLISH-T: What about parents? Didn't they object? I hear the parents say they want their kids to learn English as quickly as possible.

KINDER-T: Well we had to work a long time to help them understand how learning in the primary language would help them in English. But since they've started to see results, most parents seem really happy with our program.

7th ENGLISH-T: No matter what you say, it's going to be hard to convince me that these kids should get primary language instruction at this age. They need to spend as much time in English as possible if they are ever going to make it when they leave here.

5th/6th T: We went through this, believe me. But we knew the students could benefit from primary language instruction, so we started by looking at the numbers for each language group and then finding ways to group them. We knew we couldn't do the same thing for all students, but that we could do something better. Why waste the resources they are bringing with them?

3rd/4th T: We kept wondering how to tap into this knowlege to speed things up. And we wanted to get families more involved. You know, at this age kids really need parental guidance.

9th SOC ST-T: It seems overwhelming, but we do have some staff members who could potentially help us provide some primary language support for students with sufficient numbers, especially Russian and Chinese students.

KINDER-T: One thing that helped was going to the community. Especially in identifying people either with teaching backgrounds or who had strong schooling in their home countries.

1st/2nd-T: Yeah, we've saved you a lot of work, since we have lots of people already identified and we've been encouraging people to enroll in teacher training. Some of the people who were already teachers in their home countries just need to learn English to get certified here. So we've been trying to offer all levels of ESL classes at night for adults. I think some of your parents already are in the classes.

5th/6th-T: It took a lot of talking among ourselves and with parents to get comfortable with trying new things.

7th ENGLISH-T: Yeah, and talking between the two schools like this seemed a little strange at first, but now that we're together, I can think of other ways we might collaborate. One school district I know about provides the sixth- and seventh-grade teachers a day so they can talk about each of the students moving from one school to the other.

5th/6th-T: If we did something like that we could really make use of the portfolios we've been collecting. I'm always afraid that when we send them up with the students, they just get put in a box and never looked at again.

3rd-T: There were a lot of changes we made in assessment that have made a difference. We created a kind of placement matrix that we used to figure out what the needs of our students were.

6th LA-T: We're definitely going to need some way to identify student needs. We have kids from so many language groups. I'd guess that half of them read in their native languages and half of them don't.

ESL: This seems too overwhelming; there are too many factors to juggle.

4th-T: We know how you feel, but we think our experiences can really help you and we already know about the students and their families.

LJH-P: I think our task is clear, we need to get down to the hard work of coming up with some possible plans for reorganization.

At this stage, the LJH staff is still fairly divided about their vision for reorganization. While all believe that primary language instruction is beneficial at the elementary level, some remain unconvinced that it will work at junior high. In addition, many are reluctant to give up their academic departments, which they think they might have to do to be more like Shoreline Elementary. Understanding that different kinds of programs could be organized, they decide to come up with three plans, one for a Category IV program, one for a Category III, and one for a combination. Having various options will allow them to determine which one would best utilize existing resources and support students' academic achievement. Parents from the community and staff members from Shoreline agree to participate in the process, and they group themselves according to their inclinations regarding which type of program they think they might be most successful. The three plans they generated are described below.

PROGRAM PROPOSALS

As you read through the plans, you should take notes and pose questions regarding the issues that arise in relation to the Basic Premises of this book. We will analyze the strengths and weaknesses of the first plan. Then we will ask you to do the same for the second and third plans. We caution you that, as presented, each plan has some definite drawbacks and it is your job to discern them. To help guide you in your analysis of the plans along the five dimensions of primary language instruction, second language instruction, curriculum design, assessment practices, and community outreach, we refer you once again to the questions found on pages 235–237. With your colleagues, discuss the ways the plans could be modified or improved to better reflect the Basic Premises. Think also about how the issues raised might relate to your own setting.

Proposal A, Category IV Program

The proposed Category IV program would provide sheltered English content classes in social studies and science at each grade level, in addition to oral language and literacy-based ESL classes. No primary language instruction would be provided for any of the students. A twofold rationale for this decision is presented by the group. First, it is felt that the current staff is not sufficiently prepared to offer primary language instruction. In addition, since first language instruction couldn't be provided for all groups at this time, they think it wouldn't be fair to provide it for only one. They also think that it would be better at this stage to concentrate their energy on improving the second language program. Figure 10.2 presents an overview of the Proposal A, Category IV program plan.

Primary Language. Though no formal primary language instruction would be provided, teachers think they can still benefit from having the native language tutors the district says it will provide. These personnel would be made available in school to answer students' questions and help translate students' homework assignments, even if they did not provide instruction in the primary language. These paraprofessionals would also assist in the school's efforts to reach out to families by translating forms, documents, and newsletters into all the languages represented in the school.

Second Language. Depending on their level of proficiency, students would receive between 1 and 4 periods a day of second language instruction including sheltered content classes. All students would take two

FIGURE 10.2. Overview of Proposal A: Category IV Plan.

Primary Language
No formal instruction provided
Translation of school documents

Second Language
2 to 4 periods a day
Basic language, literacy, and two classes
in sheltered content (beginning or advanced)

Curriculum
Remain departmentalized
Sheltered classes follow core curriculum
Incorporation of learning strategy instruction

Assessment
Develop outcomes for sheltered content classes
Analysis of progress on benchmarks
Involvement of parents in assessment process

Community Outreach
Create a video portraying a typical day at Lakeview
Encourage parents to audit classes

sheltered content classes at either a beginning or advanced level. New-comers would also receive one class in language development that would focus on survival skills and basic English structure, with some inclusion of content-area vocabulary. In addition, they would receive a class focused on literacy development. Proponents of this plan consider this to be especially important since many students, while literate in their native language, need to learn a new alphabet and writing system. In order to provide sufficient numbers of sheltered classes, the ESL staff would have to work in collaboration with the science and social studies teachers who would help design and teach the sheltered classes.

Curriculum. Proponents of the Category IV plan have decided that in order to move gradually toward change, they would remain departmentalized for now, maintaining the basic curriculum for each subject area and grade level. The sheltered content classes would follow the same core curriculum. Departmental meetings would be used to coordinate topics and activities and ESL teachers would join them in these discussions. They also propose to move to trimester classes to allow for more frequent reevaluation of student progress and increase the opportunities for transition out of sheltered classes into the general education curriculum. There would not be separate sections for sheltered math in English, but they would try to assign as many students as possible to the teacher who has some interest in and experience working with second language learners.

Several members of this group have been studying overall approaches to instruction that can help improve students' academic success. The group has agreed that it would be important to include a strong schoolwide focus on learning strategies. They propose that all teachers would receive an orientation to learning strategies prior to the school year and that strategy charts would be prepared for all classrooms in the school.

Assessment. Under this plan, teachers would develop learning outcomes in literacy/oral language and for sheltered content instruction in English with benchmarks for progress included. Teachers would then get together regularly to analyze progress on benchmarks. They would establish transition criteria as they analyze data. Fearing that too much change at one time would be overwhelming, this group proposes to maintain letter grades and continue to utilize data from the district's norm-referenced tests to assess student achievement. To broaden the information available on students, they would involve parents in the assessment of student progress by designing a parent/student reflection form to be used at conferences.

Community Outreach. Advocates of this plan propose to work with the media center at a nearby community college to produce a video about Lakeview, showing a student's typical day and what the expectations are for student and parent involvement. The video would include a section about the role and importance of family members in helping students to continue to develop their understanding of school concepts in the primary language. It would be dubbed into each of the major languages at the school and used as an orientation tool for all incoming students and their parents. In addition, they would publicize an often-overlooked school policy that allows parents to sit in on, or audit, academic courses and encourage parents to attend the ESL classes on a space-available basis.

Analysis of Proposal A: Category IV Program Plan

Analysis: Primary Language. Given the numbers of students in particular language groups and the potential resources available, the decision not to provide any primary language instruction seems shortsighted. Providing at least some primary language support would allow students to better use their existing skills and knowledge. While it is positive that the native language tutors will be incorporated into the plan for community outreach, the ways in which staff propose to use them in instruction minimizes the contribution they can make. By focusing solely on translating homework assignments, they will miss opportunities for providing primary language support to extend and solidify students' content knowledge.

Analysis: Second Language. Given that there is no primary language instruction provided, a strength of this proposal is in the provision of substantial support for second language instruction. They have accounted for different aspects of language development including both content and literacy instruction and there are varied levels of second language instruction depending on students' level of proficiency. The plan also gives some general education teachers substantial contact with second language learners and vice versa. In this way they will get to learn and practice new methods. However, there is no clear expectation that all teachers will interact with second langauge learners and it appears that the ESL teacher will be given substantial responsibility for content-area teaching that is out of her area of preparation.

Analysis: Curriculum Coordination. While there will be some collaboration between the science and social studies teachers, the decision to stay compartmentalized instead of working toward more interdisciplinary approaches will make it harder to provide second language learners with a coherent program across their school day. The plan does not indicate how native language tutors will be incorporated into the instructional program and how they will actually be assigned to work with students.

Analysis: Assessment. There are several strengths of the assessment plan. One is the development of learner outcomes for literacy and oral language development in the content areas. But while the content themes are articulated, there are no outcomes designated. The inclusion of parents in the assessment process will greatly increase the teachers' understanding of students' strengths and capabilities. The decision to analyze the progress on the benchmarks is also positive, but again it is unclear how the information will be used. At the same time, the teachers have elected to stay with grades and standardized test data to assess student achievement, which diminishes the value of the other kinds of data they will be collecting.

Analysis: Community Outreach. All of the suggestions included for community outreach are positive. They indicate a willingness to try to communicate with family members and to help them become familiar and comfortable with the program at Lakeview. Given the willingness to tap community resources for this outreach, it should be possible to work to increase primary language instruction in school as well.

Proposal B: Category III Program

The staff and parents who are strong advocates of primary language development have undertaken to design a Category III program for all second language students in the building. In their plan, the intensity of primary language instruction would vary according to the numbers of speakers of each language and the resources available. Students would receive either a full class in social studies or science or more limited but regularly scheduled opportunities for primary language reinforcement. This plan would require that the district assure there will be native language tutors fluent in Vietnamese and Korean, as well as a focused community outreach to solicit members of each language community to work with the school. Another major change for the school would be to take some initial steps in assigning students to teachers in teams in order to increase the possibility of coordinating curriculum and streamlining parent outreach. Figure 10.3 presents an overview of the Proposal B, Category III Program plan.

FIGURE 10.3. Overview of Proposal B: Category III Plan.

Primary Language
> Social studies classes in Russian, science classes in Chinese
> Current events classes in Korean and Vietnamese
> Use native language tutors to review main concepts for other language group

Second Language
> 1 to 3 periods a day
> Content based language development class for beginners and literacy class for all students
> Sheltered social studies for all students except Russian speakers
> Chinese and Russian taught as foreign languages

Curriculum
> Coordination of English and social studies curriculum
> Emphasis placed on broad themes

Assessment
> Limited portfolio assessment process for English and social studies classes
> Development of rubrics and anchors for English writing
> End of year cross grade portfolio conferences
> Normed reference Test data for school accountability

Community Outreach
> Coordination of efforts between Lakeview Junior High and Shoreline Elementary
> Orientations for each major language group
> Increase opportunities for non-English speakers to participate in school governance
> Support for community-based language schools

Primary Language. Building on the expertise and qualifications of current staff members, social studies classes in Russian and science classes in Chinese would be offered at each grade level. This would be accomplished by reassigning the Russian- and Chinese-speaking teachers to teach exclusively in those languages. Though class sizes would be small, the group thought that the opportunity for intensive primary language instruction would be extremely beneficial. In addition, they propose to use the Korean and Vietnamese native language tutors to lead current events discussion classes, comprised of students from across the three grade levels. This regularly scheduled class would be offered as an elective open only to Korean or Vietnamese speakers. Discussions would be organized to tie into the main content themes of the social studies classes at each grade level. The teachers would also work cooperatively with the computer teacher to establish Internet links with students' home countries in order to tap into more resources and information in students' primary language.

For all other groups, as part of a study skills class taken by all students in the school, there would be native language tutors provided two or three times a week to review the main concepts from the academic curriculum. LJH staff would start with the people already identified by Shoreline teachers to compile a list of potential volunteers from every language represented in the building who would be able to do concept reinforcement, even if only on an occasional basis. Training would be provided for these volunteers to assure that they were working on the big ideas and broad concepts and not simply translating homework assignments. They would also receive training in using computer networks to find resources and information.

Students would also be encouraged to attend, if available, the weekend language schools being organized by churches in some of their communities. While this falls outside the framework of the regular school day, staff felt that by encouraging students to attend, they could help strengthen the message of the importance of the primary language.

Second Language. Second language learners would receive between one and three ESL classes per day. A language-development class would be offered to beginning students. This class would focus on basic structures and survival vocabulary, as well as provide some opportunities to work with content-area vocabulary. Because it would be impossible to simultaneously coordinate with all the subjects at seventh, eighth, and ninth grades, the content focus would rotate on a regular basis among different academic areas at the three grade levels. Beginners and more advanced students would receive a literacy class (instead of English language arts) and a sheltered social studies class. The only exception to this would be those students receiving content instruction in Russian. They would receive the ESL and/or the English literacy development classes, but not the sheltered social studies content class.

Another modification to the existing program would be to add beginning Russian and Chinese to the foreign language offerings. Native English-speaking students in these classes could then be paired with a native Russian or Chinese speaker in order to practice their respective second languages during lunch, free time, and after school.

Curriculum Coordination. Under this plan, all English and social studies teachers at LJH would collaborate with the ESL staff to develop a coordinated curriculum for all students in the school. They would decide on the main themes and units to utilize as the core curriculum for social studies and English at each grade level, as well as for the ESL language-development, literacy, and sheltered social studies classes. The curriculum would be based on the district curriculum, but would put greater emphasis on the broad themes such as nationalism, shared elements of civilizations, the rise and fall of civilizations, important aspects of U.S. democracy and government, and so forth. The ESL language-development and sheltered social studies classes would be organized around these themes. Second language learners receiving special education services would join three of the sheltered classes. During those periods, a special education teacher would be there to co-teach with the content teacher.

Assessment. This group has decided that a limited portfolio assessment process would be appropriate for the English and social studies classes. They would develop rubrics and anchor papers for English writing and would delineate three projects and/or papers for social studies that would be used as evidence in the portfolio. Then, through the use of planning days, they would schedule conferences at the end of the year to articulate student progress from grade to grade and teacher to teacher. The ESL teachers would also provide information regarding the progress of students in English during the assessment discussions. They propose that even though they must give standardized tests, they would use norm-referenced test data only for the school accountability report and not to measure student progress.

Community Outreach. A major feature of the community outreach plan for this proposal would be to coordinate parent orientation, meetings, and the use of interpreters between Lakeview and Shoreline. A special effort would be made to work with parents and families from languages that have only a very few speakers. With the help of community organizations, each September they would set up orientation meetings for each of the major language groups. One goal set by this group would be to work to expand the number of slots on the school's governance committee in order to accommodate representatives from as many of the language groups as possible.

They would work with existing church-based programs to support and publicize the proposed Saturday school that would focus on language and literacy development in Chinese, Korean, and Vietnamese. In addition, they would publicize opportunities for adult education and ESL classes already available at local community colleges and community centers.

Proposal C: Category III and IV Combination Program

Proponents of this combination plan think that given the current resources and numbers of languages in the school, it would be feasible to provide primary language instruction only for the Russian and Chinese students. The rest of the second language learners would receive a Category IV program, with special emphasis on sheltered content instruction. Figure 10.4 presents an overview of the Proposal C, Combined Category III and IV Program Plan.

Primary Language. Under this plan, Chinese and Russian speakers would receive two periods of native language instruction daily. One would be a grade-level content class and the other their study skills class, where students would be grouped across grade levels. In the latter class they would be able to discuss topics from their English classes and would receive help in completing their homework assignments from the Russian-speaking and Chinese teachers as well as from native language tutors.

Second Language. Because only Chinese and Russian speakers would receive primary language instruction, proponents of this plan think that a heavy emphasis would have to be placed on providing sheltered content instruction at every grade level and in all content areas for everyone else. They propose to try to offer two levels of sheltered science, social

FIGURE 10.4. Overview of Proposal C: Combined Category III and IV Program Plan.

Primary Language
For Chinese and Russian speakers only
Students would receive two periods of primary language instruction daily

Second Language
3 or 4 periods daily
Two levels of sheltered science, math, and social studies at each grade level
Some content area teachers responsible for sheltered content classes

Curriculum
Remain departmentalized, but develop school-wide global themes across content areas
Each department responsible for adapting curriculum to needs of second language learners

Assessment
Establish a student placement team
Articulation of ESL textbook skills continuum with content areas across grade levels
Use benchmarks and NRT percentile rankings to assess progress and transition
Assess all students in their primary language

Community Outreach
Offer ESL classes for adults through local community college
Orientation for families in their native language regarding available social services
Annual multicultural celebration

studies, and math classes. In Level A, beginning students from across the grade levels would be mixed. These students would receive one language/ literacy class and two content classes. Once students demonstrated sufficient proficiency they would transition to Level B and take three sheltered classes, one each in social studies, science, and math. For the rest of the day, students would be mainstreamed. As in the first plan for a Category IV program, more sections would have to be offered than is possible given the ESL allocation to the building. Therefore, one teacher in each content area would have to agree to teach sheltered classes as part of the regular load. Because Chinese and Russian students would receive content instruction in their primary language, they would receive just one period a day of ESL focused on language and literacy development. For the language and literacy class, teachers would use a commercial ESL program that includes a combined emphasis on literature studies and writing development.

This group also recognizes that a number of LJH students who will be in mainstream classes were in second language instruction at Shoreline. They think that not only should the ESL program be improved, but that all teachers in the building should learn more about how to accommodate the needs of second language learners—students currently in need of ESL services, as well as those who have been transitioned out of ESL classes. They propose to work with a local university to offer a series of three courses at LJH on second language acquisition, theories and methods, and assessment.

Curriculum Coordination. Proponents of this plan think that unless they were given an extra period of planning time, it would be too unwieldy to try to coordinate the entire curriculum at each grade level. Therefore, under this plan, LJH would remain departmentalized. They would, however, work schoolwide to develop some global themes that would be used each quarter to tie the curriculum together across grades and subject areas. As possible examples of such themes they suggest "people who've made a difference," "moving into the 21st century" and "many ways of seeing and knowing." The whole faculty would work together to finalize the themes and then devote some of their staff-development time to identifying topics and activities in each content area related to them. These would be compiled in a notebook to be given to every teacher in the building. In this way, there would be some common threads to instruction, allowing second language learners (and all students) the opportunity to meet some core concepts and vocabulary across their school day, but teachers could work more to adapt their current curriculum to meet the needs of second language learners rather than trying to change too many things at once.

Assessment. Through their discussions, staff members have realized that they will have students entering at many levels of proficiency with widely varying educational backgrounds. Therefore, they propose to establish a student placement team that would review students on entry in order to determine appropriate placement. This team would include ESL staff, a representative from each major language group, the special education teacher, and counselors.

For the language and literacy class, teachers would spend time articulating the continuum of skills from the publisher of the ESL text, by grades as well as by content themes. Benchmarks for progress, transition, and redesignations would be based on the publisher's language assessments and Normed Reference Test percentile ranking. For Russian and Chinese students, information from their progress in their primary language classes would be incorporated into their assessment profiles. Native language tutors for the other languages in the building would conduct assessments in students' primary languages each semester to evaluate their progress. In order to gain a wider view of students' success, teachers also advocate developing an observational record that would include parent input, which would be used during parent teacher conferences.

Community Outreach. Proponents of this combination program think that one of the biggest contributions they could make to the community would be to organize with a local community college to offer more ESL classes than are currently available at Shoreline for parents. They also propose to find a way to provide the Russian- and Chinese-speaking teachers a stipend to take responsibility for outreach to those two communities. They would then try to arrange for a series of presentations to be developed that would orient families to available community services. The script for the presentation would be developed in English first and then, working with representatives of the various language groups and native language tutors, it would be translated into as many languages as possible. Finally, they propose to hold a large multicultural celebration each spring where members of every group in the school would be invited to bring food, play music, and display handicrafts from their country in the school gym.

In summary, each of the plans outlined above has strengths and weakness. As you work through the analysis of each plan, remember to consider the "Key Questions" for each of the major areas described.

Decision Making on Your Own

Make a chart showing the strengths and weaknesses of each of the three proposals. For each plan, use the Premises and the key questions to help you in the analysis. Discuss your analysis with a colleague. What are major points of similarity and difference? How do the plans proposed by the Lakeview teachers relate to your own situation?

CHAPTER 11

Linda Vista—Decisions in Action

This case study of Linda Vista Elementary School in San Diego, California, is presented as an example of how one school transformed itself to better serve the needs of its linguistically diverse student population. It describes the decisions, processes, and artifacts of this schoolwide reform effort, and how a building staff can make effective decisions by applying the Basic Premises about language and learning. Several components of the reform process are presented: the decision-making process, the instructional program, supplemental and noninstructional programs, and assessment and accountability.

BACKGROUND

Linda Vista School is a large urban school serving approximately 1,000 students. The school has a satellite campus about one-half mile away from the main campus. The Linda Vista area of San Diego has traditionally been the most culturally diverse in the city and has undergone numerous changes. Through the 1960s and early 1970s the area was home to roughly equal numbers of white, African-American, and Latino families. In the early 1970s, Southeast Asian refugees moved to the area in substantial numbers and displaced many of the former residents. At one time, almost 70% of Linda Vista's enrollment was Southeast Asian. Recently, the number of Latino families moving into the area has risen. At the time of this writing the school's enrollment was 44% Asian, 40% Latino, 6% African-American, and 10% white. More than 95% of its students received free or reduced-price lunch, making the school eligible for schoolwide Title I funding. At least 77% of the students were second language speakers of English, many of them monolingual in their primary language.

Linda Vista's diverse student body presented a unique challenge to the staff. Five major languages—Hmong, Vietnamese, Lao, Spanish, and English—were represented as well as several other language groups with small numbers of students. The children of newly arrived immigrant or refugee families, often with no previous exposure to formal education, arrived at the school's doorstep on a regular basis. The staff, presented with an extraordinary opportunity to tailor a program to a distinctive student body, took up the challenge and initiated a process of site-based reform.

THE DECISION-MAKING PROCESS

The Linda Vista staff began its restructuring project before the school district officially launched its own school reform initiative. When a new principal arrived at Linda Vista, she found that the students were performing substantially below average, were assigned to classes without regard to their English language proficiency, and spent what seemed to be more time being pulled out of class for supplementary language or basic skills instruction than they spent in class. This situation called for immediate change. The first year, the staff at Linda Vista were already brainstorming and formulating a strategic plan that they began implementing the following fall. Considering the poor situation that existed at the school, this rapid planning and implementation of a schoolwide restructuring process is a testament to the potential of any staff to reinvent itself and pursue a vision given a carefully crafted decision-making process.

Rather than imposing solutions, the new principal called a faculty meeting to present data on conditions within the school. She charged the faculty with developing strategies to improve working conditions and student performance. For six months the faculty examined its beliefs about the student population, bilingual instruction, developmental education, and many other issues. They then began to meet in small groups to develop a list of need statements for the school. From these needs emerged a vision, goals and objectives, and ultimately a program based on the vision and goals.

According to most of the staff, this process proved to be extremely difficult. Teachers accustomed to working in isolation within their classrooms dreaded the prospect of modifying or scrapping their established routines in response to the vision. Others objected to the new demands on their time. A few tried to sabotage the process by starting debates over procedural matters at all staff meetings. While the opponents of the process eventually left the school, most of the other initially resistant staff eventually found the process rewarding. Individuals continued to have differences with each other over time, but conflicts became healthy and, on the whole, the staff expressed pride in their accomplishments. When asked to look at the factors critical to the success of the restructuring process, most staff point to the same factors: (a) an open process, in which all parties could express their thoughts without fear of repercussion or ridicule; (b) the involvement of all school staff, including aides, cafeteria personnel, and custodial staff; and (c) support from the assistant superintendent in charge of Linda Vista.

The importance of the open process and the involvement of all school staff in that process cannot be overemphasized in Linda Vista's restructuring story. While the open staff meetings allowed the most resistant individuals to challenge the restructuring process, they also allowed the supporters of the change to hear, respond to, and allay the fears of the more moderate resisters. In short, the openness expanded the constituency supporting reform, thereby giving the movement greater credibility within the school. The process also placed teachers, noncertificated staff, and community members at the forefront of the school's reform effort, compelling people long accustomed to following administrative dictates to step forward and assume leadership roles. The presence of respected leaders within the ranks of both certified and classified staff also contributed to the staying power of the school's restructuring effort.

The leadership role of the principal was critical. The principal initiated the process of change. She told her staff that "the need to change is not your decision, but how we change is." She then allowed staff to deliberate and set their own agenda. The principal remained directly involved in the process, however, consistently redefining the consensus reached by the staff. To some outside observers, she seemed to play too dominant a role in defining the consensus instead of letting staff reach their own conclusions, but others suggest that given the situation that existed in the beginning there may not have been any other way. Virtually all the Linda Vista staff expressed their appreciation for the principal's ability to consolidate the variety of ideas and opinions they expressed into a coherent statement of principles and plan of action. Through this process, they found that the dimensions of leadership necessary to initiate reform are distinct from those required for the sustaining process, indicating that varying styles of leadership at different times in the process may be required.

Strategic Planning

As stated above, the process of self-analysis and change began in the spring of the first year. A great risk was taken in asking staff members who were demoralized and who were unaccustomed to working together to come up with comprehensive change. At the first meeting, where the staff were presented with hard data relative to the achievement of students, degree of classroom interruptions, and pull-out instruction, teachers were asked to generate some needs statements based on these data. The initial needs statements charted by the staff were as follows: (1) more appropriate instructional/language proficiency groupings for each student; (2) less pull-out instruction during morning hours; (3) more integrated learning experiences; (4) greater equity of services to all students; (5) less labeling of special needs students; (6) a more unified staff; (7) better use of space.

It may appear that the above needs statements are very simple and perfunctory; however, these simple statements provided the springboard for the next critical step. Teachers were asked to break into groups and brainstorm a plan to meet those needs. The staff was encouraged to think creatively and not be tied down with traditional ideas, or perceived administrative restrictions.

From the outset, all group findings were recorded on chart paper, visible in the staff lounge at all times. Initially, only teachers participated in the brainstorming sessions, but gradually, with increased pressure from various staff members, classified staff became an integral part of the process. From January to June, committees formed around these issues, met on an ongoing basis, and formulated a total school plan for implementation in September. The same staff that had previously been plagued by serious morale and communication problems were now able to generate the teamwork necessary to bring about massive change.

Two significant factors contributed to this positive turnaround: the regularly changing committee membership that allowed group dynamics to shift and new leadership to continually emerge, and the constant reiteration throughout the committee work that decisions were to be arrived at through consensus. More and more ownership of the plan was taken as staff members realized that their ideas were valued. The principal also constantly redefined consensus and made it clear that all staff should be involved, not just those who were willing to work harder. This set the precedent for the schoolwide governance structure that ultimately emerged in which all staff, both certificated and classified, became active members.

Governance

In preparation for plan implementation in September, the entire staff decided on committees that would be established immediately in the fall to carry out the necessary activities for beginning the new program. Thus, the beginnings of the governance structure were emerging from the task of meeting the needs of students. The shared decision-making framework at Linda Vista evolved from an acknowledged need to restructure the educational program to benefit students. To the detriment of substantive instructional change, in many schools the change process begins with the needs of adults rather than the needs of students, resulting in power struggles among staff that ultimately fail to positively affect students in any substantial way.

At Linda Vista, a governance structure evolved, for the most part with instructional, curricular, or staff development needs in mind. Certainly conflict resolution was necessary. Working conditions were also a necessary topic in the shared decision-making process. However, these issues never overshadowed the priority of providing an excellent educational program for students.

The decision-making process took place through committee work. Each committee presented recommendations they thought important for their area to the staff for adoption or negotiation. Decisions were arrived at through consensus, although voting was necessary at times. Some committees were standing, others were recommended by the staff as needs developed. Recommendations could be initiated by the entire staff or by a committee.

Committees were negotiated at the beginning of each school year. Individual staff members then signed up for two. The next step was for the committees was to develop their proposals for the year. These proposals included composition, goals, meeting times, and self-monitoring process. They were then submitted for distribution to the entire staff. Throughout the school year, committees met, as indicated in their proposals, reported to the staff at the general meetings, and made appropriate recommendations for approval. Minutes of each committee's meetings were taken and then disseminated to the entire staff.

The process evolved over time. For example, eventually the staff decided that a point system should be initiated so that participation and responsibility were equitably distributed. Committees were weighted in relation to the breadth of their responsibility and the workload they entailed. Each staff member carried a certain number of points based on the specific assignment. This system represented the consistent development in thinking about shared responsibility. At Linda Vista, each staff member was now expected to participate on one curriculum committee and one site-responsibility committee.

Conclusions from the Restructuring Process

The experience at Linda Vista suggests that school restructuring is most successful if:

- it is a pervasive, systemic change affecting each student in the school;
- it calls for total change, rather than for changing only one aspect at a time;
- it is based on a site-based management system that requires all staff to participate;
- decisions for change are student-oriented;
- the staff is empowered by their team effort and not through individual efforts alone;
- the process for change includes nontraditional approaches;
- it provides active support and leadership by the site administrator.

THE INSTRUCTIONAL PROGRAM

Linda Vista's mission was to promote academic excellence through shared decision making, to increase teacher/staff leadership, and to maintain high expectations for all students. The staff believed that each student could learn and that everyone should be academically challenged and engaged for the entire school day. Their responsibility, then, was to ensure the best educational program possible.

Vision for Restructuring

Developing a vision for the restructuring process at Linda Vista included the following challenges: (1) meeting the diverse academic needs of each student through appropriate placement and a nongraded curriculum; (2) providing appropriate language placement and an integrated experience in an integrated setting; (3) providing each student access to all programs; (4) assessing student progress through individual authentic assessment techniques; (5) involving the parents and the community at large through an outreach program; (6) strengthening the effectiveness of the shared decision-making process.

Evolution of the Instructional Program

The decision-making process was guided by the underlying assumptions and the Basic Premises presented in Chapters 1 and 2. Through deliberation, the staff also developed several principles specific to their situation to guide their decision making. The two principles that played the most prominent roles were planning more appropriate groupings for each student and greater equity of services to all students. In some ways, these two principles were contradictory. Grouping students by their needs or language proficiency and tailoring instruction to those needs can deprive some students of certain opportunities available to other students. The Linda Vista staff found ways to balance both of these priorities within their instructional program, however. Other overriding principles to which they would adhere in developing the program included: Supplementary instruction would not be a key factor in supporting underachieving or special needs students, but rather students would receive their basic instruction within regular classroom settings; students would receive primary language instruction; all students would have access to all programs; and all students would participate in settings that were integrated by gender, ethnicity, and language.

Because of the complexity of the student population at Linda Vista, deliberation and decision making required consideration of a wide variety of variables. A first step was the staff's critical decision to move away from a deficit perspective to one that maintained high expectations for all students, and that held the same standards for all. In order to achieve this, the total school program was organized to include: (1) a nongraded curriculum for the entire school; (2) the development of an early childhood education program for all pre-kindergarten, and kindergarten and some age-6 students and special education students housed at the annex site; (3) reduced class size for all classrooms; (4) substantial weekly preparation time for each teacher; (5) a reallocation of resources in order to implement the program. Under this umbrella of principles, the specific plan developed for the school addressed all of the foregoing criteria.

The school's day was divided into two parts. The morning was devoted to first and second language instruction in the areas of literacy, social studies, and math. Limited primary language resources in the Southeast Asian language required creative thinking in order to meet the first and second language needs of students. Spanish-speaking students received a fuller bilingual program. Both of these programs are described below.

The Program for Southeast Asian Students. Given the limited resources available in the Southeast Asian languages and the importance of primary language development (Premise 2), some difficult decisions had to be made about how to offer the best possible first and second language program for these students. The decision was to offer a Category III program to Southeast Asian youngsters. Consequently, there would be a focus on English language development (Premise 3) for the Hmong, Vietnamese, and Lao students, with primary language reinforcement.

The Southeast Asian youngsters were taught in their sheltered English situation by the regular monolingual staff trained to offer sheltered instruction. Within each age grouping—early childhood, primary, middle, and upper—students in the sheltered English program were grouped homogeneously by English language proficiency in up to six proficiency levels as indicated in Figure 11.1. Figure 11.2 shows an example of upper-level rubrics used to assess progress.

For all instruction offered to limited-English-proficient students, staffing, classroom organization, and instruction were arranged so that languages were kept separated and enriched (Premise 6). Teachers used the language of instruction exclusively. This is not to say that students could not use whichever language they were comfortable with, but with consistent teacher models they soon came to respect and use the language of instruction. Using each language in this way allowed the necessary time, exposure, and intensity for strong development.

By reorganizing the limited bilingual human resources available in Hmong, Vietnamese, and Lao, primary language instructional opportunities were made possible. It was decided that one major content area could be offered in each of the these primary languages. The subject selected was social studies, an area in which culture, vocabulary, and concepts can be taught through the primary language.

The school reallocated resources to hire a certificated Hmong teacher. A Vietnamese teacher was also part of the staff along with a cadre of bilingual instructional aides. These individuals were assigned as primary language staff outside of the regular classroom. At prescribed times during the day, students were grouped for social studies primary language instruction. Math support through the primary language was organized in small groups within the regular classroom by this same cadre of staff.

The Spanish Bilingual Program. Spanish-speaking students were offered language arts, math, and social studies through their primary language while they were becoming proficient in English. English as a second language (ESL) instruction for these students was part of their regular classroom instruction, and was taught either in a team teaching situation by a monolingual English-speaking teacher or by the bilingual teacher during English language arts time. Developing clear contexts for the use of each language was also important in this program.

Student Development. It was noteworthy that in this process of change, time was not spent in the initial stages of planning and implementation bringing in experts and studying research. Keeping efforts focused within the group was necessary as the grass-roots effort took hold. More importantly, the elements that would ensure success were embedded in the ongoing process of change in organization and instruction. To ensure that high expectations were maintained, for example, an important element

FIGURE 11.1. Linda Vista Elementary, language proficiency levels.

EARLY CHILDHOOD
Sheltered
Nonsheltered
Bilingual Spanish

PRIMARY
Entry level
Sheltered A
Sheltered B
Nonsheltered
Bilingual Spanish

MIDDLE
Entry level
Sheltered A
Sheltered B
Transition A
Transition B
Nonsheltered
Bilingual Spanish

UPPER
Entry level
Sheltered A
Sheltered B
Transition A
Transition B
Nonsheltered
Bilingual Spanish

that became embedded in the program was fluidity of student movement. Planning for students to be able to move up the levels of English language proficiency when ready was one of the most important decisions the staff made in terms of raising expectations.

Students were expected to move from level to level as soon as they had met the criteria—not necessarily at the end of the semester or year. A second language team similar to the one discussed in Chapter 7 was incorporated into the process. Individual student referrals and bi-annual reviews were conducted to place or move students within the English language proficiency levels of the morning program. During these reviews,

FIGURE 11.2. Examples of upper level rubrics listings for oral language and reading.

ORAL LANGUAGE

1. Silent/Emergent Listener Speaker
- does not yet respond verbally
- minimal evidence of listening/speaking skills; expresses ideas using gestures and simple words, and is developing vocabulary

2. Limited Listener Speaker
- expresses ideas using simple words and phrases
- limited participation in class activities and group settings

3. Developing Listener Speaker
- experiences speaker, usually attentive
- occasionally takes part in class activities
- makes relevant responses
- express ideas with command of the language

5. Exceptional Listener-Speaker
- confident, effective, attentive
- actively takes part in class activities consistently in a leadership role

READING

1. Emergent Reader
- participates in shared reading
- memorizes and repeats oral language but does not connect to print
- knows some letters and is gaining awareness that letters have sounds understands "book sense"
- uses picture cues and "reads" from memory incorporating left to right knowledge
- beginning to make predictions
- ability to use prior knowledge

2. Less Experienced Reader
- has limited experience as a reader
- chooses to read very easy and familiar texts
- has difficulty with any unfamiliar material, yet is usually able to read own writing with ease
- needs a great deal of support with reading in all content areas
- is overly dependent on any one strategy when reading aloud
- rarely chooses to read for pleasure

3. Moderately Experienced Reader
- is developing fluency as a reader and reads some books with confidence
- usually most comfortable reading short books with simple narrative
- relies on re-reading favorite or familiar books
- needs help with reading in the content areas, especially using reference and information books

4. Experienced Reader
- a reader who feels comfortable with books
- is generally able to read silently and is developing confidence as a reader

5. Exceptionally Experienced Reader
- a self-motivated, confident reader who pursues his/her own interests through reading
- capable of reading in all content areas and of locating and drawing on a variety of resources to research topics independently
- is able to evaluate evidence drawn from a variety of sources
- is developing critical awareness as a reader

student performance was assessed against the school's standards through the individual portfolio.

Planning for Cross-cultural Interactions. In order to meet the criteria for providing students with a culturally, linguistically, and gender integrated experience (Premise 10), the students were heterogeneously grouped during the afternoon. A departmentalized program was offered in which students were rotated for 10-day blocks for two subjects per block. Teachers selected the subject of their choice and taught only that subject for the year. For example, a student received science and music for 10 days and then rotated to physical education and art.

A complaint often expressed by elementary school teachers is that there is not enough time to cover the entire curriculum, and that consequently subjects usually taught in the afternoon—that is, science, physical education, art, and music—do not receive adequate emphasis. It is important to note that in the above program not only were all of these subjects taught intensively (including meeting minute requirements), but additional subjects were added to the curriculum. For example, during the afternoon rotation, all students received a counseling program, as well as technology, geography, and social development. Because the morning instruction provided for the needs of all students there was no need for the remedial classes that usually prevent students from participating in many activities. A key factor of the vision, to provide equity of services and to decrease or even eliminate the labeling of students, was upheld here as all students participated in the afternoon program regardless of special needs. There were no remedial pull-out classes, and computer literacy and services such as the counseling program, often reserved for crisis intervention, were provided to all students.

The afternoon program at Linda Vista school was interdisciplinary and hands-on, and integrated writing, literature, and math into the curriculum. It was enthusiastically endorsed by the students. Students experienced a wide variety of activities and teaching styles, and most teachers knew most of the students in the school. Their enthusiastic participation was seen as evidence of its success.

Reallocation of Resources. A critical practice in any reform effort is organizational flexibility. An exemplary innovation may fail if there has not been an effort to make provisions for flexibility of staffing, student grouping, and movement. At Linda Vista, the vision dictated how resources, both financial and human, would be allocated to meet the goals set out by the staff.

In the reallocation of resources, several part-time morning teaching posts were allocated to reduce class size as well as to provide special instruction that otherwise would not have been possible within the district staffing formula. Consequently, a nontraditional design was implemented for the special education students in the resource specialist program, as well as other students who did not qualify for special education, but were older and at risk. The schedule allowed for an intensive morning program of core subjects while at the same time giving these students the opportunity to participate fully in the afternoon rotation as well as all programs available in the school. This program was called Academic Enhancement. For the 38 to 40 students in the program, five adults were available to work with them intensively. This was accomplished by teaming the resource specialist with another teacher during the morning hours. This team of teachers was complemented by two instructional aides, and an additional teacher's time for half of the instructional period. Two adjacent classrooms were utilized so that a highly intensive and individualized program was possible.

The decision to reduce class size was made not to equalize all classes, but to provide for the needs of students. Like the special education program, other classes were also maintained at much smaller size levels than most, for example, the entry-level classes for non–English speaking students were kept small so that an intensive program could be offered that would accelerate their progress.

Other Decisions Made to Support and Enhance the Vision. Throughout the restructuring process, the staff at Linda Vista continued to find ways to better meet the needs of students. The upper-level staff reorganized their math instruction to reflect a concept-based program that allowed students at all levels of math proficiency to experience a broad range of math concepts. Each of nine classrooms was a concept station. Students rotated through these concepts every 10 days to 3 weeks. Concepts ranged from basic math to geometry. This ensured that even though a student might be having difficulty with basic math, he or she would still engage in geometry. Students were assessed early in the year and after each rotation.

Other examples of ongoing improvement were the creation of a technology laboratory and the initiation of study skills and reading intervention programs. The highly successful study skills program was implemented in order to help students keep their active day organized. Standard binders and dividers were provided to each student with communication pages to parents for homework and classwork.

SUPPLEMENTAL AND NONINSTRUCTIONAL PROGRAMS

Parent and Community Outreach

The staff at Linda Vista had to make a concerted effort to change their thinking about how to involve families and the community at large. One of the largest groups represented at Linda Vista was the Hmong. Although as a people they were committed to education, Hmong culture is a highly traditional one and parents essentially assign academic responsibility to the professionals. In order to work successfully with the Hmong community, the staff had to assess their beliefs and understandings about Southeast Asian cultures. They came to understand the very dramatic differences among these cultures and the importance of earning the trust of each community. These people had suffered greatly and had left their homeland for a new and extremely different society.

It was decided that the parent and community program would be called Outreach. A commitment was made to reach out to the families on their terms and to approach this process as a developmental one. The point at which parents become part of the decision-making structure of the school would be arrived at over time and by first establishing trust.

A cadre of community aides who spoke the languages of the community was already employed at the school. However, the aides were basically involved in crisis intervention. The Outreach committee, as it came to be known, planned a totally different role for these aides. They would reach out to families through monthly home visits. These home visits were tied to a specific agenda and to various groups of students. For example, the first month of school all the new families were visited with an orientation agenda. At another time all families with at-risk students might be visited to offer specific ideas for parents about homework, discipline, and organizing time. The community aides were trusted members of the community, including clan leaders, so they were able to discuss concerns with families that other staff members might not have been able to discuss. They also made a significant contribution to bridging the language barriers.

A second major aspect of the family involvement program was the education program. A needs assessment was completed early in the year to find out what the parents thought they needed in terms of education. Several workshops throughout the year were planned based on this needs assessment. The Outreach committee first planned the agenda, often bringing in an expert to help with the lesson plan; the community aides or teachers who spoke the languages of the parents, however, would be the ones who delivered the instruction. Each workshop was conducted simultaneously in separate rooms in five languages. Understanding and communication were of primary importance (Premise 9), and transportation and child care were provided.

Over the years a rich variety of hands-on workshops were provided. Parents became more and more accustomed to and comfortable with hands-on activities and interactive sessions. Family math and reading, interactive science, and student-taught computer literacy were but a few of the offerings families experienced.

As Linda Vista's school culture evolved into one of a school community, more and more support was provided to the families. Health care and social services were coordinated by many staff members so that students and their families had access to many necessary services, information, and support. The community agencies gradually became part of the school family and were integral to the parent education program, lending their services on a regular basis. Where a closed environment had existed before, an open and accessible one was now the mode.

Eventually, parents felt the school was truly theirs. They acted as volunteers, guest speakers, and translators, and became active members of the School Site Council and Outreach committee. Parent input was always requested during the planning, implementation, and evaluation stages of the change process. For example, during the first year of piloting the new growth record as the progress reporting tool, every parent's comment about the growth record was recorded during parent conferences. These comments were the basis for continuing with the new tool and for any revisions required.

Once the families of Linda Vista school became an integral part of the school community, the web of inclusion extended to the community at large. In fact, a multifaceted partnership grew from the school's commitment to involve its community in the education process. As the community recognized the openness and success of this school, many agencies approached the school with proposals for collaboration. Linda Vista enjoyed partnerships with eight agencies: the San Diego Police Department; the County Office of Education, a nearby private school, the local YMCA, Linda Vista's McDonald's restaurant, a warehouse store, the local shopping mall and the University of San Diego.

The partners provided many valuable services to the students. For example, the warehouse store donated the seed, fertilizer, equipment, and fencing for the school's one-acre garden, which students cared for as part of their science classwork. A few years into the process, the local YMCA approached the Linda Vista staff and proposed that they use the facility for students and even offered the help of their instructors. One glitch was transportation. The local McDonald's heard of the plan and decided they could help. They wrote a grant to the McDonald's corporation to fund some buses. The grant was funded and resulted in an extensive physical education program for the students. Four days a week, physical education classes from the school were bused to the YMCA, where they participated in gymnastics, swimming, and soccer classes. Beyond the physical education program, the staff of the YMCA became part of the Linda Vista family. They were often on campus at lunch time or after school interacting with students. Many times these individuals acted as big brothers and sisters to students after school or on weekends.

During a reception for the outgoing principal of Linda Vista school, the following story was told by the executive director of the YMCA to exemplify what he felt the partnership had accomplished for him and his staff. He described how, at one point, a Hmong child had some difficulty during the swimming lessons. As a result, the parents refused to let the child return to the class until a ceremony was completed over the pool. As the executive director tells it, he would have never agreed to such an event before the partnership with Linda Vista, but after learning about and understanding the cultures represented at the school, he realized that reaching out to these parents would do much to solidify the relationship with the community. Thus, the ceremony was conducted and the child was returned to swimming class. A great deal was achieved by this simple act of acceptance.

The county office of education offered tutors from among its many employees, and video productions and the printing of many school items were but a few of the additional benefits that resulted from this partnership. The police department collaborated with the school in providing ongoing education for students and parents about gang and substance-abuse prevention. This partnership resulted in a greater trust in law enforcement in the community, since many of the sessions with police officers offered opportunities for dialogue with the community. The inherent message here is that such partnerships go beyond the specific materials and activities provided to the school. They encourage trust, develop cultural understanding, and open lines of communication.

Social Development Programs

The underpinnings of a positive school culture include a great many activities beyond actual classroom instruction. Recognition activities, discipline, conflict resolution and counseling, and other processes provide the glue that binds people together. A major foundation for social development was a comprehensive, schoolwide discipline policy that was clearly articulated to students, staff, and parents. At Linda Vista, a great emphasis was placed on the schoolwide recognition of students' individual achievements. Student achievements were celebrated at monthly assemblies where they received a variety of awards. A school bulletin board also featured the awards and the students' photos. The "Caught You Being Good" program and rewards in the counseling center were implemented to focus on positive behaviors. Many students were trained in the methods and language of conflict resolution. As conflict managers, students assisted one another, especially on the playground during recess. In all of these activities great care was taken to ensure that all students had opportunities to participate throughout the school year. In addition to the regular counseling center program that focused on developmental, preventative, and remedial counseling, Linda Vista received a mental health grant to provide support to primary age students identified as being "low risk." These students were given counseling help in the areas of self-esteem and peer relations.

In keeping with the push for continuous improvement and seeking answers to the problems plaguing African-American male students, the staff sought out and implemented the Rites of Challenge program (Mtume & Sundayo, 1988). An 8-week course for students became part of the morning social studies curriculum for 7- to 12-year-olds. The curriculum takes the students through a series of challenges, including communication with family members, withstanding negative peer pressure, and personal decision making. It also teaches African-American and African history, with parent involvement being a major component. Plans for extending these empowerment classes to provide a similar program for Latinas, another group facing serious challenges, were developed.

ASSESSMENT AND ACCOUNTABILITY

Any substantial, systemic school change must include an internal mechanism of assessment and accountability from its inception. At the very heart of the restructuring process is a foundation of student assessments embedded in the curriculum and involving the learners. It is an individual assessment, yet systematically linked to provide instructional continuity and ongoing information about students for parents and teachers, and for school accountability. Thus, the continuous progress of students becomes inextricably linked to the school's overall performance and the performance of the school professionals.

At the beginning of the restructuring planning process at Linda Vista, issues regarding assessment and accountability were consistently being

raised. In the meantime, the school's assessment committee began exploring alternative means of assessment. A natural outcome of this thinking
was the establishment of schoolwide standards reflective of the California framework but incorporating Linda Vista's six levels of English language proficiency. This process alone took two full years to accomplish.

The process of rethinking the concept of student assessment must
deal with the extremes. At one extreme is standardization such as norm-
referenced test results, grades, and so forth, which give a number, rank,
or letter representing the student's performance compared with other
students, locally or nationally. At the other extreme is an individual
teacher-developed student portfolio in which the teacher makes individual, subjective judgments about student progress.

A schoolwide alternative assessment process such as portfolio assessment lies somewhere between the above two extremes. It assesses the
actual work of students, work that is in process and reflects high-order
thinking. However, the school standardizes expectations based on its own
needs and population of students (Premise 8), thus ensuring continuity
and accountability. These standards were designed within the framework
of the larger organization, that is, district and state expectations.

The decision to incorporate portfolio assessment for language arts at
Linda Vista was an outgrowth of the many discussions about assessment.
At the beginning, the staff began maintaining portfolios for individual
students, although not systematically. This was part of the learning process and demonstrated how the experience begets the process. The next
step was to design rubrics for oral language, reading, and writing, then to
make decisions regarding the specific types of work to be included, the
students' involvement in those choices, and at what times during the year
samples would be collected.

A few years after its initiation of the school reform process, Linda Vista
School was fortunate to receive a sizable grant from the RJR Nabisco Foundation under the Next Century School project. Through this grant, the staff
decided to enhance the assessment process by an extensive technology
component, the provision for individual electronic portfolios. Teacher
computer stations were established at each of the two school campuses,
with ongoing certificated and classified staff training. The system allowed
all types of student work to be stored—oral, graphic, and written. Original
work could be electronically scanned directly from a photograph or lifted
from a video or audio tape. Each child's portfolio was maintained on the
system with the specific rubrics entered by the teacher. The individual
portfolio was then available to be accessed by the teacher or other staff
for ongoing assessment, parent conferences, and schoolwide assessment
analysis.

The collaborative decision-making process established at this school led to the next logical step in the assessment process. The staff realized that the current district student progress report was not aligned with a performance-based assessment process. Consequently, the "growth record" was developed, which reflected the students' learning growth as measured on the rubrics. A printout of the student's portfolio was attached and parents were informed about the standards the students had met. This reporting allowed the staff to focus on the achievement of the child rather than on the deficits, and helped connect both students and their parents much more intimately to the assessment process.

The staff at Linda Vista went on to conduct the same process with math standards, rubrics, tasks, and reporting. This time, the process was much easier but no less significant in informing instruction in mathematics. The cycle of improvement was now embedded at the school so that decisions about assessment practices aligned with instruction result in improved student learning.

School Accountability

One of the most dramatic decisions of the Linda Vista experience resulted from the realization that it was not enough to have created a new assessment system aligned with instruction. It was necessary to design a reporting system that could extrapolate data on a schoolwide basis. Indicators of student success, parent and staff satisfaction, school climate, and community engagement had to be designed. The first major challenge was to formulate an evaluation design that would incorporate both the district-required norm-referenced data and the performance-based results.

The school's reporting portfolio included the ASAT (Abbreviated Stanford Achievement Test) results, which were consistently mixed. The staff came to realize that even though reality dictated that these data had to be reported, they did not reflect the true progress of students. Alongside these results, the dramatic advancement of students in literacy on the performance-level rubrics was reported. Portfolios reflected major growth in writing and oral language development that a norm-referenced instrument could not possibly have demonstrated for second language learners of English. The staff-approved exemplars of student work or anchors that accompanied the portfolios provided greater inter-rater reliability to support the rubric ratings.

It was not until later that the staff developed reading strategy checklists and student observation records so that data related to the progress of students in reading could be analyzed. Hundreds of students consistently moved up the standards-based language proficiency levels described earlier.

The following data, from an assessment report completed by the district evaluation department for the report to the Next Centuries Schools project (San Diego City Schools, 1993), give a beginning trend for these performance-based data. Students' growth in the three areas measured by the Language Arts Growth Record indicated that 65%, 73%, and 65% of students advanced at least one level in oral language, written language, and reading, respectively. To advance from one level to another (e.g., Beginning Writer to Experienced Writer) was a change that indicated a substantial difference in skill level. A grade-level examination of data indicated higher percentages at the lower (K, 89%; 1–3, 60%) and upper grade levels (60%), and lower at the middle levels (fourth grade, 47%). English language proficiency data were collected from district ESL testing, with a possible 5-point score. Scores for students who had attended Linda Vista for the previous 3 years and were exited averaged 4.3. In 1991–1992, 63% English or nonsheltered level students increased approximately 63%; the following year that number was 94%.

The student attendance data included in this report give another indicator of the overall success of the Linda Vista programs. The percentage of unexcused absences declined approximately 50% each year, and for all 3 years the percentage was well below the district average. The gap between Linda Vista and the district average increased each year.

The school's accountability portfolio also provided indicators of parent and staff satisfaction. All staff, both certificated and classified, were asked to complete a survey each year. Involvement in the decision-making process, communication flow, and the entire restructuring endeavor were areas on which the respondents indicated a range of 75% to 87% agreement, with consistent increases in satisfaction over time.

Parents were asked about their satisfaction with the school in terms of how they were valued, the instructional changes, whether they felt diversity was valued, and their feelings in general about the parent outreach programs. Over time, responses increased to an 80–88% positive agreement with the school's programs and their role as parents in the education of their children.

The accountability process at Linda Vista school reflected an action research mode. Answers were not embedded in single pieces of data; rather, indicators were multifaceted and existed within a living, dynamic process. The accountability path was one that was created first and foremost by the community it served, in this case by both staff and community. It also included a feedback and reporting system to provide ongoing information about student progress as well as other important indices. Finally, and most importantly, the accountability system tightly aligned instruction, curriculum, and assessment, which were then linked closely to staff and parent accountability.

CONCLUSION

The Linda Vista community never professed to have reached any ultimate solutions. Rather, they continued to reinvent themselves, searching for answers within their community, and holding themselves accountable for them. This was a school where the visitor who entered quickly recognized the vitality of the climate. The engaged learning time was evident even approaching dismissal time. Learning was student-centered and reflected a high value placed on the diversity among students. A visitor (of which there have been thousands) saw parents on campus regularly and felt treated with genuine respect and affection.

The staff and parents at Linda Vista did not need the accolades they received to feel the worth of their endeavor, but they have been abundantly recognized. The school was named a California Distinguished School, A Next Century School, and an Apple Classroom of Tomorrow. It was recognized in *Time* and *Redbook* magazines and was the focus of several research studies. A study conducted by the Southwest Regional Laboratory of the U.S. Department of Education resulted in Linda Vista's program being named an exemplary program for limited-English-speaking students.

This case study serves as a powerful example of the decision-making processes brought together by one staff with a strong commitment. It demonstrates how a school can serve a very diverse student population at a high level of expectation for their performance, with a keen awareness that parents and the community at large must be intimately involved. We offer Linda Vista's story to you as a challenge and a vision. It was an ordinary neighborhood school with a formidable task. It transformed itself over time through a process of careful planning, intense dialogue, and commitment to children. We wish you luck in your process, because we know that if they could do it you can too!

References

Allington, R. L., & Johnston, P. (1989). Coordination, collaboration, and consistency: The redesign of compensatory and special education interventions. In R. Slavin, N. Karweit, & N. Madden (Eds.), *Effective programs for students at risk* (pp. 320–354). Boston: Allyn & Bacon.

American Association of Colleges for Teacher Education. (1988). *Teaching teachers: Facts and figures. Research about teacher education project.* Washington, DC: Author.

Anyon, J. (1980). Social class and the hidden curriculum of work. *Journal of Education, 62*(1), 67–92.

Apple, M. (1982). *Education and power.* Boston: Routledge and Kegan Paul.

Armor, D. (1976). *Analysis of the school preferred reading program in selected Los Angeles "minority schools."* (ERIC document ED130–243). Technical Report. Santa Monica, CA: Rand Corporation.

Asher, J. J. (1982). *Learning another language through actions: The complete teacher's guidebook* (2nd ed.). Los Gatos, CA: Sky Oaks Productions.

August, A., Hakuta, K., & Pompa, D. (1994). *For all students: Limited-English proficient students and goals 2000.* Discussion paper. Palo Alto, CA: Stanford University, School of Education.

Baca, L., & DeValenzuela, J. S. (1994). *Reconstructing the bilingual special education interface.* Washington, DC: National Clearinghouse for Bilingual Education.

Banks, J. A. (1994). *Multiethnic education: Theory and practice* (3rd ed.). Boston: Allyn and Bacon.

Barnes, D. (1990). Oral language and learning. In S. Hynds & D. Rubin (Eds.), *Perspectives on talk and learning* (pp. 41–54). Urbana, IL: National Council of Teachers of English.

Barrera, R. B. (1992). The cultural gap in literature based literacy instruction. *Education and Urban Society, 24,* 277–234.

Barth, F. (1969). *Ethnic groups and boundaries.* Boston: Little Brown.

Barth, R. S. (1990). *Improving schools from within: Teachers, parents, principals can make a difference.* San Francisco: Jossey-Bass.

Bennett, A., & Slaughter, H. (1983). A sociolinguistic/discourse approach to the description of the communicative competence of linguistic minority children. In C. Rivera (Ed.), *An ethnographic/sociolinguistic approach to language proficiency assessment* (pp. 2–26). Clevedon, Avon, England: Multilingual Matters.

Ben Zeev, S. (1977). The influence of bilingualism on cognitive strategy and cognitive development. *Child Development, 48,* 1007–1018.

Berman, P., Chambers, J., Gandara, P., McLaughlin, B., Minicucci, C., Nelson, Olsen, L., & Parrish, T. (1992). *Meeting the challenge of language diversity: An evaluation of programs for pupils with limited proficiency in English* (5 vols.). Berkeley, CA: BW Associates.

Brandt, R. (1989). On parents and schools: A conversation with Joyce Epstein. *Educational Leadership, 47*(2), 24–27.

Bronfenbrenner, U. (1979*). The ecology of human development: Experiment by nature and design*. Cambridge: Harvard University Press.

Brookover, W. B., et al. (1979). *School social systems and student achievement: Schools can make a difference*. New York: Praeger.

Brooks, J., & Brooks, M. (1993). *In search of understanding: The case for constructivist classroom*. Alexandria, VA: Association for Supervision and Curriculum Development.

Brown, R. (1973). Development of the first language in the human species. *American Psychologist, 28*, 97–106.

California Tomorrow. (1994). *The unfinished journey: Restructuring schools in a diverse society*. San Francisco: Author.

Campos, J., & Keatinge, B. (1984). *The Carpinteria preschool program: Title VII second year evaluation*. Washington, DC: Department of Education.

Chall, J. (1989). Learning to read: The great debate 20 years later—A response to "Debunking the great phonics myth." *Phi Delta Kappan, 70*, 521–538.

Chamot, A. U., Cummins, J., O'Malley, J. M., Kessler, C., & Wong-Fillmore, L. (1996). *Accelerating English language learning*. Glenview, IL: Scott Foresman.

Chamot, A. U., & O'Malley, J. M. (1994). *The CALLA handbook: Implementing the cognitive academic language learning approach*. Reading, MA: Addison-Wesley.

Clarke, M., & Commins, N. L. (1993). Whole language: Reform and resistance. *Language and Education, 7*(2), 79–95.

Cloud, N. (1994). Special education needs of second language students. In F. Genesee (Ed.), *Educating second language children: The whole child, the whole curriculum, the whole community* (pp. 243–277). Cambridge: Cambridge University Press.

Cohen, E. G. (1986). *Designing groupwork: Strategies for the heterogeneous classroom*. New York: Teachers College Press.

Coleman, J. S., et al. (1966). *Equality of educational opportunity*. Washington, DC: U.S. Department of Health, Education and Welfare, Office of Education, U.S. Government Printing Office.

Collier, V. P. (1987). Age and rate of acquisition of second language for academic purposes. *TESOL Quarterly, 21*(4), 617–641.

Collier, V. P. (1989). How long? A synthesis of research on academic achievement in a second language. *TESOL Quarterly, 23*(3), 509–531.

Collier, V. P. (1995). *Promoting academic success for ESL students: Understanding second language acquisition for school*. Elizabeth, NJ: New Jersey TESOL—Bilingual Educators.

Comer, J. (1984). Home-school relationships as they affect the academic success of children. *Education and Urban Society, 16*(3), 323–337.

Commins, N. L. (1989). Language and affect: Bilingual students at home and at school. *Language Arts, 66*(1), 29–43.

Commins, N. L. (1992) Parents and public schools: The experiences of four Mexican immigrant families. *Equity and Choice, 8*(2), 40–45.

Commins, N. L., & Miramontes, O. B. (1989). Perceived and actual linguistic competence: A descriptive study of four low-achieving Hispanic bilingual students. *American Educational Research Journal, 26*(4), 443–472.

Connelly, F. M., & Clandinin, D. J. (1988). *Teachers as curriculum planners: Narratives of experience.* New York: Teachers College Press.

Corson, D. (1990). *Language policy across the curriculum.* Clevedon, England: Multilingual Matters.

Cortez, C. (1986). The education of language minority students: A contextual interaction model. In *California Department of Education* (Eds.) *Beyond language: Social and cultural factors in schooling language minority students* (pp. 3–33). Los Angeles: Evaluation, Dissemination, and Assessment Center, California State University.

Crandall, J. A. (1987). *ESL through content-area instruction: Mathematics, science, social studies.* Englewood Cliffs, NJ: Prentice Hall Regents.

Crawford, J. (1989). *Bilingual education: History, politics, theory, and practice.* Trenton, NJ: Crane Publishing.

Crawford, J. (1992a). *Hold your tongue: Bilingualism and the politics of English only.* Reading, MA: Addison-Wesley.

Crawford, J. (Ed.). (1992b). *Language loyalties: A source book on the official English controversy.* Chicago: University of Chicago Press.

Cummins, J. (1979). Linguistic interdependence and the educational development of bilingual children. *Review of Educational Research, 49,* 222–251.

Cummins, J. (1986). The role of primary language development in promoting educational success for language minority students. In California State Department of Education (Ed.), *Schooling and language minority students: A theoretical framework* (pp. 3–50). Los Angeles: Evaluation, Dissemination, and Assessment Center.

Cummins, J. (1989). *Empowering minority students.* Sacramento: California Association for Bilingual Education.

Cummins, J. (1994). Knowledge, power, and identity in teaching English as a second language. In F. Genesee (Ed.), *Educating second language children: The whole child, the whole curriculum, the whole community* (pp. 33–58). Cambridge, England: Cambridge University Press.

Davies, D. (1988). Benefits and barriers to parent involvement. *Community Education Research Digest, 2*(2), 11–19.

De Avila, E. A. (1983). *Bilingualism, cognitive function and language minority group membership.* Unpublished manuscript.

De Avila, E. A., & Duncan, S. E. (1980). *Finding out/descubrimiento.* Corte Madera, CA: Linguametrics Groups.

Delgado-Gaitan, C. (1990). *Literacy for empowerment: The role of parents in children's education.* London: Falmer Press.

Delgado-Gaitan, E. (1992). School matters in the Mexican-American home. *American Educational Research Journal, 29*(3), 495–513.

Delpit. L. D. (1988). The silenced dialogue: Power and pedagogy in educating other people's children. *Harvard Educational Review, 58*(3), 280–298.

Diaz, E., Moll, L., & Mehan, H. (1986). Sociocultural resources in instruction: A context specific approach. In California Department of Education (Eds.), *Beyond language: Social and cultural factors in schooling language minority students* (pp. 187–230). Los Angeles: Evaluation, Dissemination, and Assessment Center.

Diaz, R. (1983). Thought and two languages: The impact of bilingualism on cognitive development. *Review of Research in Education, 10,* 23–54.

Dudley-Marling, C., & Searle, D. (1991). *When students have time to talk.* Portsmouth, NH: Heinemann.

Dunn, L. M. (1987). *Bilingual Hispanic children on the U.S. mainland: A review of research on their cognitive, linguistic, and scholastic development* (AGS Monograph). Circle Pines, NM: American Guidance Service.

Edelsky, C., Altwerger, B., & Flores, B. (1983). Whole language: What's the difference? Portsmouth, NH: Heinemann.

Edelsky, C., Hudelson, S., Flores, B., Barken, F., Altwerger, B., & Jilbert, K. (1983). Semilingualism and language deficit. *Applied Linguistics, 4*(1), 1–22.

Edmonds, R. (1979, October). Effective schools for the urban poor. *Educational Leadership, 37*(1), 15–18, 20–24.

Ellis, R. (1986). *Understanding second language acquisition.* Oxford: Oxford University Press.

Enright, S., & McCloskey, M. L. (1988). *Integrating English: Developing English language and literacy in the multilingual classroom.* Reading, MA: Addison-Wesley.

Epstein, J. (1984, Winter). School policy and parent involvement: Research results. *Educational Horizons,* pp. 70–72.

Epstein J., & Dauber, S. L. (1991). School programs and teacher practices of parent involvement in inner-city elementary and middle schools. *The Elementary School Journal, 91*(3), 289–305.

Erickson F., & Mohatt, G. (1982). Cultural organization of participation structures in two classrooms of Indian students. In G. Spindler (Ed.), *Doing the ethnography of schooling: Educational anthropology in action* (pp. 132–174). New York: Holt, Rinehart and Winston.

Escamilla, K. (1992). Theory to practice: A look at maintenance bilingual education classrooms. *Journal of Educational Issues of Language Minority Students, 11,* 1–23.

Escamilla, K. (1994). A sociolinguistic environment of a bilingual school: A case study introduction. *Bilingual Research Journal, 18,* 21–47.

Escamilla, K., & Medina, M. (1993). English and Spanish acquisition by limited language proficient Mexican Americans in a three year maintenance bilingual program. *Hispanic Journal of Behavior Sciences, 15,* 108–120.

Figueroa, R. A. (1989, October). Psychological testing of linguistic-minority students: Knowledge gaps and regulations. *Exceptional Children, 56*(2), 145–152.

Fine, M. (1986). Why urban adolescents drop into and out of public high school. In G. Natriello (Ed.), *School dropouts: Patterns and policies*. New York: Teachers College Press.

Follett-Lusi, S. (1994). Systemic school reform: The challenges faced by state departments of education. In R. F. Elmore & S. H. Fuhrman (Eds.), *The governance of curriculum* (pp. 109–130). Alexandria, VA: ASCD.

Freire, P. (1970). *Pedagogy of the oppressed*. New York: The Seabury Press.

Freire, P. (1985). *The politics of education: Culture, power, and liberation*. South Hadley, MA: Bergin & Garvey Publishers.

Gandara, P. (1994). The impact of the education reform movement on limited English proficient students. In B. McLeod (Ed.), *Language and learning: Educating linguistically diverse students* (pp. 45–70). Albany: SUNY Press

Garcia, E. E. (1988). Attributes of effective schools for language minority students. *Education and Urban Society, 20*(4), 387–398.

Garcia, E. E. (1991a). Bilingualism, second language acquisition, and the education of Chicano language minority students. In R. R. Valencia (Ed.), *Chicano school failure and success* (pp. 93–118). London: Falmer.

Garcia, E. E. (1991b). *Education of linguistically and culturally diverse students: Effective instructional practices* (Educational Practice Report 1). Santa Cruz: University of California.

Garcia, R. (1982). *Teaching in a pluralistic society*. New York: Harper & Row.

Genesee, F. (1994). Introduction. In F. Genesee (Ed.), *Educating second language children: The whole child, the whole curriculum, the whole community* (pp. 1–12). Cambridge: Cambridge University Press.

Gersten, R., & Woodward, J. (1994). The language-minority student and special education: Issues, trends, and paradoxes. *Exceptional Children, 60*(4): 310–322.

Gibbons, P. (1993). *Learning to learn in a second language*. Portsmouth, NH: Heinemann.

Gillet, J. W., & Gentry, J. R. (1983). Bridges between nonstandard and standard English with extensions of dictated stories. *Reading Teacher, 36*(4), 360–364.

Ginsburg, H., & Opper, S. (1979). *Piaget's theory of intellectual development*. Englewood Cliffs, NJ: Prentice-Hall.

Goodlad, J. (1984). *A place called school*. New York: McGraw-Hill.

Goodman, K. S. (1986). *What's whole in whole language*. Portsmouth, NH: Heinemann.

Gordon, J. M., & Tobias, B. A. R. (1993). *The multidimensional learning web*. Des Plaines: Illinois Resource Center.

Grant, C. A., & Sleeter, C. E. (1986). *After the school bell rings*. London: Falmer Press.

Hakuta, K. (1986). *Mirror of language: The debate on bilingualism*. New York: Basic Books.

Halliday, M. A. K. (1975). *Learning how to mean: Explorations in the development of language*. London: Edward Arnold.

Heath, S. B. (1982). *Ways with words*. Cambridge: England: Cambridge University Press.

Heath, S. B. (1986). Sociocultural context of language. In California Department of Education (Eds.), *Beyond language: Social and cultural factors in schooling language minority students* (pp. 143–186). Los Angeles: Evaluation, Dissemination, and Assessment Center, California State University.

Herrnstein, R. J., & Murray, C. (1994). *The bell curve: Intelligence and class structure in American life*. New York: Free Press.

Herzog, N. A. (1995). *Language learning strategies in an English as a second language junior high school classroom*. Unpublished doctoral dissertation. University of Colorado at Boulder.

Hirsch, E. D., Jr. (1987). *Cultural literacy: What every American needs to know*. Boston: Houghton Mifflin.

House, E. R., Emmer, C., & Lawrence, C. (1991). Cultural literacy reconsidered. In E. H. Hiebert (Ed.), *Literacy for a diverse society: Perspective, practices, and policies* (pp. 58–74). New York: Teachers College Press.

Howe, K., & Miramontes, O. B. (1992). *Ethics in special education*. New York: Teachers College Press.

Hymes, D. (1974). Ways of speaking. In R. Bauman & J. Sherzer (Eds.), *Explorations in the ethnography of speaking* (pp. 433–451). Cambridge, England: Cambridge University Press.

Kagan, S. (1986). Cooperative learning and sociocultural factors in schooling. In California Department of Education (Eds.), *Beyond language: Social and cultural factors in schooling language minority students* (pp. 231–298). Los Angeles: Evaluation, Dissemination, and Assessment Center, California State University.

Krashen, S. (1982). *Principles and practice in second language acquisition*. Oxford: Pergamon.

Krashen, S. (1985). *Inquiries & insights: Selected essays*. Hayward, CA: Alemany Press.

Krashen, S., & Biber, B. (1988). *On course: Bilingual education's success in California*. Sacramento: California Association for Bilingual Education.

Kronick, R. F., & Hargis, C. H. (1990). *Dropouts: Who drops out and why*. Springfield: Charles C. Thomas Publisher.

Kucer, S. B. (1995). Guiding bilingual students "through" the literacy process. *Language Arts, 72*(1), 20–29.

Labov, W. (1970). *Language in the inner city: Studies in the Black English vernacular*. Philadelphia: University of Pennsylvania Press.

Lambert, W. E., & Tucker, G. R. (1972). *Bilingual education of children: The St. Lambert experiment*. Rowley, MA: Newbury House.

Lareau, A. (1989). *Home advantage: Social class and parental intervention in elementary education*. London: The Falmer Press.

Larsen-Freeman, D., & Long, M. H. (1991). *An introduction to second language acquisition research*. London: Longman.

Legaretta, C. (1977). Language choice in bilingual classrooms. *TESOL Quarterly, 11*(1), 9–16.

Legaretta-Marcaida, D. (1981). Effective use of the primary language in the classroom. In California Department of Education (Eds.), *Schooling and language minority students: A theoretical framework* (pp. 83–116). Los Angeles: Evaluation, Dissemination and Assessment Center, California State University.

Lenski, G. E. (1966). *Power and privilege: A theory of social stratification.* New York: McGraw-Hill.

Lindfors, J. W. (1987). *Children's language and learning* (2nd ed.). Englewood-Cliffs, NJ: Prentice-Hall.

Linguistic Minority Research Institute. (1994, October). More LEP students receive no special services. *LMRI Newsletter, 4*(2), p. 1.

Liston, D., & Zeichner, K. (1991). *Teacher education and the social conditions of schooling.* New York: Routledge.

Lucas, R., Henze, R., & Donato, R. (1990). Promoting the success of Latino language-minority students: An exploratory study of six high schools. *Harvard Educational Review, 60*(3), 315–340.

Lyons, J. J. (1996). A report on federal English-only legislation. *NABE News, 19*(5), 1, 28–30.

McCaleb, S. P. (1994). *Building communities of learners: A collaboration among teachers, students, families and community.* New York: St Martin's Press.

McLaren, P. (1989*). Life in schools: An introduction to critical pedogogy in the foundations of education.* New York: Longman.

McDermott, R. P., & Gospodinoff, K. (1976). Achieving school failure: An anthropological approach to illiteracy and social stratification. In H. Singer & R. B. Russel (Eds.), *Theoretical models and processes of reading* (pp. 389–424). Newark, DE: International Reading Association.

McDermott, R. P., & Gospodinoff, K. (1981). Social contexts for ethnic borders and school failure. In H. T. Trueba, G. P. Guthrie, & K. H. Au (Eds.), *Culture and the bilingual classroom: Studies in classroom ethnography* (pp. 212–230). Rowley, MA: Newbury House.

McGill-Franzen, A., & Allington, R. L. (1993). Flunk'em or get them classified: The contamination of primary grade accountability data. *Educational Researcher, 22*(1), 19–22.

McLaughlin, B. (1984*). Second language acquisition in childhood: Volume 1. Preschool children* (2nd ed.). Hillsdale, NJ: Lawrence Erlbaum.

McLaughlin, M. W., & Shields, P. (1987). Involving low-income parents in the schools: A role for policy? *Phi Delta Kappan, 69,* 156–160.

McLeod, B. (1996). *School reform and student diversity: Exemplary schooling for language minority students.* Washington, DC: National Clearinghouse for Bilingual Education.

McQuillan, Patrick. (in press). *Educational opportunity in an urban American high school.* New York: SUNY Press.

Mead, G. H. (1977). *On social psychology, selected papers.* A. Strauss (Ed.). Chicago: University of Chicago Press.

Merino, B. M., & Spencer, M. (1982). The comparability of English and Spanish versions of oral language proficiency instruments. *NABE Journal, 7*(2), 1–31.

Met, M. (1994). Teaching content through a second language. In F. Genesee (Ed.), *Educating second language children: The whole child, the whole curriculum, the whole community* (pp. 159–182). Cambridge, England: Cambridge University Press.

Milk, R., Mercado, C., & Sapiens, A. (1992). *Re-thinking the education of teachers of language minority children: Developing reflective teachers for changing schools.* Washington, DC: National Clearinghouse for Bilingual Education.

Miramontes, O. (1987). Reading strategies of non-learning disabled and learning disabled Hispanic students. In S. R. Goldman, & H. T. Trueba (Eds.), *Becoming literate in English as a second language* (pp. 127–154). New York: Ablex.

Miramontes, O. B. (1990a). Organizing for effective paraprofessional services in special education: A multi-lingual/multi-ethnic instructional service (MMIS) team model. *Remedial and Special Education, 12*(12), 7–43.

Miramontes, O. B. (1990b). A comparative study of the English oral reading skills in three differently schooled groups of Hispanic students. *Journal of Reading Behavior, 22*(4), 373–394.

Miramontes, O. B. (1993a). ESL policies and school restructuring: Risks and opportunities for language minority students. *Journal of Education Issues of Language Minority Students, 12,* 77–96.

Miramontes, O. B. (1993b). Language and learning: Exploring schooling issues that impact linguistically diverse students. In D. J. Leu & C. K. Kinzer (Eds.), *Examining central issues in literacy reading, theory, and practice* (pp. 25–39). Forty-second Yearbook of The National Reading Conference. Chicago, IL: National Reading Conference.

Miramontes, O. B. (1994). Underserving linguistically diverse students: Missed opportunities in the classroom. *Educational Foundations, 8*(3), 53–74.

Miramontes, O., & Baca, L. (1993). Bilingual/multicultural education: Guidelines for speech/language and hearing impaired students. In Dolores E. Battle (Ed.), *Communication Disorders in Multicultural Populations* (pp. 1–8). Boston: Andover Medical Publishers.

Miramontes, O. B., & Commins, N. L. (1991). Redefining literacy: Discovering a community of learners. In E. Hiebert (Ed.), *Literacy for a diverse society: Perspectives, programs & policies* (pp. 75–89). New York: Teachers College Press.

Miramontes, O. B., Liston, D. P., & Fletcher, S. (in preparation). Multicultural teacher education: A case study of professional and cultural identity.

Moll, L. C. (1988). Some key issues in teaching Latino students. *Language Arts, 65*(5), 465–472.

Moll, L. C. (1990a). Introduction. In L. C. Moll (Ed.), *Vygotsky and education: Instructional implications and applications of sociohistorical psychology* (pp. 1–27). New York: Cambridge University Press.

Moll, L. C. (1990b). *Community knowledge and classroom practice: Combining resources for literacy instruction.* A handbook for teachers and planners. Arlington, VA: Development Associates, Inc.

Mtume, R., & Sundayo, J. (1988). *Rites of challenge: A passage celebration for children.* Unpublished manuscript.

Nadeau, A., & Miramontes, O. B. (1988). The reclassification of limited English proficient students: Assessing the interrelationship of selected variables. *NABE Journal, 12*(3), 219–242.

Nieto, S. (1992). *Affirming diversity: The sociopolitical context of multicultural education*. New York: Longman.

Oakes, J. (1985). *Keeping track: How schools structure inequality*. New Haven: Yale University Press.

Ochoa, A. M., Hurtado, J., Espinosa, R. W., & Zachman, J. (1987). *The empowerment of all students: A framework for the prevention of school dropouts*. San Diego: San Diego State University, Institute for Cultural Pluralism.

Ogbu, J. U., & Matute-Bianchi, M. E. (1986). Understanding sociocultural factors in education: Knowledge, identity and adjustment in schooling. In California Department of Education (Eds.), *Beyond language: Social and cultural factors in schooling language minority students* (pp. 73–142). Los Angeles: Evaluation, Dissemination, and Assessment Center.

Oller, J. W., Jr. (1980). A language factor deeper than speech: More data and theory for bilingual assessment. In J. E. Alatis (Ed.), *Current issues in bilingual education* (pp. 14–30). Washington, DC: Georgetown University Press.

Ortiz, A., & Maldonado-Colon, E. (1986). Recognizing learning disabilities in bilingual children: How to lessen inappropriate referral of language minority students to special education. *Journal of Reading, Writing, and Learning Disabilities International, 2*(1), 43–56.

Ovando, C., & Collier, V. (1985). *Bilingual and ESL classrooms: Teaching in multicultural contexts*. New York: McGraw-Hill.

Oxford, R. (1990). *Language learning strategies: What every teacher should know*. New York: Newbury House.

Padilla, A. M., et al. (1991). The English-only movement: Myth, reality, and implications for psychology. *American Psychologist, 46*(2), 120–130.

Palmer-Wolf, D. (1989). Portfolio assessment: Sampling student work. *Educational Leadership, 46*(7), 35–39.

Patterson, J. L. (1994). *Leadership for tomorrow's schools*. Alexandria, VA: Association for Supervision and Curriculum Development.

Patthey-Chavez, G. G. (1993). High school as an arena for cultural conflict: An acculturation for Latino Angelinos. *Anthropology and Education Quarterly, 24*(1), 33–60.

Paul, R. (1990). *Critical thinking: What every person needs to survive in a rapidly changing world*. In A. J. A. Binker (Ed.). Rohnert Part, CA: Center for Critical Thinking and Moral Critique, Sonoma State University.

Paulson, L., Paulson, P., & Meyer, C. (1991). What makes a portfolio a portfolio? *Educational Leadership, 48*(5), 160–163.

Perez, B., & Torres-Guzman, M. E. (1996). *Learning in two worlds: An integrated Spanish/English biliteracy approach* (2nd ed.). White Plains, NY: Longman.

Philips, S. (1983). *The invisible culture: Communication in the classroom and on the Warm Springs Indian reservation*. New York: Longman, Inc.

Piaget, J., & Inhelder, B. (1969). *The psychology of the child*. New York: Basic Books.

Porter, R. (1990). *Forked tongue: The politics of bilingual education*. New York: Basic Books.

Ramirez, J. D., & Merino, B. J. (1990). Classroom talk in English immersion, early-exit and late-exit transitional bilingual education. In R. Jacobson & C. Faltis

(Eds.), *Language distribution issues in bilingual schooling* (pp. 61–103). Clevedon, England: Multilingual Matters Ltd.

Ravitch, D., & Finn, E. C., Jr. (1987). *What do our 17-year olds know? A report on the first national assessment of history and literature.* New York: Harper and Row.

Resnick, L. B., & Klopfer, L. E. (1989). Towards a thinking curriculum: An overview. In L. B. Resnick & L. E. Klopfer (Eds.), *Toward the thinking curriculum: Current cognitive research* (pp. 1–18). Arlington, VA: Association for Supervision and Curriculum Development.

Richard-Amato, P. A. (1996). *Making it happen: Interaction in the second language classroom, from theory to practice* (2nd Ed.). New York: Addison-Wesley.

Rigney, J. W. (1978). Learning strategies: A theoretical perspective. In H. F. O'Neill, Jr. (Ed.), *Learning strategies* (pp. 165–206). New York: Academic Press.

Rossell, C. H., & Baker, K. (1966). The educational effectiveness of bilingual education. *Research in the Teaching of English, 30*(1), 7–74.

Rottier, J., & Ogan, B. (1991). *Cooperative learning in middle-level schools.* Washington, DC: National Education Association.

Rubin, J. (1975). What the "good language learner" can teach us. *TESOL Quarterly, 9*(1), 41–51.

Rueda, R., & Chan, K. S. (1980). Referential communication skill levels of moderately mentally retarded adolescents. *American Journal of Mental Deficiencies, 85*(1), 45–52.

Sagor, R. (1993). *How to conduct collaborative action research.* Alexandria, VA: Association for Supervision and Curriculum Development.

San Diego City Schools. (1993). *Next century schools assessment report.* San Diego: San Diego City Schools, Planning and Accountability Division.

Saville-Troike, M. (1979). First and second language acquisition. In H. Trueba & C. Barnett-Mizrahi (Eds.), *Bilingual multicultural education and the professional.* Boston: Newbury House.

Schermerhorn, R. A. (1970). *Comparative ethnic relations: A framework for theory and research.* New York: Random House.

Schlechty, P. C. (1991). *Schools for the 21st Century: Leadership imperatives for educational reform.* San Francisco: Jossey-Bass.

Scribner, S., & Cole, M. (1981). *The psychology of literacy.* Cambridge, MA: Harvard University Press.

Selinker, L. (1972). Interlanguage. *International Review of Applied Linguistics, 10,* 209–230.

Shannon, S. M. (1990). Transition from bilingual programs to all-English programs: Issues about and beyond language. *Linguistics and Education, 2*(4), 323–344.

Shannon, S. M. (1995). The hegemony of English: A case study of one bilingual classroom as a site of resistance. *Linguistics and Education, 7*(3), 175–199.

Shepard, L. A. (1991). Negative policies for dealing with diversity: When does assessment and diagnosis turn into sorting and segregation? In E. H. Hiebert (Ed.), *Literacy for a diverse society: Perspectives, practices, and policies* (pp. 279–298). New York: Teachers College Press.

Sinclair, R. L., & Ghory, W. (1987). *Reaching marginal students: A primary concern for school renewal.* Chicago: McCutchan.

Sizer, T. R. (1984). *Horace's compromise: The dilemma of the American high school.* Boston: Houghton Mifflin.

Skutnabb-Kangas, T. (1981). *Bilingualism or not: The education of minorities.* Clevedon, England: Multilingual Matters.

Sleeter, C. E. (1991). Introduction: Multicultural education and empowerment. In C. E. Sleeter (Ed.), *Empowerment through multicultural education.* Albany: SUNY Press.

Slobin, D. I. (1979). *Psycholinguistics.* New York: Scott Foresman.

Smith, E. (1972). Some implications for the social status of pidgin languages. In D. Smith & R. Shuy (Eds.), *Sociolinguistics in cross-cultural analysis* (pp. 47–56). Washington, DC: Georgetown University.

Smith, F. (1982). *Understanding reading* (3rd ed.). New York: Holt, Rinehart and Winston.

Snow, C. E. (1992). Perspective on second language development: Implications for bilingual education. *Educational Researcher, 21*(2), 16–19.

Snow, C. E., Barnes, W. S., Chanden, J., Goodman, I. F., & Hemphill, L. (1991). *Unfulfilled expectations: Home and school influences in literacy.* Cambridge: Harvard University Press.

Snow, M.A., Met, M., & Genesee, F. (1989). A conceptual framework for the integration of language and content in second/foreign language instruction. *TESOL Quarterly, 23*(2), 201–217.

Sobul, D. (1996, March). *Accessing success for schooled and unschooled LEP students.* Paper presented at the 25th Annual Conference of the National Association for Bilingual Education. Orlando, FL.

Stevick, E. W. (1976). *Memory, meaning and method some psychological perspectives on language learning.* Rowley, MA: Newbury House.

Swap, S. M. (1987). *Enhancing parent involvement in schools.* New York: Teachers College Press.

Teddlie, C., & Stringfield, S. (1993). *Schools make a difference: Lessons learned from a 10 year study of school effects.* New York: Teachers College Press.

Tharp, R. G., & Gallimore, R. (1990). *Rousing minds to life.* New York: Cambridge University Press.

Thonis, E. (1970). *Teaching reading to non-English speakers.* London: Collier-Macmillan.

Tikunoff, W. J., & Vazquez-Faria, J. A. (1982). Successful instruction for bilingual schooling. *Peabody Journal of Education, 59*(4), 234–271.

Tinajero, J. V., & Ada, A. F. (1993). *The power of two languages: Literacy and biliteracy for Spanish speaking students.* New York: Macmillan/McGraw-Hill.

Trueba, H. T. (1987). *Success or failure? Learning and the language minority student.* Cambridge, MA: Newbury House.

Trueba, H. T. (1989). *Raising silent voices: Educating the linguistic minorities for the 21st century.* New York: Newbury House.

Undocumented Workers Policy Research Project. (1984). *The use of public services by undocumented aliens in Texas: A study of state costs and revenues.* Policy research project report No. 60. Austin, TX: Lyndon B. Johnson School of Public Affairs, University of Texas.

U.S. Department of Education. (1990). *Staffing the multilingually impacted schools of the 1990s*. Washington, DC: Office of Bilingual and Minority Language Affairs.

U.S. Department of Education. (1994). *Goals 2000: Educate America Act*. Washington, DC: Author.

Valdez, C. M. (1989). Language minority students and educational reform: An incomplete agenda. In S. Cohen & L. Solomon (Eds.), *From the campus: Perspectives on the school reform movement* (pp. 154–169). New York: Praeger.

Valencia, R. R. (1991). *Chicano school failure and success: Research and policy agendas for the 1990*. New York: Falmer Press.

Van Allen, R., & Allen, C. (1967). *Language experience activities*. Boston: Houghton Mifflin.

Vygotsky, L. S. (1962). *Thought and language*. Cambridge: MIT Press.

Vygotsky, L. S. (1978). *Mind in society: The development of higher psychological processes*. Cambridge: Harvard University Press.

Warren-Little, J. (1994). Teachers' professional development in a climate of educational reform. In R. J. Anson (Ed.), *Systemic reform: Perspectives on personalizing education* (pp. 105–129). Washington, DC: U.S. Department of Education, Office of Educational Research and Improvement.

Wiggins, G. (1989). A true test: Toward a more authentic and equitable assessment. *Phi Delta Kappan, 70*(9), 703–713.

Wong-Fillmore, L. (1982). Instructional language as linguistic input: Second language learning in classrooms. In L. C. Wilkinson (Ed.), *Communicating in the classroom* (pp. 283–296). New York: Academic Press.

Wong-Fillmore, L. (1991). When learning a second language means losing the first. *Early Childhood Research Quarterly, 6*(3), 323–347.

Wong-Fillmore, L., & Valadez, C. (1985). Teaching bilingual learners. In M. C. Wittrock (Ed.), *Handbook of research on teaching* (pp. 648–685). Washington, D C: American Educational Research Association.

Zehler, A. M., Hopstock, P., Fleischman, J., & Greniuk, C. (1994). *An examination of the assessment of limited English proficient students*. Arlington, VA: Development Associates, Inc.

Zelazo, J. (1995). *Parent involvement in a two-way bilingual school*. Unpublished doctoral dissertation, University of Colorado, Boulder.

Zentalla, A. C. (1988). The language situation of Puerto Ricans. In S. L. McKay & A. C. Wong (Eds.), *Language diversity, problem or resource* (pp. 140–165). New York: Newbury House.

Index

About the Authors

Ofelia B. Miramontes is Associate Professor of Education at the University of Colorado, Boulder and specializes in the areas of Bilingual/ESL and Bilingual Special Education. She has been a bilingual, ESL, and special education teacher and Title VII project director. She has also worked extensively in staff development activities for bilingual and bilingual special education, teaching methods courses and helping schools develop and reorganize programs for linguistically diverse students.

Adel Nadeau was the "Principal in Residence" at the U.S. Department of Education from September 1994–May 1995. Prior to this she led an extensive and successful schoolwide reform effort at Linda Vista Elementary School in San Diego, California. Before her work in school administration, she spent many years as a teacher, Title VII director, curriculum consultant, and university professor in the area of linguistic diversity. She has returned to the San Diego Unified School District, where she is responsible for the "Humanities Curriculum." She also continues her work as a part-time professor at San Diego State University.

Nancy L. Commins has worked with linguistically diverse students in a variety of capacities over the last two decades. She has been a classroom teacher in both ESL and bilingual programs, a university professor, a bilingual program director, and a staff development consultant. Currently, she is the Director of Literacy and Language Support Services for the Boulder Valley School District in Boulder, Colorado.